£13.99

Edexcel A2 English Language and Literature

Mike Royston   Mary Jay

STUDENT BOOK

Consultants: Daniel Baker Jen Greatrex

Skills Coverage Map

Skill/specification coverage	UNIT 1	UNIT 2
Analysing unprepared prose	8-53	
Exploring genre	9-10	112-116, 126-129, 132-137
Exploring audience and purpose	9-10	
Exploring context	11	
Identifying attitudes, values and ideas	12-13	
Considering structure, form and language	14	
Writing critical analyses	15-18	
Creating a linguistic and literary framework for analysis	19-20	
Analysing written non-fiction texts	21-39	
Analysing personal letters	26-28	
Analysing journals	29-30	
Analysing political and legal documents	31-32	
Analysing investigative newspaper reports	33-34	
Analysing biographies and autobiographies	35-39	115-116
Analysing spoken non-fiction texts	40-46	
Comparing the linguistic features of speeches and writing	40-41	
Analysing live speeches	42-43	
Analysing broadcast speeches and talks	44-46	
Communicating clearly	51-53, 95-99	
Analysing and comparing plays	54-70, 81-87	
Comparing plot and setting in plays	54-58	
Comparing characterisation in plays	59-62	
Comparing the presentation of themes in plays	62-67	
Comparing stage conventions	67-70	
Analysing and comparing poems	71-80	
Considering subject matter and theme in poems	71-72, 74-75	
Considering lexis in poems	72-73, 76-77	
Considering structure in poems	73-74, 78-80	
Considering the contexts (production and reception) of texts	81-94	124-126
Choosing your own subject matter/topic/texts		103-107
Recording and researching		108-109, 117-119, 120-137
Managing your time		109-110
Writing creatively		111, 130-131, 138-141
Revising and editing		142-144
Writing a commentary on your texts		148-153

Contents

GCE A2 English Language and Literature: Introduction

Welcome to English Language and Literature at advanced level. In this course you will explore texts from both a linguistic and literary perspective taking an integrated approach, and will also create your own texts.

The kind of texts you will explore include literary, non-fiction and media texts. So, in addition to prose, drama and poetry, you will explore communication through the medium of informal and formal speech, journal entries, emails, diary extracts, radio broadcasts and blogs – taking a 'hands on' investigative approach to texts that are part of your everyday lives. At A2 you will become more independent and will be given opportunities to make personal choices and to follow your own interests and ideas.

How can I make English Language and Literature most rewarding?

To enjoy and succeed in your course you will need:

- an interest in language and how it works

- an interest in people and how they communicate with each other

- the ability to write in original, entertaining ways for readers and listeners

- an enjoyment of reading – everything from novels and stories to soap scripts and websites

- an enquiring mind that likes to find patterns in things.

What will I learn?

Unit 3 – Varieties in Language and Literature For Unit 3 you will read non-fiction prose from the late 18th century to the present day, analyse previously unseen non-fiction texts and study and compare two plays OR poetry collections

In Section A you will sample unprepared prose, both written and spoken. This section will prepare you for the unprepared question in your exam. It is important that you cover a wide-range of non-fiction genres as the exam question will include such a text.

Section B will prepare you for the part of your exam on your two chosen plays OR poetry collections. It will guide you in the skills of analysing and comparing your chosen texts and relating them to their contexts. This book cannot attempt to cover the four prescribed play pairings and the four prescribed poetry pairings in detail but it does help you to analyse and compare in the way examiners expect you to.

Unit 4 – Presenting the World. Unit 4 is the coursework unit and builds on and extends your studies and reading from AS units. You will develop your own independent reading and research skills and create your own pieces of writing.

How will I be assessed?

Unit 3 is assessed by an external exam. Unit 4 is assessed by coursework.

Unit 3
In Unit 3 you will be assessed by a 2 hour and 45 minute exam. You will be asked to:

- analyse an unprepared non-fiction text from a written or a spoken source

- write a comparative analysis of your chosen plays OR poetry collections.

Unit 4
You will complete a coursework portfolio containing three pieces of writing,

which will be worth a total of 80 marks. The work will include one piece of literary writing (21 marks), one piece of non-fiction writing (21 marks) and one analytical evaluative commentary (38 marks). You will be allowed 2500 – 3000 words for your creative texts (approximately 1500 words each) and 1000 words for you commentary covering both creative pieces.

Throughout the course you will develop your understanding of how the literary and linguistic elements of texts work, and develop your writing skills for different audiences and purposes.

How to use this book

This **Student Book** is divided into Unit 3 and Unit 4. **Unit 3** supports your work for the A2 exam 'Varieties in Language and Literature. **Unit 4** supports your work for the A2 coursework component, 'Presenting the World'.

The **Teaching and Assessment Guide** provides additional support, including commentaries and further texts, questions and exemplar responses. It can be used alongside this book.

Unit 3. Varieties in Language and Literature: an outline

Unit 3 in the **Student Book** is divided into two sections, reflecting the two sections of the exam. They are:

Section A: Unprepared Prose (pages 8-53). Section A introduces you in a systematic way to the types of non-fiction text you have to know about for the unprepared question in your exam. It covers the reading and analytical skills the examiners require you to show. The final part of this Section, part 4, gives you explicit guidance in tackling the relevant question in the exam.

Section B: Prepared Drama or Poetry (pages 54-101). Section B covers the knowledge and skills you need for the part of the exam on the two texts you have chosen in your topic area. These will be either two plays OR two collections of poetry. The final part of this Section, part 5, gives you explicit guidance in tackling the relevant question in the exam.

For Section A of Unit 3, you have to write an analysis of one unprepared non-fiction text.

For Section B of Unit 3, you have to write an essay comparing your two chosen plays OR your two chosen poetry collections.

Unit 4. Presenting the world: an outline

Unit 4 in the Student Book focuses on your coursework. It is divided into four main sections.

Section A: Approaching your coursework (pages 105–121) The first section will help you consider the types of tasks and approaches that would enable you to show your literary and linguistic expertise. This unit gives you the opportunity to work like a professional writer.

Section B: Reading and reflection (pages 122–139) This section gives you guidance on how to study your main text, develop a research plan, find wide reading and resources around your topic area and document your findings and ideas. You will also be given the opportunity to compare and contrast different genres and approaches to writing and to practise writing in different genres.

Section C: Writing your texts (pages140–149) This section gives you guidance on how to write for your literary and non-fiction tasks, how to draft, edit and revise your work and gives you some examples of writing to discuss and assess against the Assessment Objectives.

Section D: Writing your commentaries (pages 150–155) The final section gives you guidance on how to write your commentaries.

For Unit 4, you have to write a coursework folder made up of one piece of literary writing, once piece of non-fiction writing, and one analytical evaluative commentary

Unit 3: Varieties in Language and Literature

Unit Introduction

In Unit 3 of Edexcel A2 English Language and Literature you will:

- read non-fiction prose from the late 18th century to the present day
- analyse previously unseen non-fiction texts
- study and compare two plays OR two poetry collections
- relate texts to their contexts.

The course

What you will do in the exam (2 hours 45 minutes)

There are two questions. You will be asked to:

- analyse an unprepared non-fiction text from a written or a spoken source
- write a comparative analysis of your chosen plays OR poetry collections.

What will the examiners be looking for?

Examiners use three Assessment objectives (AOs). They are, in summary:

Assessment Objective	What this means in practice	Percentage of marks
AO1 Select and apply relevant concepts and approaches from integrated linguistic and literary study, using appropriate terminology and accurate, coherent written expression.	You have to use: • suitable linguistic frameworks – toolkits to examine the way spoken and written language works • suitable linguistic terms • a style of writing that is clear and fluent.	20%
AO2 Demonstrate detailed critical understanding in analysing the ways in which structure, form and language shape meanings in a range of spoken and written texts.	You have to apply to spoken and written texts: • an understanding of how their language conveys meaning • an understanding of how their form and structure convey meaning • an understanding of how language, form and structure combine to convey meaning.	40%
AO3 Use integrated approaches to explore the relationships between texts, analysing and evaluating the significance of contextual factors in their production and reception.	You have to show: • an integrated Lang-Lit approach to analysing texts • an ability to compare and contrast texts • a knowledge of the context of texts and why it is important.	40%

Examiners will also be looking for evidence of your ability to:

- transfer the skills you developed at AS to the work for A2
- show how language features influence a reader or audience
- identify and comment on attitudes, values and ideas in texts
- think for yourself.

Section A: Unprepared prose

Section A introduces you in a systematic way to the types of non-fiction prose texts, both written and spoken, that you need to know about for the unprepared question in your exam. This question will include a text chosen from a wide range of non-fiction genres. It is important to cover them all.

In the exam you have to write a critical analysis of an unprepared text. Section A takes you through the process of doing so and shows you how to meet the examiner's requirements.

Section B: Prepared drama or poetry

Section B helps you to prepare for the part of the exam on your two chosen plays OR two chosen poetry collections.

It gives you guidance in the skills of analysing and comparing these texts and relating them to their contexts. There are four prescribed play pairings and four prescribed poetry pairings on the specification. This book cannot and does not attempt to cover them all in detail. Rather, it helps you to analyse and compare in the way examiners expect and gives you plenty of practice in doing so.

How to succeed in English Language and Literature Unit 3

You can achieve a high mark on this unit by:

- using as a platform the skills you developed in Units 1 and 2: these skills are assessed again at A2
- constructing your own linguistic and literary frameworks for analysing unprepared *and* prepared texts: this is a key skill at A2, as it was at AS
- reading independently a wide range of non-fiction prose in different genres
- increasing your understanding of how texts work by writing them yourself: original writing is a tool of understanding as well as a means of expression
- enjoying your work and taking pride in it, not just 'doing it for the exam'.

A   Analysing unprepared prose

This section introduces the skills and knowledge you need for Section A of Unit 3. You will read a wide range of non-fiction prose from the late 18th century to the present day. Your work will focus first on identifying the distinctive features of written and spoken texts from different times and on relating these texts to their contexts and audiences. You will then learn how to build suitable frameworks to analyse structure, form and language in non-fiction prose. Finally, you will practise making a critical analysis of unprepared texts – that is, texts that are new to you.

Parts 1, 2 and 3 help you develop your skills of reading and analysing non-fiction. Part 4 shows you how to use these skills to tackle the exam question for Section A.

Assessment objectives

AO1 marks are awarded for selecting and applying relevant concepts and approaches from integrated linguistic and literary study, using appropriate terminology and accurate and coherent written expression (10 marks from a total of 40).

AO2 marks are awarded for demonstrating detailed critical understanding in analysing the ways in which structure, form and language shape meanings in a range of spoken and written texts (30 marks from a total of 40).

1   A foundation for Section A

Part 1 provides a foundation for your work throughout Section A. It prepares you to meet the requirements of the exam, in which you have to write a critical analysis of one unprepared non-fiction text. This could be from a written *or* a spoken source. *Note:* transcripts of spontaneous speech will not be set for the exam. The date of the text will be given.

In the course of Part 1, you will extend the knowledge of non-fiction genres you gained in Units 1 and 2 and learn to:

- appreciate the ways in which context, audience and purpose shape a text
- identify a writer's/speaker's attitudes, values and ideas
- analyse a writer's/speaker's use of structure, form and language
- plan and write a critical analysis.

The range of non-fiction

The specification for Section A requires you to read widely, both in the classroom and independently. There are no prescribed texts. The principal kinds of text, or **genres**, covered in this book are as follows.

Written texts		Spoken texts
• Diaries/Journals	• Travel writing	• Live speeches
• Letters	• Reportage: newspaper articles	• Broadcast speeches
• Autobiographies	• Reportage: eye-witness accounts	
• Biographies	• Political and legal documents	• Broadcast talks

Activity 1

1 a Review your prior reading of non-fiction by completing a copy of the table below. There will, inevitably, be some gaps in your entries. The examples were supplied by a Lang-Lit student.

Genre	Reading contexts			
	For GCSE	*For AS Unit 1*	*For AS Unit 2*	*Outside school*
Diaries/ Journals	Anne Frank's diary	'Baghdad Burning'	–	–
Letters	Wilfred Owen's letters in WW1	–	'The Oxford Book of Letters'	'Letters Home' – Sylvia Plath

b Use the list of written and spoken texts to fill in the Genre column. Put stars alongside each text to show how much you enjoyed it e.g. – ***** for 'a great deal', * for 'not at all'.

2 Compare your completed table with a partner's. Give honest reasons for your rating of three or four of the texts. How far do your preferences seem determined by the *genre* and how far by the individual text?

Genre, audience and purpose

Your work in Units 1 and 2 has shown that non-fiction texts cover a range of genres and address different audiences for different purposes. Activities 2 and 3 develop your knowledge of:

- genre conventions
- the way a writer's/speaker's audience and purpose affects their choice of genre.

Activity 2

1 There are eight written genres listed in the table on page 8. Note down the **primary audience** you would expect the writer to be addressing in each case, for example:

Diary ...   the writer himself or herself

2 Compare your ideas as a class. Then draw a continuum line with 'highly formal style' at one end and 'highly informal style' at the other. Discuss whereabouts on the line you would place each type of text. If you decide 'it depends on its purpose and/or its context', say as precisely as possible what the factors 'it depends on' are.

Activity 3

1 Read the extracts from longer texts below and on the next page. Make an initial judgement about which written or spoken genre each belongs to.

> **A**
>
> Charles Dickens was dead. He lay on the narrow green sofa – but there was enough room for him, so spare had he become – in the dining room of Gad's Hill Place. He had died in the house which he had first seen as a small boy and which his father had pointed out to him as a suitable object of his ambitions; so great was his father's hold upon his life that, forty years later, he had bought it. Now he had gone.

> **B**
>
> Four score and seven years ago our fathers brought forth on this continent a new nation, conceived in liberty and dedicated to the proposition that all men are created equal. Now we are engaged in a great civil war, testing whether that nation or any nation so conceived and so dedicated can long endure. We are met on a great battlefield of that war. We have come to dedicate a portion of that field as a final resting-place for those who here gave their lives that that nation might live.

Key terms

- genres

- primary audience

- register

- syntax

- lexis

C

As I strolled for an hour in the Park today and distantly contemplated the string of fashion – how like ants! I thought. There goes a little yellow-looking box, and two little things with four legs & one little insect driving them, and one behind the box, and something, a living insect, inside, and these little boxes & insects constituted superiority!

D

I don't know whether you agree with the Provisional Government. But I know very well that when they give you sweet speeches and make many promises they are deceiving you and the whole Russian people. The people need peace. The people need bread and land. And they give you war, hunger, no food, and the land remains with the landowners. Sailors, comrades, you must fight for the revolution, fight to the end.

E

Off Leghorn. I left Calvi on the 15th, and hope never to be in it again. I was yesterday in St Fiorenzo, and today shall be safe moored, I expect, in Leghorn; since the ship has been commissioned, this will be the first resting time we have had.

As it is all past, I may now tell you, that on the 10th of July, a shot having hit our battery, the splinters and stones struck me with great violence in the face and breast. Although the blow was so severe as to occasion a great flow of blood from my head, yet I most fortunately escaped, having only my right eye nearly deprived of its sight.

Writing in the exam

The unprepared text you are given will relate to your chosen topic area for Unit 3: 'A Sense of Place' OR 'The Individual in Society' OR 'Love and Loss' OR 'Family Relationships'. Note that you cannot answer on an unprepared text set for another topic area.

2 Work with a partner to fill in a copy of the table below. It will show your considered reasons for allocating each extract to a particular genre, in the light of what you can deduce about the writer's/speaker's intended audience and principal purpose, and your identification of lexical features, including **register**, and structural features, including **syntax**.

Extract	Probable genre	Audience	Purpose	Lexical features	Structural features
A					

Independent research

Build up a collection of non-fiction extracts from different eras and genres and consider their contexts, their main linguistic features and their impact on you as a modern reader.

3 Compare your completed tables in class discussion. Then use evidence from each extract to speculate about the period in which it was written or spoken. Some clues will come from the content. Take into account also:

- the **lexis** and register

- the grammar

- the syntax.

Context, content and style

When faced with a text you have not read before, you need to think first about its *context*. 'Context' applies to a wide range of factors influencing the production of a text. As a starting-point, though, ask yourself: when was this produced; what do I know, or what can I deduce, about its author; who is it addressing? Bear in mind that texts can have more than one audience: a published travel journal can start life as a series of jottings in a diary, a radio talk can be reproduced later in written form, a newspaper article from the 18th century can have a 21st century readership.

The next step is to explore its *content* – that is, the main theme (or themes) of the text, and what these show about the writer's/speaker's views and feelings. Context and content will be closely related. Activity 4 gives you practice in recognising context and relating it to both the content *and* style of a text.

Writing in the exam

The rubric of the question will provide details about the context of your unprepared text. Ask yourself: what can I work out from the rubric about the writer's/speaker's purposes?

Activity 4

Read texts **A** and **B** below. They are extracts from longer texts. Then refer to the annotations in the margin.

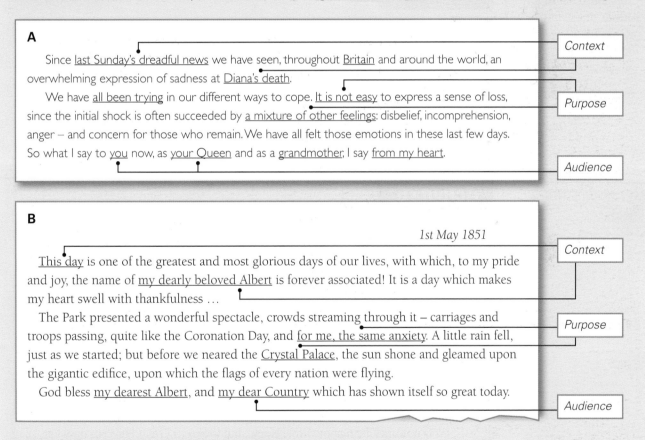

A

    Since last Sunday's dreadful news we have seen, throughout Britain and around the world, an overwhelming expression of sadness at Diana's death.

    We have all been trying in our different ways to cope. It is not easy to express a sense of loss, since the initial shock is often succeeded by a mixture of other feelings: disbelief, incomprehension, anger – and concern for those who remain. We have all felt those emotions in these last few days. So what I say to you now, as your Queen and as a grandmother, I say from my heart.

Context

Purpose

Audience

B

1st May 1851

    This day is one of the greatest and most glorious days of our lives, with which, to my pride and joy, the name of my dearly beloved Albert is forever associated! It is a day which makes my heart swell with thankfulness …

    The Park presented a wonderful spectacle, crowds streaming through it – carriages and troops passing, quite like the Coronation Day, and for me, the same anxiety. A little rain fell, just as we started; but before we neared the Crystal Palace, the sun shone and gleamed upon the gigantic edifice, upon which the flags of every nation were flying.

    God bless my dearest Albert, and my dear Country which has shown itself so great today.

Context

Purpose

Audience

1 Use the annotations to discuss with a partner:

  a each writer's/speaker's context – identity, circumstances, time and place

  b the principal purpose of each text – can you discern other purposes too?

  c the audience for each text – how do the register, lexis and form help you identify their different audiences?

2 Reshape text **A** into a diary entry and text **B** into a public speech. Write three or four sentences for each new text. You could work by yourself or with others. Then explain the changes you have made to the lexis and structure by transforming the genres of these texts. Do this either in a short written commentary or in class/group discussion.

Key terms

- attitudes
- values
- ideas

Definitions

- **Attitudes**: the writer's/speaker's personal viewpoint on the topic of the text
- **Values**: the writer's/speaker's beliefs or moral stance in relation to the topic
- **Ideas**: the writer's/speaker's viewpoint in relation to ideas of the time.

Attitudes, values and ideas

All non-fiction texts convey the **attitudes** and/or **values** and/or **ideas** of their writer or speaker. This sub-section gives you guidance in how to identify and comment on these.

These are not hard and fast categories. In practice, they will overlap, and not all texts will demonstrate each in equal proportion. Other students have found the following model helpful in planning how to write about attitudes, values and ideas in unprepared texts:

Attitudes express *emotional* and *rational* responses. ←→ **Values** express *moral* and *cultural* responses. ←→ **Ideas** express *philosophical* and *spiritual* responses.

You can apply this model to both non-literary and literary non-fiction.

Activity 5

1 Write two paragraphs about EITHER the terrorist attack on the New York World Trade Center on 11 September, 2001 OR the London bombings on 7 July, 2005. Express strong views. Choose your own audience and non-fiction genre. Include attitudes, values and ideas as defined above.

2 Compare your writing with a partner's to assess the usefulness of the model above. If you find better ways of distinguishing attitudes, values and ideas in a text, use them as you work through the rest of Section A.

Activity 6

Read texts **A** and **B**. Both are from travel journals intended for publication. Your task is to identify and comment on the attitudes, values and ideas they convey.

A

The writer, Charles Dickens, is an English visitor to Niagara Falls in 1842.

We were at the foot of the American Fall. I could see an immense torrent of water tearing headlong down from some great height, but had no idea of shape, or situation, or anything but a vague immensity. When we were seated in the little ferry-boat, and were crossing the swoln river
5 immediately before both cataracts, I began to feel what it was: but I was in a manner stunned, and unable to comprehend the vastness of the scene. It was not until I came on Table Rock, and looked – Great Heaven, on what a fall of bright-green water! – that it came upon me in its full might and majesty.
10 Then, when I felt how near to my Creator I was standing, the first effect, and the enduring one – instant and lasting – of the tremendous spectacle, was Peace. Peace of Mind: Tranquillity: Calm recollections of the Dead: Great Thoughts of Eternal Rest and Happiness: nothing of Gloom or Terror. Niagara was at once stamped upon my heart, an Image of Beauty;
15 to remain there, changeless and indelible, until its pulses cease to beat, for ever.

B

The writer, George Sala, is an English visitor to Niagara Falls in 1865.

These then were the famous Falls I had come so far to see; – 144 rods wide, 158 feet high, 1500 millions of cubic feet of water tumbling over a wall of rock every minute, a column of spray 200 – some say 300 – feet in altitude. Well, I confess that as I stood staring, there came over me a
5   sensation of bitter disappointment. And was this all? You who have seen the field of Waterloo, who have seen the Pyramids, who have seen St. Peter's, bear with me. Was this all? There was a great deal of water, a great deal of foam, a great deal of spray, and a thundering noise. This *was* all, abating the snow where I stood and the black river beneath. These were
10 the Falls of Niagara. *They looked comparatively small, and the water looked dingy.* Where was the grand effect – the light and shade? There was, it is true, a considerable amount of effervescence; but the foaminess of the Falls, together with the tinge of tawny yellow in the troubled waters, only reminded me of so much unattainable soda and sherry, and made me feel
15 thirstier than ever.

Niagra Falls

1 Fill in a copy of the table below.

	Attitudes	Values	Ideas
Dickens			
Sala			

Use your table to write two paragraphs comparing these texts in terms of their content, focusing on attitudes, values and ideas. Support your points with brief quotations, working these into your own sentences.

2 Exchange your writing with a partner's. Compare the points you made and the way you distinguished attitudes, values and ideas. If you found more to say about one text than the other, consider why.

3 Discuss briefly as a class the lexis, grammar and syntax of these texts. How do their linguistic features convey the two writers' different responses to Niagara Falls?

Key terms

- perspective
- graphological features
- emotive language
- modifiers

Definitions

Structure: the way the text is built up and made *coherent* – how the parts contribute to the whole

Form (genre): the conventions and characteristics of the text (a diary, a newspaper report, a speech, etc.) – how these contribute to the meaning and the *effect* of the piece on the reader or listener

Language: the writer's/speaker's choices of lexis and grammar – how these contribute to the meaning and establish a *perspective* for the reader or listener.

Structure, form and language

The main focus of your analysis of unprepared texts will be their structure, form (or genre) and language. You need to show how these linguistic features reflect the writer's/speaker's attitudes, values and ideas.

Units 1 and 2 have shown that these linguistic features do not exist in watertight compartments. They inter-relate. The course your analysis takes will be determined by the nature of the text and the linguistic features you find most prominent in it. For example, the *structure* of a political speech may be of greater importance in conveying meaning than the structure of a diary entry. **Graphological features** may be more important to the reader of a front page newspaper report than to the reader of a collection of published letters (but then again, if the text includes facsimiles of handwriting ...). Respond to each text on its own terms.

Activity 7

Read the text below. Your task is to show how its structure, form and language help to convey the writer's viewpoint.

This text is from a newspaper article in *The Observer* newspaper on 10 November, 1793. It gives an account of the death of Marie Antoinette, Queen of France, following the French Revolution.

EXECUTION OF
THE QUEEN OF FRANCE

HER MAJESTY had been confined in the prison of the Conciergerie since the 1st August last, in a room twelve feet long, eight feet broad, four feet under ground, and with a grated window on a level with it. Her food was of the coarsest kind, and she was constantly kept in sight by a female
5   prisoner and two light-horsemen.

On Wednesday morning she was brought into the Court to hear her sentence. Being asked if she had anything to offer against it, she answered, 'Nothing'. Her hands were tied behind her with cords, and she was conveyed to the tumbril* that waited for her. The tying of her hands was
10   also a peculiar act of cruelty, not even practised on Charlotte Corday*.

Beside her, sat the priest and executioner. Her head was bare: the hand of the hangman had already cut off those once fair tresses. Thus attended in this constrained and painful attitude, amidst two ranks of insulting and applauding ruffians, over a rugged pavement for nearly a mile, passed the
15   mother, daughter, sister, and wife of Emperors and Kings: the offspring of Maria Theresa, the descendant of the Caesars!

The procession lasted near an hour and a half; during this whole time no murmur, no sign of indignation, anger or complaint escaped her; she looked round her with a calm and dignified air. When she mounted the
20   scaffold, the same applauses and bravoes were heard again. She smiled. The executioners bound their victim to the plank which bowed her to the axe, and terminated all her sufferings.

* tumbril: cart
* Charlotte Corday: a key figure of the French Revolution, assassin of radical Jacobin Jean-Paul Marat

1 Discuss as a class the attitudes, values and ideas of the writer. Find evidence that:

   a the Queen is presented as:
- courageous
- dignified.

   b her captors are presented as:
- brutal
- indifferent to her royal ancestry.

   c the viewpoint presented is:
- sympathetic to the French monarchy
- critical of the French Republicans.

2 Explore the ways in which the structure, form and language of this text convey the writer's views and create a perspective for the reader.
Talk about:

Structure:
- the selection and ordering of detail
- the focal-point of each paragraph
- the shifts in viewpoint
- the way the climax of the story is handled.

Form (genre):
- the use of a headline
- the narrative shape, typical of reportage
- the short paragraphs, typical of reportage
- variations in sentence structure and length.

Language:
- the register, or registers, of the writing
- the use of **emotive language**
- the use of **modifiers**
- the mixing of fact and opinion.

3 Write two paragraphs about this text. Explain its context and intended audience. Then show how its main linguistic features help to convey the writer's attitudes, values and ideas.

Building up to a critical analysis

This sub-section shows you how to use the elements you have studied so far to plan a critical analysis of a substantial text.

Activity 8

1 Read the text on the next page. It is a speech by General George Patton to soldiers of the US Third Army in 1944. Patton made the speech on the eve of D (for 'deliverance') Day when the allies invaded Normandy. 'Operation Overlord', as it was known, was seen as crucial to an Allied victory in World War II.

2 Plan your analysis on a copy of the text, following the three stages on pages 16 and 17. Start your analysis by making clear statements about the context of the text and its speaker's/writer's principal purposes. Go on to link these with uses of structure, form and language. The order in which you make your points about style is up to you: the key is to be specific, not to generalise, and to illustrate what you say with quotations.

Across AS and A2

For Section A of this unit, keep referring back to the reading you did for Units 1 and 2. As you encounter new texts at A2, compare them with (for example) the reportage, biography and autobiography you read in Unit 2, and the online diaries, travel writing and autobiographical fiction you read in Unit 1. Comparison is key to increased understanding.

Writing in the exam

In Section A of the exam, the unprepared text you are given will be approximately the same length as this one. It will be related to your chosen topic area. You cannot answer on an unprepared text for another topic area. You will be writing for about 60 minutes.

You are here for three reasons. First, you are here to defend your homes and your loved ones. Second, you are here for your own self respect, because you would not want to be anywhere else. Third, you are here because you are real men and all real men like to fight.

5 When you, here, every one of you, were kids, you all admired the champion marble player, the fastest runner, the toughest boxer, the big league ball players, and the All-American football players. Americans love a winner. Americans will not tolerate a loser. Americans despise cowards. Americans play to win all of the time. I wouldn't give a hoot in hell for a man who lost and laughed. That's why

10 Americans have never lost nor will ever lose a war; for the very idea of losing is hateful to an American.

You are not all going to die. Only two per cent of you right here today would die in a major battle. Death must not be feared. Death, in time, comes to all men. Yes, every man is scared in his first battle. If he says he's not, he's a liar. Some

15 men are cowards but they fight the same as the brave men or they get the hell slammed out of them watching men fight who are just as scared as they are. The real hero is the man who fights even though he is scared. Some men get over their fright in a minute under fire. For some, it takes an hour. For some it takes days. But a real man will never let his fear of death overpower his honour, his

20 sense of duty to his country and his innate manhood.

Battle is the most magnificent competition in which a human being can indulge. It brings out all that is best and removes all that is base. Americans pride themselves on being He Men and they *are* He Men. Remember that the enemy is just as frightened as you are, and probably more so. They are not supermen…

25 Sure, we want to go home. We want this war over with. The quickest way to get it over with is to go get the bastards who started it. The quicker they are whipped, the quicker we can go home. The shortest way home is through Berlin and Tokyo. And when we get to Berlin, I am personally going to shoot that paperhanging sonofabitch Hitler. Just like I'd shoot a snake!

30 There is one great thing that you men will all be able to say after this war is over and you are home once again. You may be thankful that twenty years from now, when you are sitting by the fireplace with your grandson on your knee and he asks you what you did in the great World War II, you won't have to shift him to the other knee and say, 'Well, your granddaddy shovelled shit in Louisiana.' No, sir,

35 you can look him straight in the eye and say, 'Son, your granddaddy rode with the great Third Army and a son-of-a-goddamned-bitch named Georgie Patton!'

Stage 1

a Taking into account the *context* of this speech, deduce and note down:
- its speaker's primary audience
- its speaker's purposes (most speeches have more than one purpose: this has several).

b Remind yourself of the definitions of attitudes, values and ideas given on p 12. Then note down what the speaker says or implies about:

- war in general
- the enemy
- Americans
- Hitler
- manhood
- the coming battle
- a hero
- self-respect.

c Look over the speech as a whole and make two or three points about its structure. Focus on:

- the way it begins and ends
- the development of points from one paragraph to the next
- any major shifts in emphasis in the course of the speech.

It can be helpful to jot down opposite each paragraph a few words summarising its theme.

Key terms

- linguistic framework

Structure – overall:	Structure – specific parts of the speech:
1	1
2	2

Compare your notes up to this point as a class.

Stage 2

Now you have got a sense of the speech as a whole, imagine General Patton preparing it. There are six paragraphs. Jot down key words and phrases to use in each paragraph.

Paragraph 1	Paragraph 2	Paragraph 3
• •	• •	• •

Paragraph 4	Paragraph 5	Paragraph 6
• •	• •	• •

Stage 3

This is the key stage in your planning. You now need to relate your understanding of the context, audience and purpose of the speech, and the attitudes, values and ideas of the speaker, to his choices of language. Use the **linguistic framework** below as a focus.

Lexical choices, including register

Focus on the use and effect of:

- the continuum from **impersonal** → **personal register**
  e.g. 'Death must not be feared' → 'When you, here, every one of you, were kids'
- the continuum from **formal** → **informal lexis**
  e.g. 'innate manhood' → 'shovelled shit in Louisiana'
- **literal language**: that is, language used to state the fact of something
  e.g. 'you are real men'
- **figurative language**: that is, language used metaphorically
  e.g. 'Just like I'd shoot a snake!'
- **idioms**, **colloquialisms**, **taboo language**
  e.g. 'go get the bastards who started it'
- **deictic references (deixis)**
  e.g. 'you are here' / 'Sure, we want to go home'
- prosodic and paralinguistic features
  e.g. 'son-of-a-goddamned-bitch named Georgie Patton' / 'I wouldn't give a hoot in hell for a man who lost and laughed'

Key terms
(lexical features)

- impersonal register
- personal register
- informal language
- formal language
- literal language
- figurative language
- idioms
- colloquialisms
- taboo language
- deictic language (deixis)

Key terms
(grammatical and structural features)

- **sentence forms**
- **sentence types**
- **active voice**
- **passive voice**
- **concrete and abstract nouns**
- **premodification**
- **reiteration**
- **triadic structures**
- **syntactic parallelism**
- **personal pronouns**

Across AS and A2

The linguistic terms and concepts used in this sub-section will be familiar to you from Units 1 and 2. As you tackle new work, it is important to remind yourself what they mean and how they are applied. Get into the habit of looking back at your analytical writing for AS to find specific contexts in which you have used these terms and concepts before.

Grammar and syntax

Focus on the use and effect of:

- **sentence forms**: that is, simple, compound, complex e.g.
  - simple: 'Americans love a winner'
  - compound: 'Third, you are here because you are real men and real men like to fight'
- **sentence types**: that is, declarative, interrogative, imperative, exclamatory e.g.
  - declarative: 'You are not all going to die'
  - imperative: 'Remember that the enemy …'
- **sentence structures**: that is, sentence lengths, types of clause and phrase, use of cohesive devices – look for structural patterns at sentence level e.g.
  - short sentences in succession: paragraph 2: 'Americans … Americans … Americans…'
  - repeated syntactical structures: 'the fastest runner, the toughest boxer, the big league ball players'
  - cohesive devices: paragraph 3: 'Some men … For some … For some … But a real man'
- use of verbs – look for **active** and **passive voice** e.g. active voice predominates
- use of nouns – look for the relative frequency of **concrete** and **abstract nouns** e.g.
  - concrete: 'kids', 'runner', 'boxer'
  - abstract: 'honour', 'duty', 'manhood'
- use of modifiers – look for the extent of **premodification** and any striking uses of adjectives and adverbs e.g. 'brave men', 'real hero', limited use of premodification

Rhetorical devices characteristic of planned speeches

Focus on the use and effect of:

- **reiteration**: that is, repetition of key words and phrases e.g. paragraph 2 – 'Americans' repeated; paragraph 3 – 'every man', 'some men', 'a real man'
- patterning: that is, listing, **triadic structures** (lists of three), **syntactic parallelism** (repetition of the same grammatical structure) e.g. 'I wouldn't give a hoot in hell for a man who lost and laughed' (reinforced by alliteration); paragraph 5 – 'go home', 'can go home', 'way home'
- juxtaposition: that is, balanced or contrasting clauses and phrases e.g. 'Death must not be feared. Death, in time, comes to all men'
- discourse markers to signpost the stages of the speech for listeners e.g. discourse markers: paragraph 1 - 'First …', 'Second …', 'Third …'
- frequent and emphatic use of first and second **person pronouns** e.g.
  - second person: 'You', 'every one of you', 'you men'
  - first person singular: 'I am personally'
  - first person plural: 'we can go home'
  - third person singular: referring to himself in paragraph 6

3 Write an analysis of the way Patton's attitudes, values and ideas are conveyed by his use of structure, form and language. Do this in note form if you don't yet feel comfortable about constructing a full critical analysis.

Creating your own linguistic and literary framework to analyse a text

This sub-section gives you practice in devising your own analytical framework for Stage 3 of the process you followed in Activity 8. It leads onto Part 2 of this book where creating analytical frameworks for different written and spoken texts will be a major focus of your work.

Activity 9

Read the text below. It is a letter dated January 1918 from the playwright George Bernard Shaw to Stella Campbell. She had written to him with news of her son's death in the trenches in World War I. An army chaplain had sent her a letter of condolence, which she thought Shaw might want to see.

> Never saw it or heard about it until your letter came. It is no use: I cant be sympathetic: these things simply make me furious. I want to swear. I _do_ swear. Killed just because people are blasted fools. A chaplain, too, to say nice things about it. It is not his business to say nice things about it, but to shout that 'the voice of thy son's
> 5 blood crieth unto God from the ground'.*
>
> To hell with your chaplain and his tragic gentleness! The next shell will perhaps blow _him_ to bits; and some other chaplain will write such a nice letter to _his_ mother. Such nice letters! Such nice little notices in papers!
>
> Gratifying, isn't it. Consoling. It only needs a letter from the king to make me feel
> 10 that the shell was a blessing in disguise.
>
> No: don't show me the letter. But I should very much like to have a nice talk with that dear chaplain, that sweet sky pilot, that –
>
> No use going on like this, Stella. Wait for a week; and then I shall be very clever and broadminded again, and have forgotten all about him. I shall be quite as nice as
> 15 the chaplain.
>
> Oh damn, damn, damn, damn, damn, damn, damn, damn, DAMN, DAMN!
>
> And oh, dear, dear, dear, dear, dear, dearest!
>
> G.B.S

*a quotation from the Book of Genesis

1 Work with a partner. Discuss how the content of this letter relates to its context. Then follow the same procedure as you did for Stage 1 of Activity 8 on page 16 to identify the writer's:

- primary audience
- purposes
- attitudes, values and ideas.

End by making two or three points about the structure of the letter, saying how it reflects the writer's thoughts and feelings.

2 Follow the same procedure as you did for Stage 2 of Activity 8 on page 17. Work by yourself.

Take it further

G.B. Shaw's letter is a good example of a text which *subverts* the conventions of a genre or sub-genre – in this case, a letter of sympathy. As you work through Parts 2 and 3 of this book, be alert to the way other writers/speakers subvert or modify genre for their own purposes. Experiment yourself with genre subversion by writing an ungrateful letter of thanks, a wedding speech which predicts disaster for the happy couple, and so on.

Independent research

Collections of non-fiction you can use throughout the course include: *The New Oxford Book of English Prose*, edited by John Gross; *The Faber Book of Diaries*, edited by Simon Brett; *The Oxford Book of Letters*, edited by Frank and Anita Kermode; *The Faber Book of Reportage*, edited by John Carey; *The Penguin Book of Historic Speeches*, edited by Brian MacArthur.

3 a Discuss as a class how this letter differs in content and style from what might be expected in the circumstances. What do you deduce about:

- G.B. Shaw's personality
- his relationship with Stella Campbell?

b Construct a suitable linguistic framework for analysing the structure, form and language of the letter. Use these three headings:

- **Lexical choices**, including **register**
- **Grammar** and **syntax**
- **Genre-related points** (i.e. the use of the conventions of a personal letter)

Some of the linguistic features you choose may be the same as for Activity 8. Some will be different.

4 Draw on the work you have done in questions **1**, **2** and **3** above to write a critical analysis of this text. Write three paragraphs.

At the end, add a completed copy of the table below to show your teacher what you found straightforward, and what you found challenging, about this activity.

Critical analysis of G.B. Shaw's letter: personal evaluation	
Aspect of the task	**Comments**
Deducing context, audience and purpose	
Defining attitudes, values and ideas	
Relating structure to content	
Constructing a linguistic framework	
Analysing lexical choices	
Analysing grammar and syntax	
Analysing the conventions of the genre	
Other points	

2 Analysing written non-fiction texts

Part 2 introduces a range of written non-fiction from different times. It builds on your work in Part 1 and gives you guidance on how to:

- respond to new texts on their own terms, not simply to their genre
- identify a writer's context and audience as a starting point for analysis
- explore explicit and implicit meaning in texts
- judge the effectiveness of a text in the light of its writer's purposes
- recognise the importance of cultural as well as linguistic factors when reading texts from the past.

How to approach a new text

This sub-section shows how to approach a written text that is completely new to you. It emphasises the need to read and respond with an open mind and avoid making assumptions based on other examples of its genre you may know. To place new texts in a linguistic perspective adequate for A2, you need to go beyond the text-type categories you used for GCSE. Activities 10 and 11 below show you why this is and how to do it.

Throughout your work in this sub-section, you need to bear in mind the *variables* that influence the writing of a text. Part 1 has demonstrated how written non-fiction covers a wide range of genres. It might seem logical, therefore, to classify texts neatly by type, then go on to devise genre-based linguistic frameworks that would support an analysis of *any* newspaper article, travel journal, etc. you are faced with. Your work in Unit 2, however, has shown that there are clear pitfalls in taking this approach. The text you wrote for a reading audience may have shared some genre characteristics with other people's, but it was unique.

Activity 10 reminds you that there are many variables at work in the production of a written text. Your *reception* of it – that is, your response as a reader, either in or out of the exam – needs to take these into account.

Activity 10

1 Consider with a partner these three non-fiction genres:

   a letters   **b** biographical accounts   **c** travel journals.

   How many variables can you think of that would lead to very different texts within each of these genres?

2 Discuss the likely effect of context, audience and purpose on the content *and* style of:

   a • a letter to the editor of a current affairs magazine
   • a letter to a lover breaking off a relationship
   • a letter to a retailer placing an order.

   b • a biographical outline on the back cover of a book
   • a full-scale biographical study
   • a newspaper obituary

   c • a travel journal written in 1800
   • a travel journal written in 2000
   • a travel journal written in any era by a professional explorer.

   Each of you should then write a short extract from a text in a, b and c. Make different choices of text.

Key terms

- colloquial lexis
- non-standard punctuation
- standard punctuation
- jargon

3 Read out a selection of your extracts to the class. Then discuss how the language of texts related by genre changes according to the variables you apply. Be precise about this. Look at particular examples in your writing of:

- lexical choice
- level of formality (register)
- grammar and syntax.

4 Use your work in this activity to discuss how best to approach the genre of the particular text you are analysing. Consider the usefulness, and the limitations, of having a 'genre kit' to draw on when responding to (say) a personal diary or a report by a parliamentary commission – along the lines of:

> 'A personal diary will always include colloquial lexis, grammatically simple sentences, non-standard punctuation and frequent deictic referencing.'

… whereas …

> 'A parliamentary report will always include a highly formal register, grammatically complex sentences, standard punctuation and official jargon.'

A continuum model for written texts

An alternative to the 'genre kit' approach is to think of any non-fiction text as being somewhere on a continuum which can be represented like this:

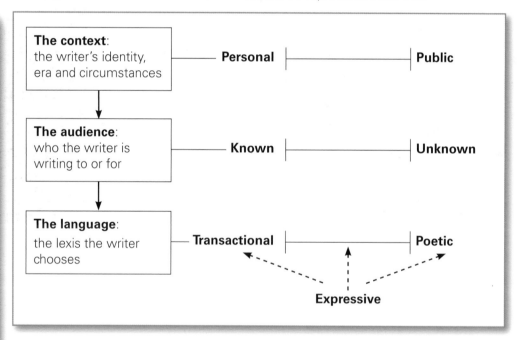

This model helps you take account of the relevant factors influencing the production of a text while remaining alert to the variables that shape its distinctive linguistic features. It is a reminder that:

> All non-fiction texts are the product of a relationship between the writer, the audience and the conventions of the chosen genre
>
> AND AT THE SAME TIME
>
> every text is individual and specific to the writer's context and the writer's purpose.

Definitions

Expressive language is informal lexis that conveys the writer's personal thoughts and feelings. It is the form of written language that comes closest to speech. It underlies all other forms of writing, as the model above shows.

Transactional language is lexis used for a practical purpose in the wider world. It is the language of fact and formality.

Poetic language is lexis used to colour and heighten description. It is the language of imagination and creative expression.

It will be helpful to use this model to begin thinking about any new non-fiction text. Try it out with a sample of texts chosen from your wider reading. Bear in mind, however, that it is a *broad* model. It will lead you in the right direction, but it will not do the job of a text-specific linguistic framework.

Same genre, different texts: an example from diary writing

Activity 11 gives you practice in using the continuum model above to place new texts in an overall linguistic perspective, from which you can move on to detailed analysis. It provides two extracts from diaries. There are strong differences between them in their contexts, audiences and use of language.

Activity 11

Read texts **A** and **B** below and on the next page.

Text **A** is taken from a diary kept by Alastair Campbell, press secretary to the former Prime Minister Tony Blair, in January 1997. He and his partner, Fiona, had accompanied the Blairs to a private dinner given by Princess Diana.

A

> I drafted a letter to Diana saying how much we had enjoyed meeting her, suggesting we meet again to carry on the discussion. Fiona was very wary of the whole thing, and TB said 'Be careful'. We agreed it
> 5 had been quite an evening. TB said I didn't have to drop him in it quite so spectacularly when he was giving all that bullshit about compassion and I said he didn't even give to beggars. He put on a cockney accent, said 'There was I chatting up this
> 10 bird, and my mate drops me in it cos he fancies her rotten. I clocked that one'.

Alastair Campbell

Text **B** is taken from a diary kept by Mary Shelley in June 1824. Her husband, the poet P.B. Shelley, died in 1822.

B

What a divine night it is! I have just returned from Kentish
Town: a calm twilight pervades the clear blue sky; the lamp-like
moon is hung out in heaven, and the bright west retains the dye
of sunset. If such weather would continue, I should write again;
5   the lamp of thought is again illuminated in my heart, and
the fire descends from heaven that kindles it. Such, my loved
Shelley, now ten years ago, at this season, did we first meet, and
these were the very scenes – that churchyard, with its sacred
tomb, was the spot where first love shone in your dear eyes. The
10   stars of heaven are now your country, and your spirit drinks
beauty and wisdom in those spheres, and I, beloved, shall one
day join you. Nature speaks to me of you. In towns and society
I do not feel your presence; but there you are with me, my own,
my unalienable!

1 Discuss with a partner where you would place each of these diary entries on the first two continuum lines:

The context: **Personal** ├──────────────────────────┤ **Public**

The audience: **Known** ├──────────────────────────┤ **Unknown**

Take into account the fact that:

a Alastair Campbell published his diaries in 2007 after Blair was replaced as Prime Minister, whereas

b Mary Shelley's diaries were not published until many years after her death.

2 Discuss with a partner where you would place each of these diary entries on the third continuum line:

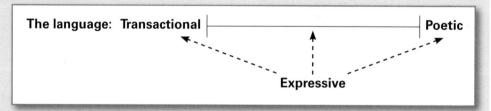

The language: Transactional ├──────────────────────────┤ **Poetic**

Expressive

Then look carefully at each writer's lexical choices. Add terms to a copy of the diagram below to describe some of the differences.

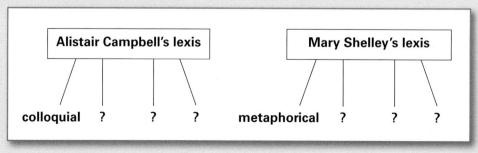

Alistair Campbell's lexis

Mary Shelley's lexis

colloquial   ?   ?   ?   metaphorical   ?   ?   ?

3 Consider as a class the extract below from the start of a critical analysis of text **A**.

> Alastair Campbell's diary entry seems to have a private purpose and audience. He records the day-by-day events of his life as Tony Blair's press secretary soon after they happened, using the 1st person pronouns 'I' and 'we' and deictic references ('Fiona was very wary of the whole thing') typical of diary writing. These create a personal perspective, an impression heightened by Campbell's use of colloquialisms such as 'giving all that bullshit' and the snippets of direct speech from those involved in the events.
>
> At the same time, Campbell seems conscious of a wider, public audience. For instance, he characterises 'TB' in a way he was unlikely to have done openly during Blair's premiership: '… my mate drops me in it cos he fancies her rotten'. Blair was often applauded for his compassion, his family values and his veneration of Princess Diana. Campbell punctures these impressions in two sentences. Blair emerges here as cynical (talking 'bullshit about compassion'), closer to his press secretary than the public would expect ('my mate'), and flirtatious towards Diana. In choosing to publish his unedited diary in 2007, Campbell's purpose may be to present a revisionist version of Blair as prime minister, as well as to present himself as being at the centre of national affairs.

Discuss how well the writer establishes the context and audience of text **A** as a basis for linguistic analysis.

4 Work as a class. Construct a suitable linguistic framework for analysing Mary Shelley's text. Start from the continuum-based model on p 22, then focus on the particulars of her use of language.

You might want to consider:

- **Context** – Mary Shelley's relationship with P.B. Shelley
- **Content** – Mary Shelley's feelings about love, nature and the afterlife
- **Audience** – self, P.B. Shelley
- **Lexis** – use of:
  - terms of address
  - figurative language
  - adjectival and adverbial modifiers
  - concrete and abstract nouns
- **Grammar** – alternation of past, present and future tenses
- **Syntax** – balanced clauses within sentences.

Key terms

- **expressive language**
- **transactional language**
- **poetic language**
- **terms of address**

Independent research

Look through collections of non-fiction grouped by genre – letters, eye-witness accounts, reportage and so on (see the suggestions for reading on pp 28, 30 and 35). Explore the sheer range and variety of individual texts within a genre in terms of their contexts, purposes and audiences. List your favourites and share them with others.

Take it further

Politicians' diaries can be rich in character revelation, gossip and linguistic invention. As well as Alastair Campbell's *The Blair Years*, some of the most interesting of recent times are Alan Clark's *Diaries*, Tony Benn's *Free at Last* and *The Diaries of Margaret Thatcher*.

An overview of the rest of Part 2

Throughout the rest of Part 2, texts will be introduced in terms of their context and audience. They move progressively along the continuum from 'personal context/known audience' to 'public context/unknown audience'.

Each sub-section is built around a group of related texts, but not simply to 'give coverage' to them. The activities vary from one sub-section to another so that you gain practice in the range of skills you need to make a full critical analysis. For example, the material on **personal letters** below guides you further in how to select features for a linguistic framework relevant to the text in question. The material on **journals** guides you in how to differentiate between, and comment on, language used in private and public contexts.

Personal context, known audience

This sub-section focuses on texts written in and about personal circumstances. They address known individuals and are not intended for publication. Activities 12, 13 and 14 help you explore the ways in which their structure, form and language are influenced by these contextual factors. You will also consider the difference between **explicit** and **implicit** meaning in non-fiction texts.

Personal letters

In analysing personal letters, your starting point is to ask 'What is this letter *for*, exactly?' A reliable indicator will be its tone and register. Tune in first to that.

Writing in the exam

Remember that for Section A of the exam the unprepared text you are given can come from *any* non-fiction genre, written or spoken. It is extremely unwise to 'guess the genre' in advance of the exam. Although four texts are provided, you have to answer on the one that relates to your chosen topic area for Unit 3.

Take it further

Write a letter of reply from Elizabeth Bibesco to Katherine Mansfield in no more than six sentences. It should EITHER express remorse and offer an apology to Katherine OR express defiance and tell Katherine not to interfere. Invent background details if you wish. Think carefully about how you will use lexis, register and tone. Then read out some of your letters in class. Judge how effective they are in expressing Elizabeth's feelings and attitude, and why.

Activity 12

Read the letter below. It was written in 1922 by the author Katherine Mansfield to Elizabeth Bibesco. Married to a foreign aristocrat, Elizabeth was trying to begin an affair with Katherine's husband, John Middleton Murray.

> Dear Princess Bibesco,
>
> I am afraid you must stop writing these little love letters to my husband while he and I live together. It is one of the things that is not done in our world.
>
> 5   You are very young. Won't you ask your husband to explain to you the impossibility of such a situation.
>
> Please do not make me have to write to you again. I do not like scolding people and I simply hate having to teach them manners.
>
>   Yours sincerely,
>
>   Katherine Mansfield.

Talk with a partner about:

- what this letter is for
- how Elizabeth is likely to have felt when she read it
- how the register, lexis and structure of Katherine's letter are carefully calculated to provoke a particular response.

Activity 13

Read the letter below. It was written in October 1868 by Charles Dickens to his sixth son, Henry, who had just gone to Cambridge University to study law.

> My dear Harry,
>
> I have your letter here this morning. I enclose you another cheque for twenty-five pounds, and I write to London by this post, ordering three dozen sherry, two dozen port, six bottles of brandy, and three dozen light claret, to be sent down to you. And I enclose a cheque in favour of the Rev. F.L. Hopkins* for £5:10:0.
>
> Now, observe attentively. We must have no shadow of debt. Square up everything that it has been necessary to buy. Let not a farthing be outstanding on any account, when we begin with your allowance. Be particular in the minutest detail.
>
> You know how hard I work for what I get, and I think you know that I never had money help from any human creature after I was a child. You know that you are one of the many heavy charges upon me, and that I trust to your exercising your abilities and improving the advantages of your past expensive education, as soon to diminish <u>this</u> charge. I say no more on that head…
>
> As your brothers have gone away one by one, I have written to each of them what I am now going to write to you. You know you have never been hampered with religious forms of restraint. But I most strongly and affectionately impress upon you the priceless value of the New Testament, and the study of that book as the one unfailing guide in your life. Deeply respecting and bowing down before the character of our Saviour, you cannot go very wrong, and will always preserve at heart a true spirit of veneration and humility. Similarly, I impress upon you the habit of saying a Christian prayer every night and morning. These things have stood by me all through my life, and remember that I tried to render the New Testament intelligible to you and lovable by you when you were a mere baby.
>
> And so God bless you.
>
> Ever your affectionate Father.

lines marked: 5, 10, 15, 20, 25

* a senior tutor at Trinity Hall, Harry's Cambridge college

1 Work with a partner.

a Imagine a 21st century father writing to his son or daughter in the same situation. What differences in the content and style of the letter would you expect? Experiment with writing a few sentences. Compare the lexis and register you use with Dickens's.

b Make deductions from the letter about the relationship between Dickens and Harry. How does Dickens's choice of lexis and register help you to do this?

c Consider what the letter shows about Dickens's values. This being a private letter, the values are not made explicit for the reader; they are implicit in what Dickens says and in the way he writes. You need to infer them from his choice and use of lexis.

Key terms

- explicit
- implicit
- capitalisation
- premodification

2 Now look carefully at the boxes below. They contain notes on some of the linguistic features of the letter. Using a copy of the passage, write these in the margin at what you think are appropriate points

Imperative sentence types	Repetition of abstractions	Repetition of grammatical structures

Use of 2nd person voice	Strong use of **premodification**

Short sentences in succession	Balance of clauses within a sentence	Use of **capitalisation**

In note form, explain the *effect* of these features in the particular part of the letter where they occur. Remember that the intended audience is Harry. Use the sentences you created yourself as a point of comparison.

Then select three or four further linguistic features you think are important to the way Dickens communicates with his son. Write them in on your copy and explain their effect in your notes.

3 As a class, use the material you have assembled to construct a suitable linguistic framework for analysing this letter. Build it around these three headings:

- Lexical choices, including register
- Grammar and syntax
- Genre-related points.

Independent research

Try to read collections of letters that will extend your knowledge and enjoyment of the genre. Include those by Ted Hughes (*Letters of Ted Hughes*, edited by Christopher Reid), Sylvia Plath *(Letters Home*, edited by Aurelia Plath) and John Betjeman (*John Betjeman's Letters*, edited by Candida Lycett Green). Letters from the 18th to 20th centurie that illuminate the social life and attitudes of the time include: *The Royal Letter Book*, edited by Herbert van Thal; *The Collected Letters of Mary Wollstonecraft*, edited by Betty T. Bennett; *The Letters of John Keats*, edited by H.E. Rollins; *The Letters of D.H. Lawrence*, edited by J.T. Boulton and *Katherine Mansfield: Selected Letters*, edited by V. O'Sullivan. The best general collection is *The Oxford Book of Letters*, edited by Frank and Anita Kermode.

Journals

The term 'journal' suggests a day-by-day record of observations, thoughts and feelings about someone's life as it is lived, the principal audience being the self. When journals are published, however, they become accessible to a wider audience – whether or not this was the writer's intention. Your analysis of them needs to take these dual audiences into account. Activity 14 helps you to do so.

Activity 14

Read the text below. It comprises extracts from a journal kept by a nursing sister, K.E. Luard, who served in France during World War I. Periodically, she sent the journal to her family in England as letters. Here she writes about the Battle of Passchendaele in July and August 1917.

Monday, July 30th, midnight, Brandhoek

Cars came for us at 5 p.m. and here we are. By the time you get this it will be history for better or worse. That we have 15 Theatre Sisters tells its own tale.

Wednesday, August 1st, midnight

It has been a pretty frightful day – 44 funerals yesterday and about as many today. After 24 hours of peace the battle seems to have broken out again; the din is so terrific I can hardly sit in this chair. Our monsters are thundering over our heads from the giants behind us, and some of theirs are coming this way. Must go and look round.

Thursday, August 2nd, 11:45 p.m.

The uproar went on all night – no one slept much. It made one realise how far up we are to have streams of shells crossing over our heads. The rain continues – all night and all day since the Push began on Monday. Can God be on our side, everyone is asking – when His (alleged!) Department always intervenes in favour of the enemy at all our best moments.

Yesterday morning Capt. C_____, V.C. and Bar. D.S.O., M.C., R.A.M.C., was brought in – badly hit in the tummy and arm and had been going about for two days with a scalp wound till he got this. Half the Regiment have been to see him – he is loved by everybody. He was quickly X-rayed, operated on, shrapnel found, holes sewn up, salined and put to bed. He is just on the border-land still; better this afternoon and perhaps going to do, but not so well tonight. He tries hard to live; he was going to get married.

Sunday, August 5th, 11:30 p.m.

Capt. C_____ died yesterday; four of us went to his funeral to-day; and a lot of the M.O.'s; two of them wheeled the stretcher and lowered him. His horse was led in front and then the pipers and masses of kilted officers followed. After the blessing one Piper came to the graveside (which was a large pit full of dead soldiers sewn up in canvas) and played a lament. Then his Colonel, who particularly loved him, stood and saluted him in his grave. It was fine, but horribly choky.

---

1 Discuss with a partner your initial reaction to this text. Then consider how far you agree with the following statements.

a The writing seems highly emotive.

b The writer's view of war seems ambivalent.

c The style seems very matter-of-fact under the circumstances.

Refer back to the continuum model for written texts on p 22. Talk about where to place this text on the three continuum lines: the context, the audience, the language.

Independent research

Read a selection of non-fiction writing by people involved in World War I. From the large amount of letters, diary writing and memoirs available, the following are highly readable and informative: *Goodbye to All That*, Robert Graves; *Memoirs of an Infantry Officer*, Siegfried Sassoon; *All Quiet on the Western Front*, Eric Remarque; *The Testament of Youth*, Vera Brittain; *The Virago Book of Women and the Great War*, edited by Joyce Marlow; *A War in Words*, edited by S. Palmer and S. Wallis; *Douglas Haig: War Diaries and Letters*, edited by Gary Sheffield and John Bourne and *Wilfred Owen: Selected Letters*, edited by John Bell.

2 a Share your responses to the text in class discussion. If people have reacted differently, be clear about why.

b Talk about what you can gather about the writer's attitudes, values and ideas. How far are they made *explicit* and how far are they *implicit* in the writing? Focus on these extracts to help you decide:

- '44 funerals yesterday and about as many today'
- 'Can God be on our side, everyone is asking'
- 'He tries hard to live; he was going to get married'
- 'Then his Colonel … stood and saluted him in his grave'.

Select two sentences from elsewhere in the text that seem predominantly 'factual'. Do they convey anything about the writer's feelings?

c This journal was not intended for publication. Do you think there would have been differences in its content and language if it had been? Try to give precise reasons for what you decide, citing specific examples of the use of lexis, register and tone.

3 Read the extract from a critical analysis of this text below.

This extract is from a mid-level analysis. Discuss as a class how the writer relates K.E. Luard's use of structure, form and language to her attitudes, values and ideas. Then add points of your own.

K.E. Luard's attitude towards her job is basically a practical one. She notes down facts – 'Cars came for us at 5 p.m.', 'no one slept much' – and puts her duties as a nurse above making observations in her journal, as when she breaks off abruptly during the bombardment on August 1st: 'Must go and look round'. The minor sentence here is typical of a diary entry. Her purpose in writing is to make a realistic record of events during the battle, as she shows by her use of grammatically simple sentences and compressed syntax: 'He tries hard to live; he was going to get married'.

However, I feel that her writing gains emotionally from being understated. Her descriptions of Capt. C____ are so moving to a modern reader because of what she implies rather than of what she actually says: 'better this afternoon and perhaps going to do, but not so well tonight'. She knows he is likely to die but does not dwell on it: 'going to do' and 'not so well' are euphemisms which cover up Capt. C____'s pain and his fight for life. The metaphor 'on the border-land still' is an example of colloquial as well as figurative lexis, as is 'horribly choky'.

Luard seems to be a woman who, perhaps because of her social background and medical training, uses language to keep her feelings in check. For example, a day on which the carnage is horrific is described in an offhand, conversational register as 'pretty frightful'. However, there are times when strong feelings break through: 'His (alleged!) Department always intervenes in favour of the enemy at all our best moments'. The capital letters here indicate Luard's Christian beliefs, but her parenthesis '(alleged!)' and the ironic exclamation suggest that her faith is being tested by the War.

Public context, targeted audience

This sub-section focuses on texts written to be published for a practical or **polemical** purpose. They include:

- official reports by Parliament, the legal profession, inspectorates, etc. – these address professionally interested parties and specific sections of the public

- investigative reports in newspapers – these address readers likely to share an interest in social issues and current affairs.

These texts target an audience selected or envisaged by the writer as opposed to a general readership. Their principal purposes are to inform and/or argue and/or persuade.

Political and legal documents

Political and legal documents are 'official' or bureaucratic texts designed to do a clearly defined job in the public domain. Activity 15 helps you explore the ways in which the structure, form and language of a parliamentary report are influenced by this fact. You will also consider how effective it is in achieving its purpose.

Activity 15

Read the text below. It is from a report by a parliamentary committee set up to investigate child labour in 1817. It concerns young chimney sweeps or, as they were then known, 'climbing boys'.

ON MONDAY MORNING, 29 March 1813, a chimney sweeper of the name of Griggs attended to sweep a small chimney in the brewhouse of Messers Calvert and Co. in Upper Thames Street; he was accompanied by one of his boys, a lad of about eight years of age, of the name of Thomas Pitt. The fire had been lighted as early as 2 o'clock the same morning, and was burning on the arrival of Griggs and his little boy at eight. The fireplace was small, and an
5 iron pipe projected from the grate some little way into the flue. This the master was acquainted with (having swept the chimneys in the brewhouse for some years), and therefore had a tile or two broken from the roof, in order that the boy might descend the chimney. He had no sooner extinguished the fire than he suffered the lad to go down; and the consequence, as might be expected, was his almost immediate death, in a state, no doubt, of inexpressible agony. The
10 flue was of the narrowest description, and must have retained heat sufficient to have prevented the child's return to the top, even supposing he had not approached the pipe belonging to the grate, which must have been nearly red hot; this however was not clearly ascertained at the inquest, though the appearance of the body would induce an opinion that he had been unavoidably pressed against the pipe. Soon after his descent, the master, who remained on the
15 top, was apprehensive that something had happened, and therefore desired him to come up; the answer of the boy was, 'I cannot come up, master, I must die here'. An alarm was given in the brewhouse immediately that he had stuck in the chimney, and a bricklayer who was at work near the spot attended, and after knocking down part of the brickwork of the chimney, just above the fireplace, made a hole sufficiently large to draw him through. A surgeon attended, but
20 all attempts to restore life were ineffectual. On inspecting the body, various burns appeared; the fleshy part of the legs and a great part of the feet more particularly were injured; those parts too by which climbing boys most effectually ascend or descend chimneys, viz. the elbows and knees, seemed burnt to the bone; from which it must be evident that the unhappy sufferer made some attempts to return as soon as the horrors of his situation became apparent.

Key terms

- **polemic(al)**
- **narrative viewpoint**
- **specialised lexis**
- **coherence**
- **modifiers**
- **modal verb forms**
- **syntactical devices**
- **minor sentences**
- **subordinate clauses**

Writing in the exam

For Section A of the exam, you need to construct and draw on a linguistic framework *appropriate to the particular text you are given*. Remember that an 'all-purpose' general framework will lead only to superficial analysis.

1 Work with a partner. Refer back to the continuum model for written texts on p 22. Talk about where to place this text on the three continuum lines printed there: the context, the audience, the language. Be precise. Make reference to the details of the text to help you decide.

2 Consider as a class how a *novelist* might use the material in this report. Talk about how the following could be handled in a piece of fiction:

- the selection of detail
- the **narrative viewpoint**
- the level of formality (register)
- the representation of speech and/or thought.

What kind of structure would you use if you were the novelist in question?

3 Look carefully at the following phrases from the report:

- 'this, however, was not clearly ascertained at the inquest, though the appearance of the body would induce an opinion that…
- 'A surgeon attended, but all attempts to restore life were ineffectual'
- 'those parts too by which climbing boys most effectually ascend or descend chimneys, viz. the elbows and knees …'

Talk about:

a how the lexis and grammar show that the purpose of the text is to give a factually accurate account of what happened

b how the structural features of the text have the same function – find examples and explain the perspective they establish for the reader

c how this perspective differs from a novelist's perspective.

4 Work as a class to select from the list of linguistic features below the most suitable ones for analysing this text. Some are to be found in the text. Others are not. Some are prominent in the text. Others are not.

Lexis and grammar – the writer's use of:

- personal register
- impersonal register
- colloquial language
- figurative language
- **specialised (or field-specific) lexis**
- proper nouns
- common nouns
- abstract nouns
- **modifiers**
- active voice
- passive voice
- **modal verb forms**

Syntactical and structural devices – the writer's use of:

- **minor sentences**
- complex sentences
- **subordinate clauses**
- interrogative sentences
- declarative sentence
- connectives (conjunctions and adverbs)
- direct speech
- indirect (reported) speech
- variations in sentence length
- balanced clauses

5 Use the linguistic framework you have now developed to write a critical analysis of this text. Begin by explaining its context, intended audience and purpose. Then relate its linguistic features to the writer's intentions, starting with the most prominent. Write three paragraphs in all. End by saying how effective it is in achieving its purpose.

Investigative newspaper reports

Investigative newspaper reports give new information. This is not presented dispassionately: the writer has a view which they mean the reader to adopt. Activity 16 helps you explore the way in which the structure, form and language of a polemical text positions the reader and guides their response.

Activity 16

Read the text below. It is taken from a report in the *Morning Post* by the investigative journalist John Hollingshead. In 1861, he was commissioned by the newspaper to write about the condition of the London poor.

The evils of overcrowding in courts* and alleys are, unhappily, not confined to the eastern end of the metropolis. There are almost as many dark holes and corners within a few yards of Regent Street or Charing Cross, which shelter almost as much sickness, crime, and poverty, as any back hiding-places in Whitechapel or Bethnal Green. We may have all hurried for years along the bright open highways, scarcely glancing at the little doorways scattered here and there between the busy shops, and yet these doorways – holes – call them by what name we will – are the entrances to many thousands of closely-packed homes. These human dwellings – human in little else but the old familiar house shape – in old central neighbourhoods, like St James's, Westminster, form square openings, reaching up to the little patch of heaven, like the shaft of a mine. The air is close and heavy, and they are dark on the clearest day. They are penal settlements, not homes, and those who visit them and consider the effect they must have on mind and morals are compelled to wonder that there is not more vice and drunkenness in the world.

The patient, hard-working poor sit in their wretched rooms, looking into each other's faces, drooping over bare shopboards, bare benches, bare tables, and half-empty grates, hoping and praying for work. They only ask to be employed. They tramp through miles of mud – they stand for hours in work-room passages – they bear rain, and cold, and hunger without murmuring, and they clear their little households of every saleable article rather than beg. When they have got their little strip of cloth, or leather, to stitch or cut into shape, they clasp it like some precious treasure, and hurry home to begin their ill-paid task. In times of plenty, they are, perhaps, a little wasteful; they look a very short way into the future; but we must think of their education and habits, and their cheerless lives. It is easy to add up their little excursions, their few dissipations, and fewer amusements, and to bring a wholesale charge of improvidence* against them when they drop dead from want; but how few would bear the trial of living where they live and come out of it prudent, thoughtful and pure!

*courts: small enclosed yards
*improvidence: wastefulness, lack of thrift

1 Work with a partner.

a Imagine you are a comfortably-off middle class reader of the *Morning Post* (it was a 'conservative' newspaper) living in the neighbourhood of Regent Street or Charing Cross. Select three or four facts from Hollingshead's report you are not likely to know.

b Talk about how Hollingshead presents these facts. Look carefully at his choice of lexis. Find examples of **connotation** – that is, words that suggest ideas and feelings beyond their literal meaning. How are these connotations intended to shape the reader's response to what is being described?

Key terms

• connotation

• external / internal viewpoint

Independent research

Read investigative and other journalism online by visiting the websites of quality newspapers. Find reports and articles from the past at the following addresses: archive.timesonline. co.uk, www.guardian.co.uk/ Archive, www.telegraph.co.uk/ archive, www.bl.uk (the British Library online newspaper archive).

2 a Share your ideas in class discussion. Then work together to fill in the table below.

Hollingshead's attitudes to the London poor	
Where they live	**How they make a living**
What his attitude is:	What his attitude is:
How his lexis states or implies his attitude:	How his lexis states or implies his attitude:

Use your completed table to consider the overall structure of this text. Does the way it is built up help readers to develop the viewpoint Hollingshead wants them to take?

b Select three sentences from different parts of the text. Look carefully at their grammar and syntax. Discuss how the structure of each sentence is designed to reflect and reinforce what it describes.

3 Take an overview of the text. Judge the effectiveness of Hollingshead's writing in arousing the reader's sympathy and admiration for the London poor. Think about:

• the balance between precise description and general observation

• the shifts between an **external** and an **internal viewpoint**

• the occasional use of metaphor and simile

• the use of syntactical patterning in paragraph 2.

Definitions

Biography – a person's life story written by someone else. Sometimes the subject is known to the writer, but normally the account given of their life is retrospective, based on research and the writer's considered opinion of the person concerned.
Autobiography – a person's life story (or parts of it) written by themselves. Prior to the 20th century, autobiographical texts were usually termed 'memoirs'.

Public context, unknown audience

This sub-section focuses on texts written for publication and intended for a general readership. In addition to travel writing, essays and historical studies, they include biography and autobiography.

The purposes of these texts vary. Broadly speaking, they are written to entertain and enlighten whoever chooses to read them. You need to use the evidence of each individual text to determine the writer's precise intentions.

Biographies

Some biographies are principally factual but most are not. Activities 17, 18 and 19 help you explore the ways in which their structure, form and language establish the writer's attitude towards his subject. You will also consider the linguistic and cultural differences between a modern text and texts written in the 18th century.

Activity 17

Read the paragraph below. It is taken from a biographical essay by Stephen Fry about his friend Peter Cook, the satirist and comedian. Cook died in 1995 of liver failure.

> Alcohol isn't a simple chemical, or if a scientist tells you it is, then he would have to confess that its effect on the human brain is bewilderingly complex. Peter never yielded to the dark side, never once turned aggressive or rude or loud or bullying or vain.
> 5 His voice often became slurred, but then it was slurred when he was sober, so that didn't mean much. He sweated a touch and one wouldn't necessarily trust him to remember lines on stage, so there's no avoiding the opinion that it was a *pity* that he used alcohol as much as he did. And of course, in the end, his liver didn't
> 10 take kindly to it either. These are all facts that can't be shirked. But, so far as I can judge, alcohol never made him a less pleasant person to be with. Everyone dies, and while it was a terrible thing that Peter Cook left the party early, those of us remaining will all be gone in the twinkling of an eye, and who is to say that, in the end, it
> 15 is better to stay long and sober than to leave early and merry?

1 Discuss with a partner the impression given here of Peter Cook. How does the writer try to present a positive, sympathetic picture of him? Think about:

- the way Stephen Fry chooses to deal with Cook's alcoholism

- the use of a personal register

- the choice of lexis in:
  - 'Peter never yielded to the dark side'
  - 'there's no avoiding the opinion that it was a *pity* he used alcohol as much as he did'
  - 'his liver didn't take kindly to it either'

- the direct address to the reader in the first and last sentences

- the use of metaphor in the last sentence.

2 Share your ideas with the class. Then, using only the information given about Peter Cook in Stephen Fry's paragraph, write two or three sentences that present a view of him as a gifted man who destroyed himself through drink.

3 Look with a partner at your own sentences. What differences are there between them and Stephen Fry's text? Is it just a matter of lexical choice – or are there also differences in voice, tone and sentence structure?

Across AS and A2

Remind yourself of the material drawn from biographies and autobiographies in the AS Student Book on pp 115–121. What did you learn about how writers position the reader and guide their response? What links did you make between a writer's sense of audience and his/her choices of lexis, register and form? Use this knowledge as you analyse the texts in Activities 17 to 21 below.

Independent research

Read a selection of biographies. Try some of the following which have proved popular with other A level students: *So Farewell Then* by Wendy E. Cook, *Six Men* by Alistair Cooke, *Ted Hughes: The Life of a Poet* by Elaine Feinstein, *Provided You Don't Kiss Me* by Duncan Hamilton, *Telling Lives* edited by E.A. Thorne, *Double Drink Story* by Caitlin Thomas, *Katherine Mansfield: A Secret Life* by Claire Tomalin, *Thomas Hardy: The Time-Torn Man* by Claire Tomalin, *The Lunar Men* by Jenny Uglow.

Writing in the exam

If your text comes from the past, the style and language will be different from modern non-fiction but your questions about it should be the same. What are the writer's purposes? What can I work out about the writer's attitudes, values and ideas? How are these conveyed by the structure, form and style? Do not become intimidated or sidetracked by linguistic difference: the examiner makes allowance for this, and texts from earlier times are *not* written in a foreign language.

Activity 18

1 Look back to Stephen Fry's text in Activity 17. Discuss as a class how the view of human life implicit in it differs from the view of human life implicit in the text below. It is from James Boswell's *Life of Dr Johnson*, published in 1791. Peter Cook suffered from alcoholism; Johnson suffered from 'morbid melancholy'.

The "morbid melancholy", which was lurking in his constitution, gathered such strength in his twentieth year, as to afflict him in a dreadful manner. While he was in Lichfield, in the college vacation of the year 1729, he felt himself overwhelmed with an horrible hypochondria, with
5 perpetual irritation, fretfulness and impatience; and with a dejection, gloom and despair, which made existence misery. From this dismal malady he never afterwards was perfectly relieved; and all his labours, all his enjoyments, were but temporary interruptions of its baleful influence. How wonderful, how unsearchable are the ways of God! Johnson, who
10 was blest with all the powers of genius and understanding in a degree far above the ordinary state of human nature, was at the same time visited with a disorder so afflictive, that they who know it by dire experience, will not envy his exalted endowments.

2 Read the extract below from a critical analysis of Boswell's text.

Boswell's attitude towards Dr Johnson's 'dismal malady' is entirely sympathetic. It is described as 'lurking in his constitution', the use of metaphor here suggesting that his illness is something independent of him which he cannot help or control. This impression is enhanced by Boswell's use of lexis drawn from the semantic field of physical, rather than mental, illness and by his use of active verbs: 'to afflict him', 'visited with a disorder'. In all probability, Boswell is not just being metaphorical here: in the 18th century, the 'morbid melancholy' which we would term "clinical depression" was thought to have a physical, not a psychological, cause.

Boswell shows how seriously this 'malady' was taken in his own day, and how much it was feared, by his choice of adjectives: 'dreadful', 'horrible', 'baleful'. These are strong modifiers, linked syntactically with equally strong abstract nouns which are given emphasis by Boswell's use of tripling: 'irritation, fretfulness and impatience', 'dejection, gloom and despair'. Boswell's attitude is that Johnson is to be deeply pitied, but, more than this, admired for the fact that his 'genius' triumphed over such a disabling 'disorder'.

Boswell attributes this not only to Johnson's resilient character but principally to God: 'How wonderful, how unsearchable are the ways of God!' This exclamatory sentence with its phrasal repetition shows the depth of Boswell's religious faith and his Christian value-system. The same impression is given by his description of Johnson as being 'blest' with a high intellect and possessing 'exalted endowments'. Nowadays we might use similar lexis about someone we admired, but 'blest' and 'endowments' have lost their religious significance. Boswell uses them literally, as a testimony to the power and goodness of God.

This extract is from a high level-commentary. Discuss as a class how the writer successfully relates Boswell's use of structure, form and language to his attitudes, values and ideas.

Writing in the exam

This commentary on Boswell's text, though not complete, is a good model of how to approach the question in Section A. It links the writer's attitudes, values and ideas relevantly to the structure, form and language of his text. Note also the detailed focus on lexical choices and the use of linguistic terminology.

Autobiographies

In autobiographies, writers give an eye-witness account of their own lives. Their viewpoint is, by definition, **subjective**. This being so, they can construct whatever version of their life they choose. Activity 19 helps you explore how two autobiographical writers, separated widely in time, use structure, form and language to engage and entertain their readers with personal experience. Activity 20 provides you with an autobiographical text from the mid-19th century to practise making a full critical analysis. This rounds off your work in Part 2.

Activity 19

Read texts **A** and **B** below. Text **A** is a passage from Lorna Sage's autobiography *Bad Blood* written in 2000. Text **B** is a passage from *An Apology for the Life of Mr Colley Cibber, Written by Himself* in 1740.

A

So the playground was hell: Chinese burns, pinches, slaps and kicks, and horrible games. I can still hear the noise of a thick wet skipping rope slapping the ground. There'd be a big girl each end and you had to leap through without tripping. Joining in was only marginally less awful than being left out. It's said (truly) that most women forget the pain of childbirth; I think that we all forget the pain of being a child at school for the first time, the sheer ineptitude, as though you'll never learn to mark out your own space. It's doubly shaming – shaming to remember as well, to feel so sorry for your scabby little self back there in small people's purgatory.

B

A great Boy, near the Head taller than myself, in some wrangle at Play had insulted me; upon which I was fool-hardy enough to give him a Box on the Ear; the Blow was soon return'd with another that brought me under him and at his Mercy. Another Lad, whom I really lov'd and thought a good-natur'd one, cry'd out with some warmth to my Antagonist (while I was down) Beat him, beat him soundly! This so amaz'd me that I lost all my Spirits to resist and burst into Tears! When the Fray was over I took my friend aside, and ask'd him, How he came to be so earnestly against me? To which, with some glouting* and sullen confusion, he reply'd, 'Because you are always jeering and making a Jest of me to every Boy in the school'. Many a Mischief have I brought upon myself by the same Folly in riper Life.

*glouting: stammering

1 Work with a partner. Talk about how each writer conveys 'the pain of being a child'. Focus on:

- the reasons why both felt sorry for themselves at school and still feel sorry for themselves as adults

- the dual perspective established in both passages: which writer uses this technique more effectively, in your opinion?

- the register and tone used in the passages: which writer conveys personal experience more vividly, in your opinion?

Share your responses with the class.

2 Then examine the spelling and punctuation in Colley Cibber's text. How great are the differences between them and the **orthography** you would find in a modern text? Do they create difficulties for you in understanding?

3 Read text C opposite from a diary written in 1718.

Decide on the meaning of the last sentence and relate it to the previous one.

The orthography of texts changes over time but Language Change is not a topic for study in this specification. Your focus should be on vocabulary (lexis) and grammar when reading for meaning.

> **C**
>
> 5
>
> *Mr Werg reported to have offered to lay with two or three men's wifes in Alnwick – one was the day before the sacrament – she asked him how he durst, when he knew he was the next day to administer sacrament and she to receive it – he replyed love was a noble passion, and God would indulge it. This sent up to London, and they say he is stopt of the living.*
>
> Rev John Thomlinson

4 In class discussion, consider the way Lorna Sage in text **A** uses:

- the first, second and third person voices
- a mixture of tenses
- a mixture of expressive language to imitate natural speech and poetic language to heighten description.

These linguistic devices are typical of much autobiographical writing. Talk about why.

Activity 20

1 Read the text opposite. It is from *Confessions of an English Opium-eater* by Thomas de Quincey, published in 1854.

2 Write a critical analysis of this text. You should analyse how effectively the writer's choices of structure, form and language convey attitudes, values and ideas in the writing. Include comment on literary and linguistic devices.

> ### Advice for planning and writing
>
> **a** Re-read the text.
>
> **b** Make notes about the attitudes, values and ideas expressed by the writer. Follow the guidance given on p 12 and throughout Parts 1 and 2.
>
> **c** Make a list of the main linguistic features of the text under three headings: structure, form and language. Follow the guidance given on pp 14 and throughout Parts 1 and 2. Then relate your choices to the notes you made in **b**, above.
>
> **d** Use the notes you have assembled so far to devise a suitable linguistic framework for analysing the text. Base this on four main aspects: **lexis**, **grammar and syntax**, **structure** and **genre-related points**. Remind yourself of the procedure you followed in Activity 8 on p 15 – use the same approach.
>
> **e** Use your linguistic framework to write your critical analysis. As you write, try to ensure that you:
>
> - consider the *content* of the text but write mainly about *style* and *language*
> - do not generalise about structure, form and language – your comments about these linguistic features should be *specific* and rooted in context
> - quote to support and illustrate every main point you make, embedding short quotations in your own sentences rather than quoting several lines
> - include some evaluation of the writer's style: that is, how *effectively* it achieves its purposes as you understand them.

Writing in the exam

Part 4 on p 47 gives detailed guidance about how your Section A answer will be assessed.

Independent research

Read a selection of autobiographies/ memoirs, both past and present. Titles popular with other A level students include: *I Know Why the Caged Bird Sings* by Maya Angelou, *Writing Home* and *Telling Tales* by Alan Bennett, *The Naked Civil Servant* by Quentin Crisp, *Chronicles* by Bob Dylan, *A Sort of Life* by Graham Greene, *Survival in Auschwitz* by Primo Levi, *The Road to Wigan Pier* by George Orwell, *Bad Blood: A Memoir* by Lorna Sage and *Memories of Being* by Virginia Woolf.

It is very long since I first took opium; so long, that if it had been a trifling incident in my life, I might have forgotten its date; but cardinal events are not to be forgotten; and, from circumstances connected with it, I remember that this inauguration into the use of opium must be referred to the spring or to the autumn of 1804; during which seasons I was in London, having come thither for the first time since my entrance at Oxford. And this event arose in the following way: from an early age I had been accustomed to wash my head in cold water at least once a day; being suddenly seized with toothache, I attributed it to some relaxation caused by a casual intermission of that practice; jumped out of bed; plunged my head into a basin of cold water, and with hair thus wetted went to sleep. The next morning, as I need hardly say, I awoke with excruciating rheumatic pains of the head and face, from which I had hardly any respite for about twenty days.

On the twenty-first day I think it was, and on a Sunday, I went out into the streets; rather to run away, if possible, from my torments, than with any distinct purpose of relief. By accident, I met a college acquaintance who recommended opium. Opium! dread agent of unimaginable pleasure and pain! I had heard of it as I had of manna or ambrosia, but no further. How unmeaning a sound was opium at that time! what solemn chords does it now strike upon my heart! what heart-quaking vibrations of sad and happy remembrances!

It was a Sunday afternoon, wet and cheerless; and a duller spectacle this earth of ours has not to show than a rainy Sunday in London. My road homewards lay through Oxford Street; and near 'the *stately pantheon*' (as Mr Wordsworth has obligingly called it) I saw a druggist's shop. The druggist (unconscious minister of celestial pleasures!), as if in sympathy with the rainy Sunday, looked dull and stupid, just as any mortal druggist might be expected to look on a rainy London Sunday; and when I asked for the tincture of opium, he gave it to me as any other man might do; and, furthermore, out of my shilling returned me what seemed to be real copper halfpence, taken out of a real wooden drawer. Nevertheless, and not withstanding all such indications of humanity, he has ever since figured in my mind as a beatific vision of an immortal druggist, sent down to earth on a special mission to myself …

Arrived at my lodgings, it may be supposed that I lost not a moment in taking the quantity prescribed. I was necessarily ignorant of the whole art and mystery of opium-taking; and what I took, I took under every disadvantage. But I took it; and in an hour, O heavens! what a revulsion! what a resurrection, from its lowest depths of the inner spirit! what an apocalypse of the world within me! That my pains vanished was now a trifle in my eyes; this negative effect was swallowed up in the immensity of those positive effects which had opened before me, in the abyss of divine enjoyment thus suddenly revealed. Here was a panacea for all human woes; here was the secret of happiness, about which philosophers had disputed for so many ages, at once discovered; happiness might now be bought for a penny, and carried in the waistcoat pocket; portable ecstacies might be had corked up in a pint-bottle; and peace of mind could be sent down by the mail.

3 Analysing spoken non-fiction texts

Part 3 introduces a range of spoken non-fiction texts from different times and shows you how to:

- analyse the distinctive features of texts addressed to a listening audience
- apply to new material the knowledge about spoken texts you gained in Units 1 and 2
- give due weight in your analysis to the fact that most live speeches and broadcasts are presentations of writing
- give due weight in your analysis to the use of prosodic features.

Speeches and writing

This sub-section asks you to revisit the coursework you did in Unit 2 to remind yourself why context and audience are key factors in shaping a spoken text. You will also compare the linguistic features of speeches and writing.

Across AS and A2

Refer back to the 'spoken' text you chose to write in Unit 2. What did you conclude about the principal differences between speech and writing? Why were context and audience so important in determining the linguistic features of spoken texts? Use your knowledge to help you analyse spoken non-fiction in this part.

Activity 21

1 Think back to the texts you created for a reading and a listening audience in Unit 2. Then fill in a copy of the table below.

Coursework texts	The context you chose	The audience you targeted	The genre and the main linguistic techniques you used
Text for a reading audience			
Text for a listening audience			

2 Use your table to discuss with a partner the chief *linguistic* differences between your texts for reading and listening audiences. Which aspects of the structure, form and language of your spoken text differentiated it most from the structure, form and language of your written text?

3 a Read around the class the five non-fiction extracts below. Some are from public speeches. Some are from written genres. Make an initial judgment about which is which.

A

Since it has pleased Providence to place me in this station, I shall do my utmost to fulfil my duty towards my country. I am very young and perhaps in many, though not in all things, inexperienced; but I am sure that very few have more real good will and more real desire
5 to do what is fit and right than I have.

B

Non-violence is the first article of my faith. It is the last article of my faith. But I had to make my choice. I had either to submit to a system which I considered has done an irreparable harm to my country or incur the risk of the mad fury of my people bursting forth when they understood the truth from my lips. I know that
5 my people have sometimes gone mad. I am deeply sorry for it.

C

The most cruel objects in these awful factories and mills are the machines. These are a danger that the children fear but can do nothing about. A factory inspector told me upon my arrival at the factory that recently a young girl had been in an incident with the carding engine. She was apparently repeatedly forced against the shaft as she was whirled round by her apron. Her right leg was torn off in the accident. I was even more shocked to discover that she is still involved in this kind of work.

5

D

You all know the reasons which have impelled me to renounce the throne. But I want you to understand that in making up my mind I did not forget my country or the Empire which, as Prince of Wales and lately as King, I have for twenty-five years tried to serve. But you must believe me when I tell you that I have found it impossible to carry the heavy burden of responsibility and to discharge my duties as King as I would wish to do without the help and support of the woman I love.

5

E

The problem of origins, human and other, is not the least whit nearer its solution. In due time the Evolution theory will have to abate its vehemence, cannot be allow'd to dominate every thing else, and will have to take its place as a segment of the circle, the cluster – as one of many theories, many thoughts, of profoundest value – and readjusting and differentiating much, yet leaving the divine secrets just as inexplicable and unreachable as before – maybe more so.

5

b Explore the stylistic characteristics of the extracts you think are from public speeches. Compare them with one extract you think is from a written genre.

Writing in the exam

The information you lacked in Activity 21 was information about *context* and *audience*. When analysing spoken texts, always start from:
- what you know, or can deduce, about the speaker
- the circumstances the speaker is in
- the audience the speaker is addressing.

Do *not* start by making general observations about style and language – along the lines of 'the listing technique is typical of speeches' or 'the speech has a formal register'.

Activity 22

1 Extracts **B**, **C** and **D** above are from public speeches. With a partner, match them with the following pieces of information:

- Lord Shaftesbury speaking in a parliamentary debate in 1856
- Mahatma Gandhi defending himself at his trial for sedition in 1922
- Edward VIII speaking in a radio broadcast in 1936.

2 Almost all public speeches, whether live or broadcast, are first written before they are delivered. Talk about how extracts **B**, **C** and **D** display some characteristic features of written texts as well as spoken ones. Then share your ideas in class discussion.

(Extract **A** is from Queen Victoria's diary for 1837. Extract **E** is from an essay by Walt Whitman written about Charles Darwin in 1869.)

Live speeches

Live speeches address a public audience in a specific public context. In an age of telecommunication, such speeches are often relayed to a wider general audience – for example, political speeches during election campaigns or at party conferences. The speakers are well aware of this wider audience and target it accordingly.

Activity 23 helps you explore a politician's use of a live speech to appeal to an audience 'in the hall' *and* a television audience. You will judge how effective the speech is in achieving its purposes by looking closely at the speaker's lexis, register and use of **rhetorical devices**.

Activity 23

Read the text below. It is from Tony Blair's platform speech at the Labour Party Conference in September 1997, after 'New Labour' had won the general election in May. The Conservatives had been in power since 1979.

It has been a very long time waiting for this moment and all I can tell you is that after eighteen long years of Opposition, I am deeply proud – privileged – to stand before you as the
5 new Labour Prime Minister of our country.

I believe in Britain. I believe in the British people. One cross on the ballot paper. One nation was reborn.

Today, I want to set an ambitious course for this
10 country: to be nothing less than the model of a twenty-first-century nation, a beacon to the world. It means drawing deep into the richness of the British character. Creative. Compassionate. Outward-looking. Old British values, but a new
15 British confidence.

We can never be the biggest. We may never again be the mightiest. But we can be the best. The best place to live. The best place to bring up children, the best place to lead a fulfilled life, the
20 best place to grow old. …

[speech continues for 5 pages]

You remember how your parents, like mine, used to say to you: 'Just do your best'. Well, let us do our best. On May 1st, the people entrusted me with the task of leading their country into a new
25 century. That was your challenge to me. And proudly, humbly, I accepted it.

Today, I issue a challenge to you. Help us make Britain that beacon shining throughout the world. Unite behind our mission to modernise our
30 country for all our people. For there is a place for all the people in new Britain, and there is a role for all the people in its creation. Believe in us as much as we believe in you.

Give just as much to our country as we all of
35 us intend to give. Give your all. Make this the giving age.

'By the strength of our common endeavour, we achieve more together than we can alone'. On May 1st 1997, it wasn't just the Tories who were
40 defeated. Fear of change was defeated. Cynicism was defeated. Did I not say it would be a battle of hope against fear? On May 1st 1997, fear lost. Hope won. The Giving Age began.

1 Work in a group. Imagine you are Blair and his advisers meeting in advance to decide on the 'keynotes' of the speech. Use evidence from the text to fill in a diagram like the one below showing the keynote themes you want to include.

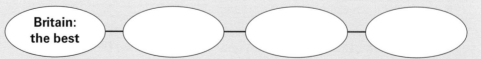

Britain: the best

Put these in what you think was their order of importance to New Labour.

2 a Share your ideas in class discussion. Then take three keynotes you agree about. Look through the speech carefully and list all the single words and phrases that relate to each of these keynotes. Put them in three separate columns.

b How frequently do these keynote words and phrases appear? Do they appear in specific parts of the speech or are they 'threaded through' it? Depending on your answer, decide on two clear statements you are now able to make about the structure of the speech.

3 Work with a partner.

a Take turns to read Blair's speech aloud, paragraph by paragraph. Deliberately exaggerate its prosodic and paralinguistic features to bring them out as strongly as possible. Then discuss the extent to which this speech depends for its impact upon live performance. Cite particular uses of **prosodics**: volume, pitch, tone, pace and stress.

b Look at the five rhetorical devices listed below which are commonly used in platform speeches. You will recognise them from your work in Unit 2.

Superlative adjectives	First person pronouns	Syntactic parallelism
Positive **abstract vocabulary**	Words and phrases that assume shared values	

Find examples in Blair's speech of the devices listed. Discuss their intended effect on listeners in the contexts where they appear.

Then identify up to five more rhetorical devices in the speech and make brief notes about:

- the effect they are intended to have
- their effectiveness in context.

4 Share your ideas with the class. Have you found any rhetorical devices that seem designed to make a particular impact on a *television* audience?

5 Work together to reshape the first 10 lines of the speech, down to 'the best place to live', into an article by Tony Blair for a quality newspaper. Leave the content unchanged. Use the grammar, syntax and punctuation you would expect to find in a written text for a general adult readership.

6 Write two or three paragraphs comparing and contrasting the language of Blair's speech with the newspaper article you wrote. Comment on their linguistic features and the effect these are intended to have on their respective audiences.

Key terms

- rhetorical devices
- prosodics
- superlative adjectives
- syntactic parallelism
- abstract vocabulary

Writing in the exam

If the text you are given is from a live speech, the aspects of structure, form and language covered in Activity 23 are likely to be prominent in it. Refer back to the AS Student Book pages 130–132 to reinforce your understanding of how rhetorical devices can be used in speeches.

Broadcast speeches

Broadcast speeches target a TV or radio audience in order to inform and/or persuade. Activity 24 helps you explore the way a speaker on the radio uses structure and lexis adapted to that medium to influence a listening audience. You will also consider the speaker's use of prosodic features and the effects they achieve.

Activity 24

Read the text below. It is from a speech transmitted by German radio to Britain in November 1942. The speaker, John Amery, was strongly opposed to Churchill's government and to the allies.

Listeners will wonder what an Englishman is doing on the German radio tonight. You can imagine that before taking this step I hoped that someone better qualified than me would come forward. I dared to believe that some ray of common sense would guide the counsels of Mr Churchill's government. Unfortunately this has not been the case.

5   For two years, living in a neutral country, I have been able to see through the haze of propaganda to reach something which my conscience tells me is the truth. That is why I come forward tonight without any political label, without any bias, but just simply as an Englishman to say to you: a crime is being committed against civilization. Not only the priceless heritage of our fathers, of our seamen, of our Empire builders, is being thrown

10 away in a war that serves no British interests – but our alliance leader Stalin dreams of nothing but the destruction of the heritage of our fathers.

    Morally this is a stain on our honour; practically it can only lead sooner or later to disaster and Communism in Great Britain, to a disintegration of all the values we cherish most. It is not the government, the members of Parliament, to whom the ultimate

15 decision belongs. It is up to you to go forward sure of your sacred right of free opinion, sure of your patriotism. It is up to you to decide that this has lasted long enough, that our boys are dying to serve no British interest but for the interests of a small clique of unscrupulous men.

    There is more than enough room in the world for Germany and Britain. Your leaders

20 say Germany seeks world domination. Did it ever occur to your mind that this is but another trick of that long-planned strategy of Jewish propaganda, intended to thwart Germany's commanding position on the continent, to which she is, after all, entitled? However fantastic it may sound, the German Army is at this moment the only thing that stands between Communism and you, the only protection that exists for private property.

25 If that rampart collapsed your liberties would be a vague souvenir of a happy past.

1 Work with a partner. Explore the speaker's attitudes, values and ideas by considering how far his speech bears out the following:

John Amery is:

a a British patriot

b convinced that Churchill is a Communist

c more concerned about money than the survival of Britain

d not saying what he really thinks.

What do you think Amery's agenda is?

2 Share your ideas in class discussion. Then show how Amery's attitudes, values and ideas are conveyed to listeners by his use of:

- terms of address: 'You can imagine', 'our alliance leader Stalin', 'our boys', 'Your leaders'

- shifts in perspective in the course of the speech

- emotive and connotative language

- abstract lexis.

3 Work in a small group. Imagine you are Amery preparing to broadcast this speech. On a photocopy of the text, write instructions about the use you will make of prosodics as you deliver it. Think about: tone, pitch, pace, volume and stress. Annotate the text in your own way.

Read the speech to another group and listen to their version. Explain what you were trying to achieve. Judge the effect and the effectiveness of your readings.

John Amery

Writing in the exam

If the unprepared text you are given in Section A is from a radio or TV speech, focus strongly on this contextual factor as you make your analysis. Activities 24 and 25 remind you that speakers adapt their language to the medium and their sense of audience. In the exam, you need to show how.

Broadcast talks

Broadcast talks are less formal than speeches. Rather than addressing 'the public at large', the speaker will address an imagined listener as if in conversation. For example, the talk from which the next extract is taken begins: 'The other night, here in London, I did something I hadn't done for many months – I went to a cinema'. This is not to say, however, that the register of a broadcast talk will remain intimate or informal throughout.

Writing in the exam

The instruction for this task reproduces the wording of the Section A question.

J. B. Priestley

Activity 25

1 Read the text on the next page. It is taken from a BBC radio talk by J.B. Priestley in June 1940.

2 Write a critical analysis of this text. You should analyse how effectively the speaker's choices of structure, form and language convey attitudes, values and ideas in the writing.

Follow the **Advice for planning and writing a critical analysis** in Activity 20 on p 38.

It's a fact – and cold print could prove it – that about Hitler and the Nazis I have always held the same opinion – the opinion that they were evil, and that the time must come when either we must destroy them or they must destroy us; they were no more to be compromised with than typhoid fever
5   is to be compromised with. You might as well try to come to an amicable settlement with a pack of ravening wolves. My feeling from the first, I think, had nothing to do with economics and politics, but was really moral – or, if you like, religious. Here, in these cruel figures who emerged from the underworld, who promptly destroyed the cultural life of their country,
10   turned workers into serfs again, trained boys to be brutes, brushed away the last specks of honour, organised two new government departments – one for systematic lying; the other for equally systematic torture; and even perverted and poisoned the life of the family, so that school children became spies at the very dinner table – here, I say, was something that cut
15   deeper than the economic disagreements and political differences.

Here, I felt, was the growing corruption, the darkening despair of our modern world, shaping itself into one vast dark face – a German dark face, that would call to other dark faces elsewhere. Every nation has two faces – a bright face and a dark face. I had always been ready to love the
20   bright face of Germany which speaks to us of beautiful music, profound philosophy, Gothic romance, young men and maidens wandering through the enchanted forests. I had been to Germany before the last war, walking from one little inn to another in the Rhineland. After the war I went back, and wrote in praise of the noble Rhine, the wet lilac and the rust-
25   coloured Castle of Heidelberg, the carpets of flowers and the ice-green torrents of the Bavarian Alps. But after the Nazis came, I went no more. The bright face had gone, and in its place was a vast dark face with its broken promises and endless deceit, its swaggering Storm Troopers and dreaded Gestapo, its bloodstained basements where youths were hardened
30   by the torture of decent elderly folk – the terror and the shame, not just their shame, but our shame, the shame of the whole watching world, of the concentration camps.

4 Tackling Section A of the exam

Part 4 gives you advice about how to prepare for and perform well in Section A of the exam. It shows you how to:

- base your answer firmly on the wording of the question

- plan your answer so that it meets the two assessment objectives, AO1 and AO2

- build up your answer in a systematic and detailed way

- use quotation effectively so that your answer is specific, not general

- write your answer in a clear and fluent style.

What you have to do in the exam: a summary

1 You will read a non-fiction prose passage you have not seen before. It could be from a written or a spoken source, though it will *not* be a transcript of spontaneous speech. It could come from any time between the late 18th century and the present day. You choose the passage that relates to your topic area.

2 You have to identify and comment on the attitudes, values and ideas expressed by the writer or speaker.

3 You have to analyse the use of structure, form and language and show how these convey the attitudes, values and ideas of the writer or speaker.

4 You have to express your opinion about how effectively the writer or speaker achieves their purposes in the passage.

Learn by heart points **2**, **3** and **4**. If you base your exam answer on them you will have done everything the question asks you to do.

Planning your answer

Stage 1: How to read and annotate the passage

Read carefully the information you are given about the *context* of the passage. Underline anything that seems important: its date, facts about the writer/speaker, clues about its intended audience, whether it has a private or a public purpose and so on.

Then read the passage straight through, slowly, without annotating.

Read the passage again, paragraph by paragraph. Annotate it lightly as you read. Activity 26 on the next page illustrates a way of doing this.

Assessment objectives

Examiners use two assessment objectives for Section A. They are:
AO1 – Select and apply relevant concepts and approaches from integrated linguistic and literary study, using appropriate terminology and accurate, coherent written expression.
AO2 – Demonstrate detailed critical understanding in analysing the ways in which structure, form and language shape meanings in a range of spoken and written texts.

Writing in the exam

The exam question will be worded as follows: Write a critical analysis of the text you have read. You should analyse how effectively the writer's or speaker's choices of structure, form and language convey attitudes, values and ideas in the writing. In your response you should demonstrate your knowledge and understanding of literary and linguistic concepts.

Activity 26

1 Read the annotated paragraph below. It is the first half of an unprepared exam text in the topic area 'The Individual in Society'.

autobiographical

sketches of people he knew?

general public readership

The passage below is an extract from the memoir *Some People by Harold Nicolson, published in 1927. He was a journalist who went on to become a distinguished politician.*

between the wars

attitude

specific content

How fortuitous and yet how formative are the admirations which our school life thrusts upon us! With no man have I had less in common than with J.D. Marstock, and yet for years he exercised upon me an influence which, though

attitude

5 negative, was intense. How clean he was, how straight, how manly! How proud we were of him, how modest he was about himself! And then those eyes – those frank and honest eyes!

a note of irony

public school context

'One can see,' my tutor said, 'that Marstock has never had a mean or nasty thought.' It took me six years to realise that

10 Marstock, although stuffed with opinions, had never had a thought at all.

attitude

I can visualise him best as he appeared when head of the school, when captain of football. A tall figure, he seemed, in his black and orange jersey striped like a wasp. Upon his

unflattering simile

JDM is vain

15 carefully oiled hair was stuck a little velvet cap with a gold tassel: he would walk away from the field, his large red hands pendant, a little mud upon his large red knees. He would pause for a moment and speak to a group of lower boys.

satirical?

'Yes, Marstock – no, Marstock' they would answer, and then

20 he would smile democratically, and walk on – a slight lilt in his gait betraying that he was not unconscious of how much he was observed.

vanity, again

2 Annotate with a partner the rest of the passage on the facing page. You will each need a copy of it. Try to pick out:

- words and phrases that show Nicolson's attitudes, values and ideas

- linguistic features that convey Nicolson's attitudes, values and ideas – look at lexical choices, any uses of figurative language, grammatical constructions, tone, sentence types and forms, punctuation

- structural features at text level that convey Nicolson's attitudes, values and ideas – look at the writer's viewpoint, how the whole passage is built up, the use of paragraphs, cohesive devices to link sentences and paragraphs, the beginning and the ending.

3 Discuss as a class what you have come up with. Justify the points you have made. Add any annotations you think are important.

Those wide open eyes that looked life straight, if unseeingly, in the face were fixed in front of him upon that distant clump of Wellingtonians, upon the two red towers of the college emerging behind. His cheeks, a little purple in the cold, showed traces of that eczema which so often accompanies adolescent youth. But it was not an ugly face. A large and fleshy nose: a thin mouth:
5 a well-formed chin: a younger and plumper Viscount Grey.

Under the great gate he went and across the quadrangle. He must first look in upon the Sixth Form room, a room reserved apparently for prefects who were seldom in the Sixth. He sank into a deck chair by the fire. The other prefects spoke to him about conditions in the Blucher dormitory and the date of the pancake run. Yes, he would have to tell the Master about the Blucher, and there
10 was no reason why they should not have the run on Tuesday. And then out under the great gate again and across through pine trees to Mr Kempthorne's house. There on the floor would be his basin ready for him and a can of hot water beside it. And he had ordered that seed-cake. The smell of cocoa met him as he entered the passage. Seed-cake, and cocoa, and Pears soap, and the soft hum of a kettle on the gas: then work for two hours and then prayers. He would read the roll-call
15 himself that evening. Oh yes! and afterwards there was a boy to be caned. The basket work of his armchair creaked as he leant forward for the towel.

Stage 2: How to turn annotations into a writing plan

Activity 27

1 Look over all the annotations on your copy of the Nicolson passage. Now group them together under the following headings.

   a The context of the passage – genre (type of writing), purpose, audience.

   b The writer's attitudes towards his subject – focus on key themes.

   c The writer's values and ideas – philosophical, moral, cultural (remember that these are likely to be implicit rather than stated explicitly).

   d The writer's use of lexis.

   e The writer's use of form and structure.

   f The effectiveness of the passage in achieving its purpose.

2 Compare the way you have grouped your annotations with a partner's. Explain how you have worked and discuss what you found most difficult. Make any changes you think are necessary.

3 Write a critical analysis of the Nicolson passage based on your six-part plan. Remember that 'critical' means 'using the concepts and terms of literary criticism and comment'; it does not mean 'criticising the way the passage is written'.

   You could base the order of your paragraphs on **a** to **e** above. Alternatively, you could integrate points about attitudes, values and ideas with points about structure, form and language. This second method is preferable if you feel confident enough to use it.

Using AO1 and AO2 to assess and improve your answer

Activity 28

1 Look at the mark-bands below. They show you the descriptors for the top bands of AO1 and AO2.

AO1 Band 3	AO2 Band 5
• Applies a significant range of relevant linguistic and literary concepts and approaches from integrated linguistic and literary study • Employs a wide range of terminology accurately • Writes with control, fluency and coherence.	• Engages fully and critically with the attitudes, values and ideas in the text, exploring, where appropriate, subtle, implied or embedded meanings • Demonstrates secure understanding of an extensive range of features of structure, form and language • Takes a precise and incisive analytical approach, exploring in detail a wide range of connections between features and their effects.

Discuss as a class the precise meaning of these six bullet points. Pick out the examiner's key words in each case.

2 Go through your analysis of the Nicolson passage. Judge your work first against the descriptors for Band 3 of AO1, then against the descriptors for Band 5 of AO2. Write at the bottom of your work:

AO1
• I met the following requirements …
• I still need to meet the following requirements …

AO2
• I met the following requirements …
• I still need to meet the following requirements …

Use the examiner's key words to help you decide what to say. Use your own words to say it. Your teacher can show whether they agree with you when they mark your analysis.

3 Use your own and your teacher's assessment to draw up a list of your main targets for the next time you practise an exam answer. Base these targets on the mark-bands for AO1 and AO2. Your list might look like this:

Targets for next time	
What I need to do …	**… to meet these assessment targets …**
1 Increase my use of literary terms	AO1, bullet point 1
2 Give a clearer structure to my answer as a whole	AO2, bullet point 3
3 Differentiate more clearly between attitudes, values and ideas	AO2, bullet point 1
4 Say more about the structure of the passage and how the writer uses it to convey A/V/I	AO2, bullet point 2

Improving your style and expression

This sub-section helps you to write clearly and fluently and to include in your answer an adequate range of linguistic/literary terms.

Activity 29

1 Read the extract below from an answer on the Nicolson passage.

> Harold Nicolson doesn't like public schools and the way they are run. You can tell this from the sarcastic way he says about the captain J.D. Marstock, 'how modest he was about himself!'. Later on he is shown as not being modest at all, as in the quote:
>
> 5   'he was not unconscious of how much he was observed'. 'Not unconscious' shows he actually liked being observed. He liked being looked up to by the 'lower boys', as we see from the way Nicolson quotes them sucking up to him 'Yes, Marstock – no, Marstock'. Public schools breed this sort of unhealthy hero worship. Just as they breed bullying, as we see
>
> 10 from the way Marstock is looking forward to caning a boy: 'Oh yes! and afterwards there was a boy to be caned'. The exclamation mark shows Marstock thought this was a highlight of his day. Nicolson is being very critical of a public school, of its bullying as well as its snobbery, there is a lot of sarcasm running right throughout his writing.

2 Rewrite this extract. Keep the same points, but try to:

- use a wider vocabulary

- include more critical terms

- improve the fluency of the style.

3 Read the short passage below. It is an extract from a diary written by Jane Welsh Carlyle in 1855. Then write about it as if you are in the exam, relating attitudes, values and ideas to uses of structure, form and language. Take no more than 20 minutes.

> A stormy day within doors, so I walked out early, and walked, walked, walked. If peace and quietness be not in one's own power, one can always give oneself at least bodily fatigue – no such bad succeedaneum* after all. Life gets to look for me like
> 5 a sort of kaleidoscope – a few things of different colours – black predominating, which fate shakes into new and ever new combinations, but always the same things over again. To-day has been so like a day I still remember out of ten years ago; the same still dreamy October weather, the same tumult of mind contrasting
> 10 with the outer stillness; the same causes for that tumult. Then, as now, I had walked, walked, walked with no aim but to tire myself.

*succeedaneum: therapy

4 Exchange your writing with a partner's. Compare the points you have made and the way you have expressed them. Be constructively critical of each other's work. Use AO1 and AO2 as a starting point and then focus on your choices of language, including linguistic/literary terms.

Activity 30

1 Read as a class the extract below from an analysis of the Jane Carlyle passage.

The writer is depressed. It has been 'a stormy day within doors', the metaphor suggesting that her family life is troubled. This impression is strengthened by her syntactically-balanced reference to 'the same tumult of mind ... the same causes for that tumult' ten years before and, in particular, by her use of the simile:

'Life gets to look for me like a sort of kaleidoscope ... black predominating'.

She conveys the extent of her mental 'tumult' by drawing a contrast between her inner turbulence and 'the dreamy October weather' outside, in which she 'walked, walked, walked' to find some peace of mind through tiring herself out. The emphatic repetition of the verb implies that the situation 'within doors' is serious and that she is determined to find relief from it through 'bodily fatigue'. It seems to work, as her rather wry, self-conscious reflection 'no such bad succeedaneum after all' shows.

This being the writer's personal diary, she confides her feelings frankly. However, there seems to be a limit to what she is able or willing to make explicit to herself even in this private context: 'so like a day I still remember ... the same causes'. Perhaps the reasons for her lack of 'peace and quietness' at home run so deep that she cannot bring herself to inspect them. There are strong suggestions, in fact, that she feels helpless to change things. She states categorically that a remedy is 'not in one's power', and her metaphor of 'fate' shaking the kaleidoscope of her life into 'new and ever newer combinations' gives the impression that she lacks power or volition over personal circumstances. Her fatalism is further suggested by her adverbial modifier 'one can always give oneself <u>at least</u> bodily fatigue' and her emphasis on 'always the same things over again' where the lexis reflects her frustration: she says the same thing in three different ways.

2 Evaluate as a class this writer's style and expression. How well does it meet the requirements of AO1 Band 3?

AO1 Band 3	AO2 Band 5
• Applies a significant range of relevant linguistic and literary concepts and approaches from integrated linguistic and literary study • Employs a wide range of terminology accurately • Writes with control, fluency and coherence.	• Engages fully and critically with the attitudes, values and ideas in the text, exploring, where appropriate, subtle, implied or embedded meanings • Demonstrates secure understanding of an extensive range of features of structure, form and language • Takes a precise and incisive analytical approach, exploring in detail a wide range of connections between features and their effects.

3 Now read the examiner's comments below on this analysis. Remember that it is not a full answer.

Were this level of response to be sustained throughout an answer in Section A, it would meet the requirements of the top band of AO1 and of the top band of AO2.

AO1: The response includes a very good range of points, all of them rooted clearly in linguistic and literary concepts. The approach is integrated, so that, for instance, the writer is able to respond both to figurative language and to syntactical structure in her first paragraph. There is a confident command of terminology. It is used accurately ('the emphatic repetition of the verb' ...'suggested by her adverbial modifier') and succinctly. The general vocabulary is wide and appropriately employed: 'She conveys the extent of ...', 'She states categorically that ...', 'her rather wry, self-conscious reflection'. This is a mature and fluently-written response which would be placed at the top of Band 3.

AO2: On the whole, the response engages authoritatively with the attitudes and feelings in the text, identifying the fatalistic outlook of the writer and suggesting that this passage is only partly typical of much diary writing. In paragraph 2 the writer comes dangerously close to speculation ('Perhaps the reasons ...'): it may have been better to relate the reticence in the text to its Victorian context. Structure, form and language are dealt with very well and in a specific way; it is pleasing that the response avoids generalisation. A strong feature is the embedding of quotation, so that the reader is kept continually in touch with the text and the writer can make pertinent reference to it throughout. The approach is analytical rather than narrative or discursive and, at times, incisive. This response would be placed in the middle of Band 5.

---

4 Finally, consider as a class the way the response to the Jane Carlyle passage employs reference and quotation. Use the examiner's comment on this as a starting point. Then discuss how far quotation achieves the following purposes within the response as a whole:

- to foreground the text

- to illustrate specific points about the text

- to help develop the analysis from point to point

- to make the writing more concise by integrating quotation into sentences

- to help give overall coherence to the writing.

Try to make your own use of quotation achieve all these purposes in your exam answer.

B Analysing prepared plays and poetry

This section introduces the prescribed plays and poems for Section B of Unit 3. You have to study EITHER a pair of plays OR a pair of poetry collections. These are linked to a topic area: 'A Sense of Place', 'The Individual in Society', 'Love and Loss', or 'Family Relationships'.

The main focus of your work will be a comparison of language techniques and literary devices in your paired texts. In making comparisons, you need to identify and comment on the contextual factors that influence the way your texts are written and received (see AO3 in the Assessment objectives box below).

Parts 1 and 3 below deal with prescribed plays. Parts 2 and 4 deal with prescribed poems. Part 5 shows you how to meet the requirements of the Section B exam for both plays and poems.

Assessment objectives

AO1 marks are awarded for selecting and applying relevant concepts and approaches from integrated linguistic and literary study, using appropriate terminology and accurate and coherent written expression (10 marks from a total of 60).

AO2 marks are awarded for demonstrating detailed critical understanding in analysing the ways in which structure, form and language shape meanings in a range of spoken and written texts (10 marks from a total of 60).

AO3 marks are awarded for using integrated approaches to explore relationships between texts, analysing and evaluating the significance of contextual factors in their production and reception (40 marks from a total of 60).

Across AS and A2

Refer back to Analysing Voices in Drama in Unit 1, particularly the 'key questions' about scripted plays on pp 39–40 of the AS Student Book. Your analysis of plays in Unit 3 will be a comparative one, but your detailed exploration of lexical, structural and prosodic features in drama at AS provides a platform for your work at A2. It also reminds you that, in making comparisons between plays, general points must be supported by specific textual analysis.

1 Comparing the key features of plays

Part 1 gives you guidance in making literary and linguistic connections between your chosen plays. It shows how to compare the ways in which your dramatists:

- make use of plot and setting
- construct character
- present themes
- make use of stage conventions.

Each sub-section below uses a different pairing from the specification to illustrate comparison of these key features of drama. The material can be readily adapted to the study of other pairs of plays.

Comparing the use of plot and setting

This sub-section helps you explore the use dramatists make of plot and setting to construct a theatrical narrative. It takes as its focus the pairing of *Translations* by Brian Friel and *Stuff Happens* by David Hare, in the topic area 'A Sense of Place'. Activities 31, 32, 34 and 36 can be used for any pair of prescribed plays.

Setting and context

Activity 31

1 Read with a partner the following stage directions from *Translations* and *Stuff Happens*.

From *Translations*:

> Act 1, Scene 1:
>
> The hedge-school is held in a disused barn or hay-shed or byre. Along the back wall are the remains of five or six stalls – wooden posts and chains – where cows were once milked and bedded. A double door, left, large enough to allow a cart to enter. A window right. A wooden stairway without a banister leads to the upstairs living-quarters (off) of the schoolmaster and his son … At the door is a pail of water and a soiled towel. The room is comfortless and functional – there is no trace of a woman's hand.

(line 5 marked in margin)

From *Stuff Happens*:

> Act 1, Scene 1:
>
> As the audience arrives, the cast are already assembling on stage. Then the lights change and one of the Actors speaks.

> Act 1, Scene 2:
>
> Another Actor steps forward.

> Act 1, Scene 4:
>
> Bush, fastidiously punctual, is already in place, sitting alone at the head of a torpedo-shaped table.

> Act 1, Scene 7:
>
> The War Cabinet – including Bush, Rice, Wolfowitz, Powell, Tenet, Cheney and Rumsfeld, now in casual clothes – assemble at Camp David.

Scene from *Stuff Happens*

Decide which of the following descriptions could apply to one or both of these plays, on the evidence of the stage directions:

- a play about political events
- a play with a conventional set and staging
- a play set in the recent past
- a **domestic drama**
- a play set in the distant past
- a play with social themes
- a play with an unconventional set and staging
- a **public drama**

2 Share your responses with the class. Then read aloud the first 10–12 pages of your two chosen plays.

Key terms

- psychological drama
- public drama
- domestic drama
- theatrical time

3 a Fill in a copy of the table below.

The setting of plays	*Translations* OR your 1st play	*Stuff Happens* OR your 2nd play
What the setting suggests about the play's social context	Comments: Evidence:	Comments: Evidence:
The perspective (or viewpoint) in which the audience sees events	Comments: Evidence:	Comments: Evidence:
What kind of play this seems to be, e.g. a tragedy, a comedy, a **psychological drama**, a play of ideas, etc.	Comments: Evidence:	Comments: Evidence:

b Consider the titles of your two plays. Can you relate them to what you have decided about their setting and viewpoint in **a** above?

Activity 32

1 Look over the first Act of *each* of your plays. Compare the dramatists' use of plot and setting by discussing as a class:

a the way the plot develops in each play. Does it:
  - follow an unbroken linear course (like the links in a chain) or is it divided into distinct episodes
  - follow real time (by the clock) or **theatrical time**
  - move into the inner lives of the characters or in a more social direction
  - move towards conflict or away from it?

b how the setting is important to the plot of each play. Does it act as:
  - a 'backdrop' to events
  - a means of clarifying events to the audience
  - an integral part of events
  - a combination of these?

Support your ideas with textual reference and explanation.

2 From the second Act of *each* of your plays, choose a short episode which you think marks an important development in the plot. This could be, for example, when:

  - new information is revealed about the past

  - new information, which is likely to affect the future is revealed

  - a character is shown in a new light

  - a relationship between two characters takes a new turn.

Put yourself in the place of a theatre director. Make brief notes about how you would present these episodes on stage, making the audience aware of the play's changed (or changing) focus.

3 Share your ideas in small group discussion. You could direct other group members to act the episodes in the way you see them.

4 Working as a class, take an overview of your two plays. Discuss and make notes about:

  - how the social context of each play relates to its themes as you understand them

  - how the setting(s) of each play help clarify these themes to the audience.

Present your notes in a comparative way. You could use two columns, parallel boxes, paired segments of a circle and so on.

Take it further

Choose two or three short episodes from your plays and annotate them as if you are a director planning a performance. Focus on the use of setting and staging – positioning, interaction between characters, moves on stage, the pace and rhythm of lines and so on. Taking this approach to the text as a *script* will teach you a lot about your dramatists' techniques.

Complication and conflict

Activity 33

1 Read the extracts from *Translations* and *Stuff Happens* below.

From *Translations*:

> *The following night.*
>
> *This scene may be played in the schoolroom, but it would be preferable to lose – by lighting – as much of the schoolroom as possible, and to play the scene down front in a vaguely 'outside' area.*
>
> MAIRE: O my God, that leap across the ditch nearly killed me.
> YOLLAND: I could scarcely keep up with you.
> MAIRE: Wait till I get my breath back.
> YOLLAND: We must have looked as if we were being chased.
> *They now realise they are alone and holding hands – the beginnings of embarrassment. The hands disengage. They begin to drift apart. Pause.*
> MAIRE: Manus'll wonder where I've got to.
> YOLLAND: I wonder did anyone notice us leave.
> *Pause. Slightly further apart.*
> MAIRE: The grass must be wet. My feet are soaking.
> YOLLAND: Your feet must be wet. The grass is soaking.
> *Another pause. Another few paces apart. They are now a long distance apart from one another.*
> *(Indicating himself)* George.
> *Maire nods:* Yes – yes. Then:
> MAIRE: Lieutenant George.

From *Stuff Happens*:

> *The Security Council arrives. Also the foreign ministers and their ambassadors.*
>
> AN ACTOR: On February 5th Colin Powell goes to the UN to demonstrate the US government's case for 'imminent threat'. He calls it his 'Adlai Stevenson moment'. The Head of a White House Communications team, Dan Bartlett, has a different name for the same occasion:
> BARTLETT: We call it 'the Powell buy-in'.
> *Powell is at the UN making his presentation.*
> POWELL: My colleagues, every statement I make today is backed up by sources, solid sources. These are not assertions. What we're giving you are facts and conclusions based on solid intelligence.
> AN ACTOR: In fact, Powell has spent the last four days angrily throwing out most of the two-hundred-minute speech Cheney, the CIA and the Pentagon have given him to read.
> *At once Powell is back in his own office.*
> POWELL: This is just garbage! What is this stuff? Who gave us this garbage? Does anybody believe this garbage? I'm not saying this shit!
> *Powell returns to the UN.*
> Mr President, Mr Secretary General, distinguished colleagues, I cannot tell you everything that we know. But what I can share with you, when combined with what all of us have learned over the years, is deeply troubling.

2 These extracts mark major turning points in the plays' plots. Discuss with a partner why they do so, and in what ways. You might consider:

- the different social/cultural backgrounds of Maire and Yolland

- Brian Friel's stage directions at the start of this Scene

- Colin Powell's relationship with President Bush before and after this point

- David Hare's stage directions in this Scene.

3 Share your ideas in a class discussion. Then consider how each dramatist makes the issue of *language* central to :

a these extracts
b *Translations* and *Stuff Happens* as a whole.

Talk about:

- the linguistic barrier between Maire and Yolland in the extract

- the way in which different languages create complication and conflict in *Translations*

- the differences between Colin Powell's public and private language in the extract

- the way in which the language of politics and diplomacy creates complication and conflict in *Stuff Happens*.

Activity 34

1 Working in a small group, select a major turning point in the plot of each of your plays. It should be an episode where conflict is EITHER heightened OR resolved. Read aloud your chosen episodes.

2 Fill in a copy of the table below, either by yourself or in your group.

Conflict in the play	1st play	2nd play
Main causes of the conflict	Comments: Evidence:	Comments: Evidence:
How the conflict is presented on stage	Comments: Evidence:	Comments: Evidence:
Consequences of the conflict	Comments: Evidence:	Comments: Evidence:

3 In class discussion, explore the way in which the plots of your plays as a whole move towards conflict OR move towards the resolution of conflict. Quote from each text to illustrate your comparative points.

Endings

Activity 35

1 Read aloud the endings of *Translations* (from 'HUGH: Take care, Owen. To remember everything is a form of madness') and *Stuff Happens* (Scene 24).

Then consider as a class:
- each dramatist's reasons for his choice of ending
- how each ending gives the audience a perspective on the events and themes of the whole play
- whether, as a reader/viewer, you find these endings effective.

2 a Discuss with a partner alternative ways in which Friel and Hare could have ended their plays. (Both dramatists, in fact, changed their original endings in the course of rehearsal. Hare did so several times.)

b Justify one or both of your alternative endings in class discussion. Explain:
- how consistent it is with the direction in which the play has been moving
- how it leaves the audience feeling about the play's main characters
- how it gives emphasis to a key theme, or key themes, in the play as a whole.

Take it further

Rewrite the ending of one or both of your plays. Annotate your writing to show the effects you were trying to achieve and the thinking behind them.

Activity 36

Adapt Activity 35 to your plays.

Comparing techniques of characterisation

This sub-section helps you explore the way dramatists construct their characters and present them to the audience. It takes as its focus the pairing of *Othello* by William Shakespeare and *Equus* by Peter Shaffer, in the topic area 'The Individual in Society'. Activities 38, 39, 41 and 43 can be used for any pair of prescribed plays.

Remember that 'character' is an object of the dramatist's craft. Characters in plays are not real people. '**Characterisation**' is the craft that creates character.

Key terms

• **characterisation**

• **idiolect**

• **blank verse**

Idiolect

Activity 37

Read the extracts from *Othello* and *Equus* below.

From *Othello*:

> OTHELLO: O blood, Iago, blood!
>
> IAGO: Patience I say, your mind perhaps may change.
>
> OTHELLO: Never, Iago. Like to the Pontic sea,
> 5   Whose icy current, and compulsive course,
>   Ne'er feels retiring ebb, but keeps due on
>   To the Propontic, and the Hellespont:
>   Even so my bloody thoughts, with violent pace
>   Shall ne'er look back, ne'er ebb to humble love,
>   Till that a capable and wide revenge
> 10   Swallow them up. Now by yond marble heaven,
>   In the due reverence of a sacred vow,
>   I here engage my words.

From *Equus*:

> ALAN: Stay, Equus. No one said Go! … That's it. He's
>   good. Equus the Godslave, Faithful and True. Into my
>   hands he commends himself – naked in his chinkle-
>   chankle. [*He punches* NUGGET] Stop it! … He wants to
> 5   go so badly.
> DYSART: Go, then. Leave me behind. Ride away now, Alan!
>   … Now you are alone with Equus.
> [*ALAN stiffens his body*]
> ALAN [*ritually*]: Equus – son of Fleckwus – son of Neckwus
> 10   … *Walk* …Here we go. The King rides out on Equus,
>   mightiest of horses. Only I can ride him. He lets me turn
>   him this way and that. His neck comes out of my body. It
>   lifts, in the dark. Equus, my God-slave! … Now the King
>   commands you. Tonight, we ride against them all.

1 Working in a small group, compare and contrast the **idiolects** (distinctive styles of speech, unique to the individual) of Othello and Alan in the extracts. Focus on the following points:

In *Othello*:

– the register (level of formality) of Othello's speech
– the grammatically complex sentence structures Othello uses
– Othello's lexical choices, for example 'Like to the Pontic sea', 'ne'er ebb to humble love', 'Swallow them up'
– the medium of **blank verse**.

In *Equus*:

– the register (level of formality) of Alan's speech
– the grammatically simple sentence structures Alan uses
– Alan's lexical choices, for example, 'Godslave, Faithful and True', 'The King rides out on Equus, mightiest of horses'
– the medium of prose.

2 Share your ideas in class discussion. What does the lexis of Othello and Alan suggest about their personalities? How does it show them to be gripped by powerful feelings in the above extracts?

Activity 38

Choose a central character from each of your plays. With the help of your teacher, select a speech or a passage of dialogue that typifies their language use. Adapt Activity 37 to your plays, devising suitable comparative questions about the use of idiolect.

Take it further

Put yourself into role as a/the central character in one of your plays. Imagine a meeting with a/the central character from your other play. Write the dialogue, trying to reproduce their idiolects faithfully. Then make an analysis of the way in which you have characterised them through your choice and use of language.

Activity 39

1 Working with a partner, choose a character from each of your plays whose idiolect *contrasts* with that of the character you discussed in Activity 38. Show the main contrasts by filling in two copies of the table below, one for your first play and one for your second. Base your analysis on specific extracts from each play.

1st play – extract on page 59	Character A	Character B
Idiolect: lexical choices	Comments: Evidence:	Comments: Evidence:
Idiolect: grammar and syntax	Comments: Evidence:	Comments: Evidence:
Idiolect: register and prosodic features	Comments: Evidence:	Comments: Evidence:

How do these differences in idiolect reflect the relationship between Characters A and B? Consider why their relationship is important to the play as a whole.

2 Share your ideas in class discussion. Then turn attention to the character you regard as central in each of your plays. Othello speaks differently in a public context from the way he speaks in a private one. Alan in *Equus* has one register he uses with Dysart and another register he uses with Equus.

Consider variations in the speech style of the central character in each of your plays. Why do they speak differently in different contexts or at different points? As a starting point, discuss these possible reasons:

- they are shown to have a public face and a private face
- they are shown to have an outer life and an inner life
- they are shown in the course of the play to develop a new, or changed, identity.

Interaction

Activity 40

Working with a partner, read the extract below from near the end of *Equus*.

JILL: See, it's all shut. There's just us … Let's sit down. Come on.
[*They sit together on the same bench, left*]
Hallo.
5 ALAN: [quickly] Hallo.
[*She kisses him lightly. He responds. Suddenly a faint trampling of hooves, off-stage, makes him jump up*]
JILL: What is it?
10 [*He turns his head upstage, listening*]
Relax. There's no one here. Come here.
[*She touches his hand. He turns to her again*]
You're very gentle. I love that …
ALAN: So are you … I mean …

[*He kisses her spontaneously. The hooves trample again, harder. He breaks away from her abruptly towards the upstage corner*] 15
JILL: [rising] What is it?
ALAN: Nothing! …
JILL: [gently] Take your sweater off. 20
ALAN: What?
JILL: I will if you will.
[*He stares at her. A pause*]
ALAN: You're … You're very …
JILL: So are you … [Pause] Come here. 25
[*He goes to her. She comes to him. They meet in the middle, and hold each other, and embrace*]
ALAN [*to* DYSART]: She put her mouth in mine. It was lovely. *Oh, it was lovely!*

1 Consider how the language of this extract creates the relationship between Alan and Jill for the audience. Focus on:

- the register and tone of each speaker
- the main sentence types used by each speaker
- the use of **ellipses**, pauses and other **non-fluency features**
- the dramatist's use of a **sub-text**.

2 Share your responses in class discussion. Then discuss how this interaction between Alan and Jill creates tension and suspense for the audience. Why is it a key episode in *Equus*?

3 Read aloud the extract from Act 5, Scene 2 of *Othello*, beginning at line 23 ('DESDEMONA: Who's there? Othello?') and ending on line 41 ('OTHELLO: And for that thou diest').

Compare and contrast the linguistic features of this extract with those of the extract from *Equus* above. How does the interaction between Othello and Desdemona create tension and suspense for the audience? Why is it a key episode in *Othello*?

Activity 41

With the help of your teacher, choose short extracts from near the end of each of your plays that show an important stage in the relationship between two major characters. Adapt Activity 40 in order to compare:

- their main linguistic features
- the importance of your extracts to the play as a whole.

Key terms

- ellipsis (ellipses)
- non-fluency features
- sub-text

Sympathetic or unsympathetic portrayals?

Activity 42

1 Working on *Othello* in a small group, discuss your personal responses to

a Iago   **b** Cassio.

Do you find Shakespeare's portrayal of them to be sympathetic, unsympathetic or balanced between the two?

Now divide your group. Sub-group 1 should argue a case for seeing each of them as being presented sympathetically. Sub-group 2 should argue a case for the opposite. Refer to particular passages in the text to support your case.

2 **a** Discuss as a class the evidence you find in the text for Shakespeare's portrayal of Othello being:

- essentially sympathetic
- essentially unsympathetic.

If you have watched a DVD of the play in performance, refer to that too.

b Consider how your view of Othello is bound up with the *language* Shakespeare gives him. Use his dying speech in the play, as printed opposite as a reference point:

> OTHELLO: … then must you speak
>   Of one that lov'd not wisely, but too well:
>   Of one not easily jealous, but being wrought,
>   Perplex'd in the extreme; of one whose hand
> 5   Like the base Indian, threw a pearl away,
>   Richer than all his tribe: of one whose subdued eyes,
>   Albeit unused to the melting mood,
>   Drops tears as fast as the Arabian trees
>   Their medicinal gum; set you down this,
> 10 And say besides, that in Aleppo once,
>   Where a malignant and a turban'd Turk
>   Beat a Venetian, and traduc'd the state,
>   I took by the throat the curcumcised dog,
>   And smote him thus.   [*Stabs himself*]

Take it further

Make a 'sympathy grid' for each of your plays. Place the leading characters on it to show how sympathetically/ unsympathetically you feel they are portrayed. Provide a key to explain your decisions.

Look closely at the two registers here: that of the soldier and that of the lover.

a malignant and a turban'd Turk	a pearl / Richer than all his tribe
took by the throat the circumcised dog	melting mood
smote him thus	Drops tears as fast as the Arabian trees / Their medicinal gum

c Has Othello's language changed in the course of the play? How do you respond to his next lines: 'I kiss'd thee ere I killed thee, no way but this, / Killing myself, to die upon a kiss'?

d It has been said that Othello is 'perplex'd in the extreme' because he can think and express himself in only one dimension. Do you think this is a valid point? Does it affect your sympathy for him, or lack of it, in the play?

3 Compare your response to Shakespeare's portrayal of Othello with your response to Peter Shaffer's portrayal of Alan Strang.

Discuss in a small group how far you see Alan as being:

- 'perplex'd in the extreme'
- unable to communicate, verbally and emotionally, in a normal way
- a victim of his background and upbringing
- a psychotic killer

Does Shaffer make you feel sympathetic to Alan in the play as a whole? If there is disagreement about this, be clear about how you respond to the dramatist's *characterisation* of him rather than to his 'character'.

Activity 43

Adapt Activity 42 in order to compare the dramatists' presentation of central characters in your plays. How sympathetic do you find their portrayals to be? Your exploration should be text-based and balanced: it is rarely the case that leading characters in drama are presented in a black and white way.

Comparing the presentation of themes

This sub-section helps you explore the way dramatists present their themes to the audience. It takes as its focus the pairing of *All My Sons* by Arthur Miller and *A Doll's House* by Henrik Ibsen, in the topic area 'Family Relationships'. Activities 45, 47 and 49 can be used for any pair of prescribed plays.

Plot or theme?

The plot of a play is its story or narrative. Its themes are the ideas about human life, which the plot is used to explore. The audience *interprets* a play's themes from:

- the plot the dramatist presents them with
- the way he or she presents it.

Activity 44

1 Read the extracts from *A Doll's House* and *All My Sons* opposite. You will need a copy of the extracts to highlight and annotate.

Highlight any parts of these two texts that develop, or give new information about, the plays' plots. Then use a different highlighter to mark any parts that reveal or convey the plays' themes.

From *A Doll's House*:

NORA: We'll drink champagne until dawn! [*Calls*] And, Helen! Put out some macaroons! Lots of macaroons, for once!

HELMER [*takes her hand in his*]: Now, now, now. Don't get so excited. Where's my little songbird, the one I know?

NORA: All right. Go and sit down – and you too, Dr Rank. I'll be with you in a minute. Christine, you must help me put my hair up.

RANK [*quietly, as they go*]: There's nothing wrong, is there? I mean, she isn't, she isn't er – expecting?

HELMER: Good heavens, no, my dear chap. She just gets scared like a child sometimes – I told you before – [*They go out, right*]

NORA: Well?

MRS LINDE: He's left town.

NORA: I saw it from your face.

MRS LINDE: He'll be back tomorrow morning. I left a note for him.

NORA: You needn't have bothered. You can't stop anything now. Anyway, it's too wonderful, really, in a way – sitting here and waiting for the miracle to happen.

MRS LINDE: Waiting for what?

NORA: Oh, you wouldn't understand. Go in and join them. I'll be with you in a moment.

MRS LINDE goes into the dining-room

NORA [*stands for a moment as though collecting herself. Then she looks at her watch*]: Five o'clock. Seven hours till midnight. Then another twenty-four hours till midnight tomorrow. And then the tarantella will be finished. Twenty-four and seven? Thirty-one hours to live.

HELMER [*appears in the doorway*, right]: What's happened to my little songbird?

NORA [*rushes to him with her arms wide*]: Your songbird is here!

From *All My Sons*:

CHRIS: Dad! Dad!

KELLER [*trying to hush him*]: I didn't kill anybody!

CHRIS: Then explain it to me. What did you do? Explain it to me or I'll tear you to pieces.

KELLER [*horrified at his overwhelming fury*]: Don't, Chris, don't –

CHRIS: I want to know what you did, now what did you do? You had a hundred and twenty cracked engine-heads, now what did you do?

KELLER: If you're going to hang me, then I –

CHRIS: I'm listening. God Almighty, I'm listening!

KELLER [*their movements now are those of subtle pursuit and escape. KELLER keeps a step out of Chris's range as he talks*]: You're a boy, what could I do! I'm in business, a man is in business; a hundred and twenty cracked, you're out of business; you got a process, the process don't work you're out of business; you don't know how to operate, your stuff is no good; they close you up, they tear up your contracts, what the hell's it to them? You lay forty years into a business, what could I do, let them take forty years, let them take my life away? [*His voice cracking*] … Chris … Chris, I did it for you, it was a chance and I took it for you. I'm sixty-one years old, when would I have another chance to make something for you? Sixty-one years old you don't get another chance, do ya?

CHRIS: You knew they wouldn't even hold up in the air.

2 Compare your highlightings in class discussion. Then add boxes in the margin noting your response to the themes. They could include:

A Doll's House Theme of the middle-class woman trapped by marriage and social convention suggested by 'What's happened to my little songbird?' / 'Your little songbird's here'.

All My Sons Theme of family loyalty versus responsibility to wider society suggested by 'I didn't kill anybody' and 'Chris … Chris, I did it for you'.

Try to create two or three further boxes for each extract. They should be based on your responses to:

- the character's lexis, including imagery (figurative language)
- contrasts between characters and their idiolects
- the repetition of key words and phrases.

3 Working in a small group, use your copies of the extracts to compare the way Ibsen and Miller reveal and convey their plays' themes. What similarities or differences do you find in the techniques they use? Make careful notes. Then report back your ideas to the class.

Key term

- juxtaposition

Activity 45

With the help of your teacher, choose two extracts, one from each of your plays, that reveal and convey key themes. On a copy of these, make annotations in the way suggested in stages 1 and 2 of Activity 44 on page 62. Then adapt stage 3 of Activity 44 to your plays, ensuring that your notes are comparative.

Use of dialogue

A play's themes emerge from the dialogue the dramatist gives his characters to speak. Dialogue can be described linguistically as a **juxtaposition** of idiolects – that is, the setting of one character's lexis and speech style against another's. Out of these interactions the main issues and ideas of the play come into focus for the audience.

Activity 46

1 Read aloud the extracts from *A Doll's House* below and *All My Sons* on the facing page.

From *A Doll's House*:

> NORA [*quickly*]: He must never see that letter. Tear it up. I'll find the money somehow –
> KROGSTAD: I'm sorry, Mrs Helmer, I thought I'd explained –
> NORA: Oh, I don't mean the money I owe you. Let me know how much
> 5   you want from my husband and I'll find it for you.
> KROGSTAD: I'm not asking your husband for money.
> NORA: What do you want, then?
> KROGSTAD: I'll tell you. I want to get on my feet again, Mrs Helmer.
> I want to get to the top. And your husband's going to help me. For
> 10   eighteen months now, my record's been clean. I've been in hard straits
> all that time: I was content to fight my way back inch by inch. Now I've
> been chucked back into the mud, and I'm not going to be satisfied with
> just getting back my job. I'm going to get to the top, I tell you. I'm going
> to get back into the bank, and it's going to be higher up. Your husband's
> 15   going to create a new job for me –
> NORA: He'll never do that!
> KROGSTAD: Oh, yes, he will. I know him. He won't dare to risk a scandal.
> And once I'm in there with him, you'll see! Within a year I'll be his
> right-hand man. It'll be Nils Krogstad who'll be running that bank, not
> 20   Torvald Helmer!
> NORA: That will never happen.
> KROGSTAD: Are you thinking of – ?
> NORA: Now I *have* the courage.
> KROGSTAD: Oh, you can't frighten me. A pampered little pretty
> 25   like you –
> NORA: You'll see! You'll see!
> KROGSTAD: Under the ice? Down in the cold, black water? And then, in
> the spring, to float up again, unrecognizable, hairless – ?
> NORA: You can't frighten me.
> 30   KROGSTAD: And you can't frighten me.

From *All My Sons*:

> MOTHER: I had a terrible night. [*She stops moving*] I never had a night
>   like that.
> CHRIS [*looking at Keller*]: What was it, mom? Did you dream?
> MOTHER: More, more than a dream.
> 5 CHRIS [*hesitantly*]: About Larry?
> MOTHER: I was fast asleep, and – [*Raising her arm over the audience*]
>   Remember the way he used to fly low past the house when he was in
>   training? When we used to see his face in the cockpit going by? Only
>   high up. Way, way up, where the clouds are. He was so real I could
> 10   reach out and touch him. And suddenly he started to fall. And crying,
>   crying to me … Mom, Mom! I could hear him like he was in the room.
>   Mom! … it was his voice! If I could only – [*Breaks off, allowing her
>   outstretched hand to fall*] I woke up and it was so funny – The wind …
>   it was like the roaring of his engine. I came out here … I must have
> 15   been half asleep. I could hear that roaring like he was going by. The tree
>   snapped right in front of me – and I like – came awake. [*She is looking
>   at the tree. She suddenly realizes something, turns with a reprimanding
>   finger shaking slightly at Keller*] See? We should never have planted that
>   tree. I said so in the first place; it was too soon to plant a tree for him.
> 20 CHRIS [*alarmed*]: Too soon!
> MOTHER [*angering*]: We rushed into it. Everybody was in such a hurry to
>   bury him. I *said* not to plant it yet. [*To Keller*]: I *told* you to - !
> CHRIS: Mother, Mother! [*She looks into his face*] The wind blew it down.
>   What significance has that got? What are you talking about? Mother,
> 25   please … Don't go through it all again, will you? It's no good, it doesn't
>   accomplish anything. I've been thinking, y'know? – maybe we ought to
>   put our minds to forgetting him?
> MOTHER: That's the third time you've said that this week.
> CHRIS: Because it's not right; we never took up our lives again. We're like
> 30   at a railroad station waiting for a train that never comes in.

2 Working in a small group, copy and fill in the tables below. Look carefully at the characters' lexical choices, register, syntax and use of prosodics before you make your entries.

A Doll's House – themes explored through dialogue
Nora and Krogstad
Nora's preoccupations:
How her use of language reflects these:
Krogstad's preoccupations:
How his use of language reflects these:

All My Sons – themes explored through dialogue
Mother and Chris
Mother's preoccupations:
How her use of language reflects these:
Chris's preoccupations:
How his use of language reflects these:

3 Share your responses in class discussion. Then set these extracts in the context of the plays as a whole. Talk about:

- which linguistic features are typical of each character's idiolect – how do these convey their attitudes and feelings?

- what kind of relationship is created here between the characters – how is this used to illustrate major themes in the play?

Key terms

- parallel plot
- parallel action
- symbols
- motifs
- sub-plot

4 Choose one further extract from *A Doll's House* and one further extract from *All My Sons*. They should be taken from near the end of the plays.

Work as a class to explore:

a what the dialogue reveals about major themes

b how its linguistic features help to convey these themes to the audience.

Use the same approach as in stage 2 of this activity. Then discuss the similarities/differences in the way Ibsen and Miller use dialogue to give the audience a perspective on the themes they deal with.

Take it further

Irrespective of the plays you are studying, make a comparative analysis of the uses of language by Krogstad and Mother in the extracts on pp 64–65. Relate your comments to what the language reveals about their personalities.

Activity 47

Adapt Activity 46 to your plays. With the help of your teacher, select two pairs of passages: one from before the midway point of your plays and one from near the end. It is important that you:

- focus on the linguistic features of the dialogue, not just on 'character'
- relate your comments on the extracts to themes of your plays
- make comparative points about the techniques used by your two dramatists.

Use of patterning, symbols and motifs

A play's themes are highlighted by the dramatist's use of structural patterns – for instance, **parallel plots**, **parallel action** across Acts and Scenes, and characters who mirror other characters to show similarity or difference. Visual **symbols** and verbal **motifs** also create a play's structural pattern, helping the audience to interpret themes clearly and imaginatively.

Activity 48

1 Discuss in a small group these questions about Ibsen's use of structural patterns in *A Doll's House*:

a How does the **sub-plot** centring on Krogstad and Mrs Linde give the audience a perspective on the relationship between Helmer and Nora? What thematic points does Ibsen convey by using this structural parallel?

b What contrasts in character are there between:

- Helmer and Krogstad
- Nora and Mrs Linde?

What thematic points does Ibsen convey by using these character contrasts?

c What contrasts are there between the endings of Act 1, Act 2 and Act 3? What thematic points does Ibsen convey by using this structural contrast?

2 Share your ideas in class discussion. Make sure that you not only *describe* the structural patterns you have found but also *explain* how they are used to convey themes.

3 Discuss these questions about Miller's use of structural patterns in *All My Sons*:

a How does the contrast between Joe Keller's life and that of his business partner Steve give the audience a perspective on Joe? What thematic points does Miller convey by using this contrast?

b What parallels and oppositions are there between Chris and George as sons in relation to their fathers? What thematic points does Miller convey by making the audience aware of these?

c What contrasts in character are there between Mother and Ann? What thematic points does Miller convey by using this character contrast?

4 Working with a partner, copy and complete the tables below.

Symbols and motifs used by Ibsen in *A Doll's House*	Symbols and motifs used by Miller in *All My Sons*
Symbol: The tarantella	**Symbol:** Larry's tree
Motif: The idea of entrapment – a doll in a doll's house = Nora, Christine (?) – 'I shall watch over you'	**Motif:** The idea of 'sons' – both individually and collectively = Larry, Chris and the dead pilots – 'I guess they were all my sons'

Try to make up to three further entries in each table. Then join up with another pair. Share your ideas. Discuss how the symbols and motifs in each play:

- highlight key themes and ideas
- gain meaning and importance by repetition
- help to give clarity and coherence to the dramatic structure.

Activity 49

Adapt Activity 48 to your plays. With the help of your teacher, devise suitable questions about structural patterns in stages 1 and 2. The exploration of symbols and motifs in stage 3 is directly relevant to all the prescribed plays.

The structural patterning of a play depends upon the dramatist and the techniques he decides to use. Ibsen and Miller use similar structural devices. Not all the paired dramatists do. Ensure that you take a comparative approach in order to identify similarities OR differences in their techniques.

Comparing the use of stage conventions

This sub-section helps you explore the way dramatists use stage conventions to realise their plays on stage and create a perspective for the audience. It takes as its focus the pairing of *The Glass Menagerie* by Tennessee Williams and *Betrayal* by Harold Pinter, in the topic area 'Love and Loss'. Activities 50, 52 and 54 can be used for any pair of prescribed plays.

> **Writing in the exam**
>
> The kind of structural features covered in this sub-section are most clearly illustrated in the theatre. They are much harder to recognise by simply reading the text. It is, therefore, highly desirable that you see live or recorded performances as you prepare for the exam. It is a good strategy to refer briefly to productions of your plays as you develop your answer in Section B.

Scene setting and the dramatist's purposes

Activity 50

1 Read the dramatists' notes/stage directions for *The Glass Menagerie* and *Betrayal* below.

From *The Glass Menagerie*:

> The Wingfield apartment is in the rear of the building, one of those vast hive-like conglomerations of cellular living-units that flower as warty growths in overcrowded urban centres of lower-middle-class population and are symptomatic of the impulse of this largest and fundamentally enslaved section of American society to avoid fluidity and differentiation and to exist and function as one interfused mass of automatism.
>
> The apartment faces an alley and is entered by a fire-escape, a structure whose name is a touch of accidental poetic truth, for all of these large buildings are always burning with the slow and implacable fires of human desperation. The fire-escape is included in the set – that is, the landing of it and steps descending from it.
>
> The scene is memory and is therefore non-realistic. Memory takes a lot of poetic licence. It omits some details; others are exaggerated, according to the emotional value of the articles it touches, for memory is seated predominantly in the heart. The interior is therefore rather dim and poetic.

(line numbers: 5, 10, 15, 20)

From *Betrayal*:

> Scene 1: Pub. 1977. Spring.
> Scene 2: Jerry's House. Study. 1977. Spring.
> Scene 3: Flat. 1975. Winter.
> Scene 4: Robert and Emma's House. Living Room. 1974. Autumn.
> Scene 5: Hotel Room. Venice. 1973. Summer.
> Scene 6: Flat. 1973. Summer.
> Scene 7: Restaurant. 1973. Summer.
> Scene 8: Flat. 1971. Summer.
> Scene 9: Robert and Emma's House. Bedroom. 1968. Winter.

(line numbers: 5, 10)

1 Imagine you know nothing whatever about these two plays. Discuss with a partner:

- what *kind* of play the dramatist's notes/stage directions lead you to expect in each case
- what differences there are in the nature of the information given here to the director and actors
- what you can infer about the two dramatists' purposes.

Share your ideas in a class discussion.

Now read the openings of *The Glass Menagerie* and *Betrayal* below.

From *The Glass Menagerie*:

> The narrator is an undisguised convention of the play. He takes whatever licence with dramatic convention is convenient to his purposes …
>
> TOM: Yes, I have tricks in my pocket, I have things up my sleeve. But I am the opposite of a stage magician. He gives you illusion that has the appearance of truth. I give you truth in the pleasant disguise of illusion.
>
> To begin with, I turn back time. I reverse it to that quaint period, the thirties, when the huge middle class of America was matriculating in a school for the blind. Their eyes had failed them, or they had failed their eyes, and so they were having their fingers pressed forcibly down on the fiery Braille alphabet of a dissolving economy.
>
> In Spain there was Guernica. Here there were disturbances of labour, sometimes pretty violent, in otherwise peaceful cities such as Chicago, Cleveland, Saint Louis …This is the social background of the play. [MUSIC]

(line numbers: 5, 10, 15, 20)

From *Betrayal*:

> Pub. 1977. Spring.
> Noon. *EMMA is sitting at a corner table. JERRY approaches her with drinks, a pint of bitter for him, a glass of wine for her.*
>
> *He sits. They smile, toast each other silently, drink. He sits back and looks at her.*
>
> JERRY: Well …
> EMMA: How are you?
> JERRY: All right.
> EMMA: You look well.
> JERRY: Well, I'm not all that well, really.
> EMMA: Why? What's the matter?
> JERRY: Hangover. [He raises his glass] Cheers. [He drinks] How are you?
> EMMA: I'm fine. [She looks round the bar, back at him] Just like old times.

(line numbers: 5, 10, 15)

2 Discuss the questions below.

a For what purpose do you think Tennessee Williams is using the stage convention of a narrator here? What kind of perspective does Tom give the audience on the events that are about to be shown?

b How does the opening of *Betrayal* dispense with some of the usual stage conventions of drama? How does this affect the audience's response?

3 Read aloud the first five pages of your plays. Then copy the table below and fill in the relevant parts.

Use of stage conventions at the beginning of plays	
1st play	**2nd play**
Usual conventions:	Usual conventions:
Unusual conventions:	Unusual conventions:
Dramatist's possible purposes:	Dramatist's possible purposes:

Use your tables to explore in class discussion the main stage conventions used in your plays *as a whole*. How do these compare and contrast? Do you find them effective in achieving the dramatists' purposes? Be precise about this. Make a comparative list and illustrate your points with textual reference.

Chronology

Dramatists sometimes disrupt the chronology of 'real time' for their own purposes. This is particularly the case in plays where 'the scene is memory', as Tennessee Williams notes about *The Glass Menagerie* (see p 68).

Activity 51

1 Working with a partner, re-read:

- Scene 9 and Scene 1 of *Betrayal* in that order
- Scene 7 of *The Glass Menagerie*.

Use these Scenes to consider the way each dramatist presents the theme of memory, love and loss to the audience.

In *Betrayal*, focus your discussion on:

- how the lexis of Jerry and Emma changes in the course of the play
- how time is shown to change people who believe themselves in love
- how memory is shown to be selective and sometimes distorting.

In *The Glass Menagerie*, focus your discussion on:
- how Laura's lexis changes in the course of Scene 7
- how time is shown to change people who believe themselves in love
- how memory is shown to be selective and sometimes distorting.

2 Join up with another pair. Compare your ideas and then report them back to the class.

Key terms

• stage
  conventions

• narrator

• chronology

• dual / multiple
  time scheme

Activity 52

1 Working in a small group, devise three clear statements about the dramatists' use of chronology or a 'time scheme' in your plays. Use the statements below to start you thinking.

The dramatist may:

- introduce gaps in time between Scenes or episodes
- use flashbacks
- use chronology to show the influence of the past on the present
- construct a dual or multiple time scheme
- present time subjectively, from inside the mind of a character.

2 Contribute your statements to class discussion. Then relate them to what you consider to be your dramatists' purposes. Consider:

- how the handling of chronology positions the audience in relation to the events and characters
- how the handling of chronology gives a distinctive shape or structure to the play as a whole
- how successful the handling of chronology is (or might be) in the theatre.

Theatrical effects and effectiveness

Activity 53

1 Working in a small group, make director's notes for a production of *Betrayal*. Use the following headings to help clarify your thinking.

- Set (or sets)
- Continuity between scenes
- How to indicate the movement of time 'backwards' from 1977 to 1968
- Use of lighting
- Use of music and/or sound.

Then plan in detail how to present Scene 7 on stage. You could give a rehearsed performance to another group and act as an audience for theirs.

2 Read aloud as a class Scene 3 of *The Glass Menagerie*. Then discuss how to present it on stage, making use of the theatrical effects Tennessee Williams specifies. These include:

- a fluid, 'transparent' set
- the screen device
- varied lighting effects
- music.

3 Review your work in stages 1 and 2 of this activity. Then discuss as a class whether *Betrayal* and *The Glass Menagerie* need to be experienced in the theatre to:

a fully understand the dramatists' intentions
b judge their effectiveness as plays.

Take it further

Write stage manager's notes for a production of one or both of your plays. Think about how technical effects could help convey major themes to an audience watching the play(s) for the first time.

Activity 54

Adapt Activity 53 to your plays. With the help of your teacher, make amendments to the table for stage 1 and choose a suitable Scene/episode for stage 2.

2 Comparing the key features of poems

Part 2 gives you guidance in making literary and linguistic connections between your chosen poems. It shows how to compare the ways in which your poets:

- present themes
- use lexis
- use structure.

Each sub-section below uses a different pairing from the specification to illustrate comparison of these key features of poetry. The material can be readily adapted to the study of other pairings.

Areas of comparison: an overview

This sub-section helps you identify the main areas of comparison you need to consider when working on your poems. It takes as its focus the pairing of *The Wife of Bath's Prologue and Tale* by Geoffrey Chaucer and *Selected Poems* by Tony Harrison, in the topic area 'Family Relationships'. Activities 55, 57 and 59 can be used for any poetry pairing.

Subject matter or theme?

A poem's **subject matter** is what it describes. Its **themes** are the ideas about human life that the poet uses the subject matter to explore. The reader *interprets* a poem's themes from the subject matter and the way the poet presents it.

Across AS and A2

Refer back to Analysing Voices in Poetry in Unit 1, particularly the 'key questions' about poems on pp 49–50 of the AS Student Book. Your analysis of poems in Unit 3 will be a comparative one, but your detailed exploration of lexis, structure and the use of voice in poetry at AS provides a platform for your work at A2. It also reminds you that, in making comparisons between poems, general points must be supported by specific textual analysis.

Activity 55

1 Read the poem by Tony Harrison and the extract from *The Wife of Bath's Prologue* below.

The Wife of Bath's Prologue

To chirche was myn housbonde born a-morwe
With neghebours, that for him maden sorew;
And Jankin, our clerk, was oon of tho.
As help me God! whan that I saugh him go
5 After the beere, me thoughte he hadde a paire
Of legges and of feet so clene and faire
That al myn herte I yaf unto his hoold.
He was, I trowe, a twenty winter oold,
And I was fourty, if I shal seye sooth;
10 But yet I hadde alwey a coltes tooth.
Gat-toothed I was, and that bicam me weel;
I hadde the prente of seinte Venus seel.
As help me God! I was a lusty oon,
And faire, and riche, and yong, and wel bigon;
15 And trewly, as mine housboundes tolde me,
I hadde the best *quoniam* mighte be.

Geoffrey Chaucer

Long Distance II

Though my mother was already two years dead
Dad kept her slippers warming by the gas,
put hot water bottles her side of the bed
and still went to renew her transport pass.

5 You couldn't just drop in. You had to phone.
He'd put you off an hour to give him time
to clear away her things and look alone
as though his still raw love was such a crime.

He couldn't risk my blight of disbelief
10 though sure that very soon he'd hear her key
scrape in the rusted lock and end his grief.
He *knew* she'd just popped out to get the tea.

I believe life ends with death, and that is all.
you haven't both gone shopping; just the same,
15 in my new black leather phone book, there's your name
and the disconnected number I still call.

Tony Harrison

2 a Both texts are 'about' marriage. Working with a partner, summarise the marital situations being described by Chaucer and Harrison here.

b Consider these statements about each text.

In *The Wife of Bath's Prologue*:
- the Wife is attracted to Jankin at her husband's funeral
- the Wife is a full-blooded, promiscuous woman
- sexual appetites are stronger than moral doctrines about chastity and fidelity.

In *Long Distance II*:
- Harrison's father cannot adapt to life without his wife
- love is stronger than death
- Harrison wants to believe he will meet his dead parents again.

Decide which statements apply to the subject matter of the poems and which to their themes.

3 Share your ideas in class discussion. Then create your own definitions of subject matter and theme to help you differentiate between them in future work. Use two more extracts/poems by Chaucer and Harrison to illustrate these.

Take it further

Write your own modern version of the extract from *The Wife of Bath's Tale* on p 73 in either free verse or prose. Use a glossary to help you. Try to keep the racy, colloquial feel of the original and bring out the Wife's extrovert character.

Activity 56

With the help of your teacher, choose from your collections two poems by different poets which are related in subject matter. Adapt Activity 55 to help you differentiate between their subject matter and theme.

Lexis

In studying poems, the lexical features you need to focus on are:

- your poets' lexical choices (remember that a poet starts with a blank page)
- your poets' use of register and tone
- your poets' use of figurative language
- your poets' use of **phonological features** – that is, the way the sound of words helps to convey meaning.

You will relate these lexical features to your poets' presentation of themes.

Activity 57

1 Re-read the texts by Chaucer and Harrison in Activity 55. Compare the register and tone used in them by completing the table below.

Use of register and tone	Chaucer	Harrison
Whose voice do we hear?		
What register does the voice use?		
What perspective (or viewpoint) is created for the reader?		

2 Compare your entries with a partner's. Then work together to comment on the *effect on the reader* of the following uses of figurative language:

Chaucer
- 'al myn herte I yaf unto his hoold'
- 'I hadde alwey a coltes tooth'
- 'the prente of seinte Venus seel'

Harrison
- 'as though his still raw love was such a crime'
- 'my blight of disbelief'
- 'Long Distance'

How does the figurative language add depth of feeling to each poet's exploration of his theme?

3 Share your responses in class discussion. Then turn your attention to the use of **vernacular** lexis in these texts. Compare the impressions given by the use of idioms and colloquialisms in:

Chaucer:
a 'As help me God!'
b 'I was a lusty oon'
c 'I hadde the best *quoniam* may be'

Harrison:
a 'warming by the gas'
b 'You couldn't just drop in'
c 'popped out to get the tea

Consider the kind of social and cultural context each poet is creating here. What attitudes on the part of Chaucer towards the Wife, and on the part of Harrison towards his parents, does the vernacular language suggest? How does the use of phonological features – for instance, **onomatopoeia** and **alliteration** – help to convey these attitudes more strongly?

> **Key terms**
>
> • **phonological features**
>
> • **vernacular**
>
> • **onomatopoeia**
>
> • **alliteration**
>
> • **subject matter**
>
> • **theme**

Activity 58

Adapt stages 1 and 2 of Activity 57 to two poems by different poets in your collection. Work in a small group to devise appropriate questions on the use of register and figurative language. Then exchange these with another group and discuss your answers. Hold a plenary discussion about how your poets' attitudes towards their subjects is conveyed by their lexical choices.

Structure

In studying poems, the structural features you need to comment on are:

*   your poets' choice of genre (sonnet, ballad, narrative poem, blank verse, rhymed couplets, etc.)
*   your poets' use of grammar and syntax
*   your poets' use of rhyme and rhythm
*   your poets' use of rhetorical patterns within a poem.

Relate these structural features to your poets' presentation of theme.

Activity 59

Read the poem by Tony Harrison and the extract from *The Wife of Bath's Tale* below.

Turns

I thought it made me look more 'working class'
(as if a bit of chequered cloth could bridge that gap!)
I did a turn in it before the glass.
My mother said: *It suits you, your dad's cap.*
5 (She preferred me to wear suits and part my hair:
You're every bit as good as that lot are!)

All the pension queue came out to stare.
Dad was sprawled beside the postbox (still VR),
his cap turned inside up beside his head,
10 smudged H A H in purple Indian ink
and Brylcreem slicks displayed so folks might think
he wanted charity for dropping dead.

He never begged. For nowt! Death's reticence
crowns his life's, and *me*, I'm opening my trap
15 to busk the class that broke him for the pence
that splash like brackish tears into our cap.

Tony Harrison

The Wife of Bath's Tale

Greet was the wo the knight hadde in his thought,
Whan he was with his wyf abedde ybrought;
He walweth and he turneth to and fro.
His olde wyf lay smilinge evermore,
5 And seyde, 'O deer housbonde, *benedictee!*
Fareth every knight thus with hys wyf as ye?
Is this the lawe of King Arthures hous?
Is every knight of his so dangerous?
I am youre owene love and eek your wyf;
10 I am she which that saved hath youre lyf,
And, certes, yet ne dide I yow nevere unright;
Why fare ye thus with me this firste night?
Ye faren lyk a man had lost his wit.
Where is my gilt? For Goddes love, tel me it,
15 And it shal be amended, if I may'.
'Amended?' quoth this knight, 'alas, nay, nay!'

Geoffrey Chaucer

Make brief notes describing each poet's use of structure. Use these headings:

- the narrative form: one narrative voice and some quoted speech
- the narrative viewpoint
- couplets / stanzas
- **iambic pentameter**
- simple / complex rhyme scheme
- structural contrasts within the extract/poem.

2 Working as a class, compare the *use* each poet makes of these structural features by copying and completing the table below.

Structural features and the poet's purposes			
Harrison's purposes	**Use of structural features**	**Chaucer's purposes**	**Use of structural features**
To characterise his mother and father		To characterise the Loathly Lady and the young knight	
To compare and contrast himself with his mother		To present the Wife's view of their relationship	
To convey his view about the working class		To amuse the reader	

Make sure that you relate the structural features you identify to their *effect* within each text.

Key terms

- **iambic pentameter**
- **part-rhyme**
- **persona**
- **cosonance**
- **assonance**

Activity 60

With the help of your teacher, choose two poems by different poets from your collections which compare OR contrast particularly well in their use of structural features. Annotate a copy of them in the way described in stage 1 of Activity 59. Then adapt the table in stage 2 to relate these features to the poets' purposes as you understand them.

Comparing the presentation of themes

This sub-section helps you explore the way poets present their themes to the reader. It takes as its focus *Selected Poems by Thom Gunn and Ted Hughes* and T.S. Eliot's *The Wasteland and Other Poems*, in the topic area 'The Individual in Society'. Activity 62 can be used for any poetry pairing.

An integrated approach

Themes in poems are created and conveyed through language. You need, therefore, to *integrate* your comments on a poet's themes and linguistic techniques rather than try to treat them separately. This is particularly important when you are making comparisons: it is easy to slip into generalising about how poems are alike and unlike and forget about the language. Activity 61 shows you how to guard against this.

Activity 61

Read the two poems below.

Snowdrop

Now is the globe shrunk tight
Round the mouse's dulled wintering heart.
Weasel and crow, as if moulded in brass,
Move through an outer darkness
5   Not in their right minds,
With the other deaths. She, too, pursues her ends,
Brutal as the stars of this month,
Her pale head heavy as metal.

Ted Hughes

Landscapes   I. New Hampshire

Children's voices in the orchard
Between the blossom- and the fruit-time:
Golden head, crimson head,
Between the green tip and the root.
5   Black wing, brown wing, hover over;
Twenty years and the spring is over;
To-day grieves, to-morrow grieves,
Cover me over, light-in-leaves;
Golden head, black wing,
10   Cling, swing,
Spring, sing,
Swing up into the apple-tree.

T.S. Eliot

1 a Working with a partner, remind yourself how to distinguish between subject matter and theme in a poem (see p 71). Then devise one sentence summarising Hughes's theme in *Snowdrop* and one sentence summarising Eliot's theme in *Landscapes: New Hampshire*.

b Compare the poets' use of lexis and structure to present their themes. Focus on:
- Hughes's use of figurative lexis to describe the snowdrop and the creatures
- Eliot's use of figurative lexis to describe time
- the use of **part-rhyme** and rhythm in *Snowdrop*
- the use of rhyme and rhythm in *Landscapes: New Hampshire*
- the use of voice (including register and tone) in both poems.

2 Share your ideas in class discussion. Then read aloud *In Praise of Cities* by Thom Gunn and *Preludes* by T.S. Eliot. Discuss your initial responses to them. What themes do they seem to deal with? How do these themes compare and contrast?

Think about:
- Main impressions given of city life
- The poet's use of second person voice/**persona** and viewpoint
- The poet's use of extended metaphor (semantic field)
- The poet's use of connotative lexis

Use your completed notes to make clear, comparative points about:
- the main themes of each poem, and, *as an integral part of this*,
- the main linguistic techniques used to explore and convey them.

3 Read *Wind* by Ted Hughes. Discuss in a small group how Hughes develops the themes of:
- the power of nature and the elements
- the powerlessness of man in the face of these.

Then consider the main linguistic techniques Hughes uses to convey his themes to the reader. Focus on the use and effect of:
- figurative language (the poem is dense with metaphors and similes)
- first and third person voice and viewpoint
- connotative lexis
- phonological features (the poem makes strong use of onomatopoeia, alliteration, **consonance** and **assonance**).

4 Share your ideas in class discussion. Then compare the impression Hughes gives of nature with the impression Gunn and Eliot give of urban life. You will find the differences to be extreme. Discuss why by exploring how Gunn and Eliot and Hughes look at life from different perspectives. Refer to the following poems to develop your ideas further:
- Thom Gunn: *On the Move*
- T.S. Eliot: *The Love Song of J. Alfred Prufrock*
- Ted Hughes: *The Horses*

Activity 62

Choose two poems from your collection which explore similar themes. Adapt Activity 61 in order to practise taking an integrated approach to analysing and comparing them.

Comparing the use of lexis

Take it further

Read the first two parts of T.S. Eliot's poem *The Waste Land*. Make a comparison between his use of lexis there and his use of lexis in *Landscapes: New Hampshire*. How do you account for the differences?

This sub-section helps you explore the way poets use lexis to:

- create a distinctive voice
- construct patterns of imagery.

It takes as its focus *Metaphysical Poetry* and *Selected Poems* by Sylvia Plath, in the topic area 'Love and Loss'. Activity 63 is self-contained and will be useful to all students.

Voice, register and tone

All poems have a voice. Activity 63 illustrates how poets create a voice appropriate to their theme and how they use it to position the reader.

Activity 63

1 Read aloud the poems by John Donne and Sylvia Plath below.

Batter my Heart

Batter my heart, three-personed God, for you
As yet but knock, breathe, shine and seek to mend;
That I may rise and stand, o'erthrow me, and bend
Your force to break, blow, burn and make me new.
5 I, like a usurped town, to'another due,
Labour to'admit you; but oh, to no end;
Reason, your viceroy in me, me should defend,
But is captived, and proves weak or untrue;
Yet dearly I love you, and would be loved fain*,
10 But am betrothed unto your enemy.
Divorce me, untie, or break that knot again,
Take me to you, imprison me, for I,
Except you enthral* me, never shall be free,
Nor ever chaste, except you ravish me.

John Donne

* fain: in return
*enthral: enslave

Crossing the Water

Black lake, black boat, two black, cut-paper people.
Where do the black trees go that drink here?
Their shadows must cover Canada.

A little light is filtering from the water flowers.
5 Their leaves do not wish us to hurry:
They are round and flat and full of dark advice.
Cold worlds shake from the oar.

The spirit of blackness is in us, it is in the fishes.
A snag is lifting a valedictory*, pale hand;
10 Stars open among the lilies.
Are you not blinded by such expressionless sirens*?

This is the silence of astounded souls.

Sylvia Plath

*valedictory: bidding farewell
* sirens: dangerous rocks

In class discussion, explore each poet's creation and use of voice. Use the questions below to help you.

On *Batter my Heart*:

- Who is Donne addressing?
- How would you describe his tone of voice?
- Why does he want to be 'battered', 'o'erthrown', 'divorced', 'imprisoned', 'enthralled' and 'ravished'? What do all these verbs have in common?
- How do the phonological features of Donne's language emphasise its meaning? (Choose two or three examples.)

On *Crossing the Water*:

- Who do you think Plath is addressing?
- How would you describe her tone of voice?
- Look carefully at the adjectival **modifiers** in the poem: what do they have in common?
- How do the phonological features of Plath's language emphasise its meaning? (Choose two or three examples.)

Take it further

Read Sylvia Plath's poems *Daddy* and *Tulips*. Compare and contrast her use of voice, register and tone in them with her use of these linguistic features in *Crossing the Water*.

2 Each poet uses a conversational form. How useful is it in making an analysis to describe their registers as 'conversational', 'colloquial' or 'informal'?

Choose adjectives from the box below that you could apply more specifically to the tone and register of these voices:

personal	intimate	confidential	exclamatory	dramatic
argumentative	beseeching	bewildered	imperative	interrogative

Quote from the poems to justify your choices. What do you think each poet's purpose is in **positioning** the reader as a listener to a conversation (or in the case of *Crossing the Water*, perhaps, as an addressee)?

Key terms

- **modifiers**
- **positioning**
- **semantic field**
- **extended metaphor**

Activity 64

Read the poem below.

Life

I made a posy while the day ran by:
Here will I smell my remnant out, and tie
    My life within this band.
But time did beckon to the flowers, and they
5 By noon most cunningly did steal away,
    And withered in my hand.

My hand was next to them, and then my heart:
I took, without more thinking, in good part
    Time's gentle admonition:
10 Who did so sweetly death's sad taste convey,
Making my mind to smell my fatal day,
    Yet sug'ring the suspicion.

Farewell, dear flowers, sweetly your time ye spent,
Fit, while ye lived, for smell or ornament,
15   And after death for cures.
I follow straight without complaints or grief,
Since if my scent be good, I care not, if
    It be as short as yours.

George Herbert

Take it further

Write your own 'metaphysical' poem. Choose an everyday subject and explore it through the use of extended metaphor, unusual connections between ideas and a highly formal structure. If you wish, you could write a parody of Herbert's poem 'Life' – 'I made a _____ as the day ran by', etc.

Patterns of imagery

In poetry, single metaphors and similes colour a visual description or illuminate an idea. When metaphors and similes are *extended* and built up into a pattern that runs throughout a poem, the *semantic field* they create becomes the poem's main structural principle. It constructs meaning rather than 'embellishes' or 'adds to' it.

1. Working with a partner, explore how Herbert uses the extended metaphor of flowers to reflect on life. Make notes on how:

- The poet establishes his theme in stanza 1 e.g. 'I made a posy while the day ran by'; 'By noon…did steal away / And withered in my hand'.

- The poet develops his theme in stanza 2 e.g. 'I took…in good part/ Time's gentle admonition'; 'to smell my fatal day./Yet sug'ring the suspicion'

- The poet concludes his theme in stanza 3 e.g. 'sweetly the time ye spent'; 'if my scent be good, I care not if / It be as short as yours'

2 Share your responses in class discussion. Use your completed table to show how:

- different aspects of flowers are included in the pattern of imagery – their appearance, their smell, their use as decoration, their use in medicine, etc.

- the semantic field *develops* and gives depth to the theme as the poem goes on.

3 Re-read John Donne's sonnet *Batter my Heart* on p 76. Working in a small group, make your own table to show how Donne uses the extended metaphor of a town under siege to develop his theme of the need for Christian salvation.

Comparing the use of structure

This sub-section helps you explore the way poets shape and construct their poems to match their intentions and create a perspective for the reader. It takes as its focus *Thomas Hardy: Poems* and *The Best-loved Poems of John Betjeman* in the topic area 'A Sense of Place'. Activities 65 and 67 are self-contained and will be useful to all students. Activities 66 and 68 can be used for any poetry pairing.

Genre

The first choice a poet makes is of genre. Activity 65 shows you how the structural features of a chosen genre help to convey the poet's theme and guide the reader's response.

Activity 65

Read aloud the poem below.

Death in Leamington

She died in the upstairs bedroom
　　By the light of the ev'ning star
That shone through the plate glass window
　　From over Leamington Spa.

5　Beside her the lonely crochet
　　Lay patiently and unstirred,
But the fingers that would have work'd it
　　Were dead as the spoken word.

And Nurse came in with the tea-things
10　　Breast high 'mid the stands and chairs –
But Nurse was alone with her own little soul,
　　And the things were alone with theirs.

She bolted the big round window,
15　　She let the blinds unroll,
She set a match to the mantle,
　　She covered the fire with coal.

And "Tea!" she said in a tiny voice
　　"Wake up! It's nearly *five*."
Oh! Chintzy, chintzy cheeriness,　　　　　　20
　　Half dead and half alive!

Do you know that the stucco is peeling?
　　Do you know that the heart will stop?
From those yellow Italianate arches
　　Can you hear the plaster drop?　　　　　25

Nurse looked at the silent bedstead,
　　At the gray, decaying face,
As the calm of a Leamington ev'ning
　　Drifted into the place.

She moved the table of bottles　　　　　　30
　　Away from the bed to the wall;
And tiptoeing gently over the stairs
　　Turned down the gas in the hall.

John Betjeman

1 Explore the poem's themes with a partner. As a starting point, decide how far you agree with the three statements below.

　a The old woman dies and no one mourns her: the poem is about the loneliness of age.

　b The dead woman's house is decaying from neglect: the poem is a lament for the passing of a way of life.

　c The Nurse treats the old woman with condescension and indifference: the poem is about the lack of care of 'carers'.

2 Justify your ideas about theme in class discussion. Then turn your attention to the poem's form and structure. Discuss these questions:

　• What kind of subject matter do you associate with ballads?

　• What form and structure do traditional ballads have? Think about stanza forms, rhyme schemes, rhythm and voice/viewpoint.

　• In what ways does *Death in Leamington* seem like a traditional ballad, and in what ways does it seem different?

　Betjeman said that he deliberately used the **ballad** form for this poem but modified some of its traditional features to match his 'modern' theme (the poem was published in 1955). Consider how successful he is in doing so.

Read aloud the poem below. It was written in 1915: its title refers to World War I.

In Time of 'The Breaking of Nations'

I

Only a man harrowing clods
　　In a slow silent walk
5　With an old horse that stumbles and nods
　　Half asleep as they stalk.

II

Only thin smoke without flame
　　From the heaps of couch-grass;
10　Yet this will go onward the same
　　Though Dynasties pass.

III

Yonder a maid and her wight*
　　Come whispering by:
15　War's annals will cloud into night
　　Ere their story die.

Thomas Hardy

*wight: lover

3 Discuss as a class:

  a the poem's theme

  b how Hardy uses the **lyric** genre to present and convey his theme

  c why Hardy may have chosen to use the form and structure of a lyric, normally associated with love poetry, for a poem related to war.

Thomas Hardy

Activity 66

With the help of your teacher, choose several poems from your collections that differ significantly in their form and structure. Compare the way in which their structural features relate to their themes and guide the reader's response.

Structure and meaning

Analysing structure in poems is difficult. It is an aspect of meaning that often gets overlooked. Activity 67 shows you how to use close reading to identify specific structural features and see them as an essential part of the way a poem communicates its themes.

Activity 67

1 Read aloud the following poem and then working with a partner, use the questions on the next page to help you interrogate the poem.

The Self-Unseeing

Here is the ancient floor
Footworn and hollowed and thin,
Here was the former door
Where the dead feet walked in.

5　She sat here in her chair,
Smiling into the fire;
He who played stood there,
Bowing it* higher and higher.

Childlike, I danced in a dream;
10　Blessings emblazoned that day;
Everything glowed with a gleam;
Yet we were looking away!

Thomas Hardy

*Bowing it: playing the violin

Key terms

• ballad

• lyric

1 a Stanza 1:
  - Where is 'here'? Where is the poet situated in stanza 1?
  - Why is the door a 'former' door? Why are the feet 'dead'?

b Stanza 2:
  - Who is 'she'? Who is 'he'?
  - What stage in the speaker's life is being described here?

c Stanza 3:
  - What perspective does the speaker establish in stanza 3?
  - How do you interpret line 12?

d Whole poem:
  - What significance do you attach to the poem's title?
  - How would you summarise the poem's theme in one sentence?

2 Share your responses with another pair. Then explore the following structural features of the poem in relation to the development of its theme.

a Stanza 1:
  - The speaker's voice is musing aloud. How does the structure of the stanza help to convey this impression?
  - What is the effect on the reader of juxtaposing 'dead' and 'feet' in line 4?
  - How would you describe the rhythm of stanza 1?: Lively, Sombre, Regular, Uneven, Excited, Subdued?
  - Stanza 1 is lightly punctuated. How does this affect the way it sounds when read aloud? How is this effect enhanced by the short lines?

b Stanza 2:
  - As in stanza 1, the speaker uses deictic references ('here', 'there'). What perspective does this give the reader?

  - Lines 5 and 6 are identical in structure to lines 7 and 8. What impression does this give of the relationship between 'she' and 'he'?
  - The lines in stanza 2 are strongly rhymed, as are lines throughout the poem. Why do you think the poet has chosen to use a strict, formal **rhyme scheme**?

c Stanza 3:
  - The first word of line 9 is given strong emphasis. How? Why is it one of the key words in the poem as a whole?
  - 'Emblazoned' is a prominent verb in line 10 and in the whole poem. How does the poet give it prominence? What ideas does this word suggest?
  - 'glowed with a gleam' in line 11 is alliterative. What is the effect on the reader of this phonological feature?
  - 'Yet' is given prominence by its placing at the beginning of line 12. Why is it a key word in the poem? Why does the poem end with an exclamation?

3 Share your responses in class discussion. Then make a class list of the structural features you have been exploring – for instance: the order of lines and the patterns they form; rhythm; rhyme scheme; changes in tense and perspective, etc.

It is important to include on your list the typical *effects on the reader* of the features you note down. When writing an analysis, it is never enough just to *describe* structural features; you always need to comment on their *purpose and effect*.

4 Read *Slough* by John Betjeman. After identifying its theme, analyse its structural features in the way you have done with Hardy's *The Self-Unseeing*. Work as a class or in a group. End your discussion by comparing the way these two poets use structure to create meaning. There are many similarities.

Key terms

- rhyme scheme

Take it further

Read poems by Hardy and Betjeman about the passing of time and the changes it brings. Start with 'Friends Beyond' by Hardy and 'Youth and Age on Beaulieu River' by Betjeman. Compare the way in which they use structural features to explore and convey the themes of past and present, youth and age, transience and permanence, etc.

Activity 68

With the help of your teacher, choose one poem by each of your poets and use the close reading method shown in Activity 67 to relate their structural features to their themes.

3 Comparing plays in their contexts

For Section B you need to research the contexts in which your plays were written and received. There are two main kinds of context:

- the context of **production**, which concerns the writing of the plays
- the context of **reception**, which concerns the way audiences and readers respond to them.

You should build these **contextual factors** into a comparison of your plays.

Part 3 helps you to plan, carry out and apply your research. It shows you how to:

- identify the contexts relevant to a study of plays
- relate plays to their historical, social and cultural contexts
- relate plays to their theatrical and literary contexts.

The sub-sections below use between them the full range of paired plays in the specification to illustrate how to explore contextual factors. You will benefit from reading them all. Draw on the material and the approaches taken to guide your work.

Assessment objectives

AO3 emphasises that you need to consider 'the significance of contextual factors' in both 'the production and reception' of play texts. This AO counts for two-thirds of the marks for Section B. The highest band rewards 'an incisive and evaluative approach to a range of relevant contextual factors'.

The context of production

This sub-section helps you relate plays to:

- the events of the time in which they are set
- the social and cultural climate of the time when they were written.

Activities 70 and 72 can be used for any pair of plays.

Historical background: *Translations* and *Stuff Happens*

Translations by Brian Friel is set in 1833. Its focus is the making of the first Ordnance Survey map of Ireland. *Stuff Happens* by David Hare is set between 1975 and 2005. Its focus is the build-up to the Iraq War. Each dramatist bases his plot on real historical events.

Activity 69

1 Work in a small group. Between you, find out about the following events in 18th and 19th century Irish history:

- the Rebellion (or 'Rising') of the United Irishmen against British rule in 1798
- the Act of Union passed by the British government in 1800
- the Spring Rice Report to the British government in 1824, advocating a general survey of Ireland
- the setting up by the British government of National Schools in Ireland in the 1830s
- the Irish Potato Famine of 1845.

Research sources include: *The Great Shame*, Keneally, Chatto 1998; *Irish History and Culture*, ed Orel, Portmanock 2004.

2 Work in a small group. Between you, find out about the following events in 20th and 21st century American history:

- the fall of Saigon in 1975 during the Vietnam War
- the terrorist attack on the New York World Trade Center in 2001
- the invasion of Iraq in March 2003
- the end of the military offensive against Iraq in April 2003
- the execution of Saddam Hussein in 2006.

Research sources include: *Terrorism and US Foreign Policy*, Pillon, USA 2005; *usforeignpolicy. about.com*.

Key terms

- production
- reception
- contextual factors
- manifesto
- social realism
- heightened language
- social and ethical problems

Writing in the exam

The focus of your comparative analysis will be the structure, form and language of your plays. Contextual factors should be included in this comparison but should not dominate it. Bear in mind that an historical approach to context will not be as central to other pairings as it is to *Translations* and *Stuff Happens*.

3 Share your findings with the class. Then explore the ways Brian Friel and David Hare *use* history in their plays. You might consider:

- how far they just reproduce history and how far they reshape it for their own purposes
- whether *Translations* and *Stuff Happens* are 'documentary' plays about historical events or plays about individuals and communities
- what view of the British in *Translations*, and of politicians in *Stuff Happens*, is presented by the dramatists. Do they persuade you to share it?

4 Read the notes below for a comparative analysis of the use of historical background in *Translations* and *Stuff Happens*.

Translations	Stuff Happens
Friel bases his plot on imagined characters	Hare bases his plot on real-life characters
Friel's play shows Irish history at a crossroads – the British are pursuing a policy of colonial oppression, which will lead to the Troubles of the 20th century	Hare's play shows global history at a crossroads – the Bush doctrine of 'pre-emptive strikes' and 'regime change' will lead to a future holocaust, the play suggests
Friel's play is a domestic drama about a family and a close-knit community – the characters are portrayed as rounded individuals	Hare's play is explicitly political throughout – characters have only a public, not a private, dimension
Political themes emerge out of characters' relationships – they are not presented as the dramatist's **manifesto**	Political themes are dominant and often presented in the form of argument or debate – the dramatist has a clear manifesto

Discuss the use made here of research into historical context. Note how it is used to *interpret* the plays rather than just 'fill in their background'.

Activity 70

Adapt Activity 69 to your plays. With the help of your teacher, first decide:

- what historical background material will be relevant to a comparative study of them
- what research sources to use.

Undertake your research. Then hold a similar discussion to that outlined in stage 3 of Activity 69, focusing on the way your dramatists *use* historical background to present their themes to an audience.

Social and cultural background: *A Doll's House* and *All My Sons*

A Doll's House is set in a small-town middle class household in Norway in the 1870s. *All My Sons* is set in a small-town community in middle America in 1947. Each dramatist deals explicitly with social themes. Ibsen's focus is on the way 19th-century married couples, particularly wives, are locked into unfulfilling relationships by social convention and rigid moral codes. Miller's focus is on the way a morally decent man puts making money above his responsibilities to the community to which he belongs.

Activity 71

Ibsen and Miller belong to the '**social realism**' school of drama. Much of the relevant social context is, therefore, presented in the plays themselves. This activity shows you how to identify and use it.

1 Work in a small group. Re-read the following parts of *A Doll's House*:

- Act 1, pp 1–5 (of the prescribed Oxford edition)
- Act 2, pp 62–66
- Act 3, pp 78–86
- the alternative 'German' ending, pp 87–88.

Discuss the social themes you can identify here. How do you think Ibsen wants you to respond to:

- the way Helmer treats Nora, and the way she reacts to him, in Act 1?
- Christine Linde's decision to marry Krogstad in Act 2 and her motives?
- Nora's decision to leave Helmer and her children at the end of the play?
- the alternative ending, which the dramatist later called a 'barbaric outrage'?

2 Work in a small group. Re-read the following parts of *All My Sons*:

- Act 1, pp115–118 (of the prescribed Penguin edition)
- Act 1, pp121–122
- Act 2, pp156–158
- Act 3, pp166–171.

Discuss the social themes you can identify here. How do you think Miller wants you to respond to:

- Joe Keller's account of his and Steve's business operation in Act 1?
- Chris's conversation with Ann about his war experiences and 'the rat race' in Act 1?
- Chris's argument with Joe at the end of Act 2?
- Chris's argument with Joe at the end of Act 3?

3 Share your responses with the class. Then compare the ways Ibsen and Miller give prominence to the themes you have discussed by the dramatic techniques they use. Find examples in both plays of their use of:

- significant revelations from the past
- parallel situations and relationships
- dramatic climaxes that take the form of confrontations
- characters' use of **heightened language** to signal 'key moments'.

4 Work in a group.

Between you, research each dramatist's own comments on the social themes of his play. The best print sources are shown in the Independent Research box.

Relevant material online includes: a review of the first London performance of *A Doll's House* in June 1889 (*The Times*) and an article in *The New York Times* for June 22, 1956, 'Arthur Miller Admits Helping Communist-Front Groups in '40s'. (Miller was under investigation by his government for Un-American Activities during the 1950s.)

5 Adapt Activity 71 to your plays. With the help of your teacher, choose suitable extracts for stages 1 and 2 and suitable research sources for stage 4. Remember that your purpose is to compare the way your dramatists *make use of* social context, as shown in stage 3.

Take it further

Both Ibsen and Miller have been labelled 'problem playwrights' – in other words, principally concerned with examining *social and ethical problems* in their plays – at the expense of the 'social realism' they claimed for themselves. Do you think this is a fair judgement? Write or discuss your response.

Independent research

See: *The Oxford Ibsen* (London, 1960–77) – it contains Ibsen's notes on *A Doll's House* and a critical introduction; Miller's *Collected Plays* (Cresset Press, 1958) – it contains Miller's extensive introduction to *All My Sons*.
See: *Ibsen: the Critical Heritage*, Egan (ed) (Routledge, 1972); and *Arthur Miller*, Welland (Oliver & Boyd, 1961).

Writing in the exam

Bear in mind that social and cultural context will be mainly presented in the plays themselves. Take care not to 'import' into your comparison of them social history that has only a general bearing on the plays.

The context of reception

This sub-section helps you explore:

- the reception of plays by audiences over time
- the reception of plays by literary critics and other readers.

Activities 74 and 76 can be used for any pair of plays.

Theatrical reception: *The Glass Menagerie* and *Betrayal*

Both these plays have had a mixed theatrical reception. First produced in 1945, *The Glass Menagerie* was greeted enthusiastically by audiences and theatre critics who praised its 'raw emotional power' and its 'technical ingenuity'. First produced in 1978, *Betrayal* was given a largely hostile reception by audiences and theatre critics who saw it as 'gimmicky' and 'banal … it leaves us feeling a little despairing, a little titillated, a little bored and a lot frustrated'. Since then, the theatrical response to each play has, generally speaking, reversed.

Activity 72

1 Work in a small group. Read the extracts from reviews of these plays on this and the facing page.

A 'Menagerie' full of stars, silhouettes and weird sounds

Memory, which is notorious for playing tricks on people, pulls off some doozies* in the narcoticized* production of Tennessee Williams's 'The Glass Menagerie' which opened last night at the Ethel Barrymore Theater. As staged by David Leveaux, this revival suggests that to recall the past is to see life as if it had occurred underwater, in some viscous sea through which people swim slowly and blindly.

Folks drown in this treacherous element. Unfortunately, that includes the show's luminous but misdirected stars: the two-time Oscar winner Jessica Lange, who brings a sleepy, neurotic sensuality to the role of the vital and domineering Amanda Wingfield, and Christian Slater, who plays her poetical son, Tom, as a red-hot roughneck. Within its first 15 minutes, you feel the entire production sinking into a watery grave…

The ensemble is asked to compete with mood music that suggests someone playing popular tunes on the rims of water-filled glasses through an amplifier. Worse, much of the action occurs behind lacy curtains, so the cast members are often seen only in silhouette. The overall visual effect is rather like that of an Italian Vogue, proclaiming that the 1940s are back in fashion …

It could be argued (by a deconstructionist in a really good mood) that since everyone in 'The Glass Menagerie' is lonely, the medley of conflicting acting styles appropriately underscores the characters' isolation. But the sum effect is without emotional impact. The situation is hardly improved by Mr Leveaux's having all the Wingfields caressing, kissing and clutching one another as much as they do. Incest is not what Williams had in mind here, even as a subtext.

Ben Brantley, *The New York Times*

*doozies: bizarre moments
*narcoticized: doped-up

When the why usurps what next

This is the first important revival of a piece disgracefully undervalued when it appeared 13 years ago. Harold Pinter has admittedly written more forcefully; but none of his plays, not even 'The Caretaker' or 'Old Times', has the emotional density of 'Betrayal'. As David Leveaux's wary production confirms, there is hardly a line into which desire, pain, alarm, sorrow, rage and some kind of blend of feelings has not been compressed like volatile gas in a cylinder less stable than it looks.

What upset the reviewers in 1978 was that the plot harked back to a theatrical period when dramatists were obsessed by love triangles which, if not eternal, were certainly interminable. Yet since the story started after a man's affair with his best friend's wife had finished, ended with its beginning, and in between lopped this way and that through time, 'Betrayal' was also dismissed as gimmicky.

The answer is that Pinter's narrative method takes "what next?" out of the spectator's mind and replaces it with the rather deeper "how?" and "why?". Why did love pass? How did these people cope with the lies, the evasions, the sudden dangers, the panic, and the contradictory feelings behind their own deftly engineered masks? The play's subject is not sex, not even adultery, but the politics of betrayal and the damage it inflicts on all involved

Cheryl Campell has mastered the art of doing little yet implying much. When Robert discovers the affair, her Emma has only to become very still to suggest the dread within. Again, there is no mistaking the bleak grief behind the tight smiles when, at the play's start and the story's end, she realises she has lost both men. There, on her face, is what betrayal has meant. It is just one of many quietly eloquent* moments in a riveting evening.

Benedict Nightingale, *The Times*

*eloquent: expressive

2 In your group:

a Compare your own response to the plays, and/or productions of them you have seen, with these reviewers' responses.

b Discuss how much you have learned about the plays by reading comments made from an audience's perspective. Consider whether either reviewer has:

- given you new insights into the dramatists' intentions

- resolved any uncertainties you may have had about the plays

- changed your opinion of the plays.

3 Find out more about the stage history and theatrical reception of *The Glass Menagerie* and *Betrayal* by reading reviews from the following online sources:

- On *The Glass Menagerie*:
- *The New York Times*, April 2, 1945
- *The New York Times*, March 23, 2005
- *The Guardian*, February 14, 2008

- On *Betrayal*:
- *The Times*, January 23, 1991
- *The Guardian*, June 6, 2007
- *The New York Times*, July 27, 2008

Compare the reviewers' opinions. What do they show of the range and variety of the plays' theatrical reception over time? How could you make use of them in a comparative analysis of the plays?

Activity 73

Adapt Activity 73 to your plays. Go online to research their theatrical reception: quality newspapers reproduce their theatre reviews in full. As in stage 2 above, you should focus on how reviewers influence *your* view of the plays when seen from an audience's perspective.

Take it further

Write a review of your ideal production of *The Glass Menagerie, Betrayal* OR one of your own plays. Bring out the way in which the staging, set, technical effects and acting combined to realise the dramatist's intentions for the audience. Comment favourably on your own performance in one of the leading roles.

Literary critical reception: *Othello* and *Equus*

Othello was written in 1601–2, *Equus* in 1973. Both have been seen by critics and readers as 'disturbing' plays. In the case of *Othello*, this is because a black man kills his white wife, after being provoked into a jealous rage by the 'motiveless malignity' (Coleridge) of a lieutenant who has been described as 'the embodiment of evil'. In the case of *Equus*, it is because a repressed teenager viciously blinds a group of horses, ostensibly without motive, and is privately envied by the psychiatrist whose task is to return him to 'normality' ("That boy has known a passion more ferocious than I have felt in any second of my life").

Literary criticism of both plays has centred on the theme of the 'outsider' in society. Othello's story raises questions about race and racism. Alan Strang's story raises questions about mental disturbance and the way people express their sexuality. The material used below illustrates the range of critical debate.

Activity 74

1 Read the extracts from different critics of *Equus* below.

A

'Equus' seems to me to contain every bit as much phoney baloney and pseudo-profundity as such other of Shaffer's hits as 'Amadeus' and 'The Royal Hunt of the Sun' … Strang is just a
5 classic mixed-up kid, lonely, sexually confused, and with a love of horses which has become disastrously tangled up with his mother's hard-line Christianity … [The play contains] absurd and dangerous psychobabble, inspired by that
10 most dodgy of 60's gurus R.D. Laing, in which we are asked to believe that the mentally ill are vouched an insight, and a passion, denied to the boringly sane.

CHARLES SPENCER

B

Son of a pious mother and an atheist father, Alan developed an early obsession with Christian sado-masochism; while a wild ride on the sea coast gave him
5 a parallel fixation on horses. The two obsessions merge into his private cult of "Equus", and on taking a weekend stable job, he consummates his worship
10 in orgiastic night riding. But when a girl takes him back to the stable to make love, he sees this as an act of sacrilege: and, believing that the eyes of Equus will reduce him to permanent impotence, he
15 blinds every horse in the stable.

Irving Wardle

C

In the play's loose-seeming yet taut and economical structure there is a progressive demonstration of the hollowness and self-questioning of Dysart, the psychiatrist who is charged with the job of mental restoration. Shaffer does not make the elementary mistake, any more
5 than R.D. Laing does, of romanticizing madness into a vision of the truth denied to the 'sane', but he does show us Alan's particular brand of insanity as a legitimate and valuable response to experience which brings its own benefits and has to be emasculated by society in the cause of its own self-preservation.

John Russell Taylor

2 Discuss as a class:

a how these critics interpret the play differently, and what evidence they give

b how far they react to the play as a **theatrical** experience

c how far you share their views.

3 Read the extracts from different critics of *Othello* below.

A

The moral, sure, of this Fable is very instructive. First, this may be a caution to all Maidens of Quality how, without their Parents consent, they run away with a Blackamoor. Secondly, this
5 *may be a warning to all good Wives that they look well to their Linnen. Thirdly, this may be a lesson to Husbands, that before their jealousie be Tragical the proofs may be Mathematical.*

Thomas Rymer (1693)

B

Othello must not be conceived as a negro, but a high and chivalrous Moorish chief. Jealousy does not strike me as the point in his passion; I take it to be rather an agony
5 that the creature, whom he believed angelic, with whom he had garnered up his heart, and whom he could not help still loving, should be proved impure and worthless. It was the struggle *not* to love her – 'But
10 yet the *pity* of it, Iago! – O Iago! The *pity* of it, Iago'. There is no ferocity in Othello; his mind is majestic and composed. He deliberately determines to die; and speaks his last speech with a view of showing his
15 attachment to the Venetian state, though it had superseded him.

S.T. Coleridge (1835)

C

The superficial disproportion between black skin and white skin conquers the inward, unseen 'marriage of true minds'. Similarly, with the disproportion between youth and age: 'She must change for youth';
5 being sated with his body she will find the error of her choice. The tragedy becomes a tragedy of loss of faith. And, such is the nature of Othello's heroic temperament, the loss of faith means the loss of all meaning and all value, all sense of light: 'I have no
10 wife.? O insupportable! O heavy hour! / Methinks it should be now a huge eclipse / Of sun and moon'.

G.K. HUNTER

4 Discuss as a class:

a how you see the issue of Othello's colour

b how you see the issue of Iago's motivation

c how you see the issue of Othello's 'heroic temperament'.

Activity 75

Adapt Activity 75 to your plays. With the help of your teacher, build up a collection of literary critical reception. *Select* key points from them. As in stages 2 and 3 above, you should focus on how critical reception affects *your* view of the plays when seen from a literary perspective.

Independent research

Make a short list of the issues about *Equus* and *Othello* you want to find out how critics have reacted to. This will focus your research and help you make best use of it. Especially with *Othello*, there is a huge amount of literary criticism available and it is easy to lose sight of the wood for the trees. The best resource to start with is *Othello: a sourcebook*, Hadfield, Routledge 2004, which presents extracts from critical reception over the last 300 years with clear notes to guide you through it.

4 Comparing poems in their contexts

For Section B you need to research the contexts in which your poems were written and received. There are two main kinds of context:

- the context of **production**, which concerns the writing of the poems
- the context of **reception**, which concerns the way readers respond to them.

You need to build these **contextual factors** into a comparison of your poems.

Part 4 helps you to plan, carry out and apply your research. It shows you how to:

- identify the contexts relevant to a study of poems
- relate poems to their social and cultural contexts
- relate poems to their literary and critical contexts.

The sub-sections below use between them the full range of paired poetry collections in the specification to illustrate how to explore contextual factors. You will benefit from reading them all. Draw on the material and the approaches taken to guide your work.

The context of production

This sub-section helps you relate poems to:

- the social and cultural background against which they were written
- the literary traditions within which they can be placed
- the context of the poet's life and writing.

Social background: *The Wife of Bath's Prologue and Tale* and *Selected Poems: Tony Harrison*

Chaucer wrote *The Canterbury Tales* during the 1380s and 1390s. They are set against a background of medieval life and society of which the middle-class Wife of Bath is one vivid example. Harrison's *Selected Poems* were written between 1965 and 2000. They are often strongly autobiographical and make frequent reference to his family life and upbringing in a working-class community in Leeds.

In exploring the use of social background by these poets, you need to remember that the Wife of Bath is a fictional character created for a long narrative poem. On the other hand, Harrison normally writes in the first person, using a persona and a voice that is recognisably his own. Social 'background' can be found principally in the poems themselves, as Activity 77 shows.

Activity 76

1 Read the extract opposite from near the beginning of *The Wife of Bath's Tale*.

2 Use a glossary to help you understand this extract in full. Work with a partner. Discuss and note down the impressions given here of the social life of a well-to-do middle-class woman in medieval times. Consider:

   - how the Wife spends most of her time
   - the Wife's friends and neighbours and the part they play in her life
   - the Wife's entertainments
   - the Wife's frequent references to religious customs and festivals
   - how the Wife likes to dress, and why.

3 Read the poem by Tony Harrison below.

4 Work with a partner. Discuss and note down the impressions given here of:

   a the 'gentlemen'
   b the 'dumb'.

   Consider:
   - how Harrison presents the convict and the tin miners
   - how Harrison presents the 'stout upholders of the law' and the 'gentlemen'
   - why Harrison uses Cornish dialect at the end of the poem
   - why this poem can be read as being about class differences
   - the voice Harrison uses and what it shows about his attitudes.

   Then compare and contrast the impressions of social and cultural life given by Chaucer and Harrison.

5 Put these texts into the context of what you already know from your study of *The Wife of Bath's Prologue and Tale* and *Selected Poems: Tony Harrison*. Relate their social themes to other parts of Chaucer's poem and other poems by Harrison. Your emphasis should be on how the poets *use* social background to explore their themes.

   Then research further the social context of these texts. Refer to the Independent Research box.

And so bifel that ones in a Lente –
So often times I to my gossib wente,
For evere yet I loved to be gay,
And for to walke in March, Averill, and May   5
Fro hous to hous, to heere sondry talis –
That Jankin clerk, and my gossib dame Alis,
And I myself, into the feeldes wente.
Myn housbonde was at Londoun al that Lente;
I had the bettre leyser for to pleye,   10
And for to se, and eek for to be seye
Of lusty folk. What wiste I wher my grace
Was shapen for to be, or in what place?
Therfore I made my visitaciouns
To vigiles and eek to processiouns,   15
To preching eek, and to thise pilgrimages,
To pleyes of miracles, and to mariages,
And wered upon my gaye scarlet gites.

National Trust

Bottomless pits. There's one in Castleton,
and stout upholders of our law and order
one day thought its depth worth wagering on
and borrowed a convict hush-hush from his warder
and winched him down; and back, flayed, grey, mad, dumb.   5

Not even a good flogging made him holler!

O gentlemen, a better way to plumb
the depths of Britain's dangling a scholar,
say, here at the booming shaft at Towanroath*,
now National Trust, a place where they got tin,   10
those gentlemen who silenced the man's oath
and killed the language that they swore it in.

The dumb go down in history and disappear
And not one gentleman's been brought to book:

Mes den hep tavas a-gollas y dyr   15

(Cornish) – 'the tongueless man gets his land took.'

*a former tin mine in Cornwall

Independent research

For Chaucer, the best sources are: *An Introduction to Chaucer*, Hussey, Spearing and Winney, Cambridge; and *The Cambridge Chaucer Companion*, ed Boitani and Mann, Cambridge.
For Harrison, the best sources are: radio3/johntusainterview/ram/ajtharrison.ram; *Tony Harrison*, Kelleher, Northcote House 1996 – 'Writers and their Work' series; and *Tony Harrison*, Loiner, Byrne, Clarendon Press 1997.

Key terms

- production
- reception
- contextual factors

Activity 77

Adapt Activity 77 to your poems. Choose one poem by each of your poets which illustrates their *use* of social and cultural context particularly well. Analyse and compare them in the way shown in stages 1 to 4 above. Then, with the help of your teacher, find suitable research sources and use them to develop your thinking about the importance of social and cultural contexts to your poetry pairing.

Literary background: *The Waste Land and Other Poems: T.S. Eliot* and *Selected Poems: Thom Gunn and Ted Hughes*

Two of the major publishing dates of the 20th century were 1917 when T.S. Eliot brought out his first volume of verse, *Prufrock and Other Observations*, and 1957 when Ted Hughes brought out his first volume of verse, *The Hawk in the Rain*. In exploring the literary context of these poets, you need to look at the new departures in modern poetry that they represented rather than at the influences on them of other writers. Both Eliot and Hughes seemed highly original at the time. Activity 79 illustrates why.

Activity 78

Read aloud the extract below from A.E. Housman's poem *The Shropshire Lad*. It was published in 1891. This is a 'love song'.

Now read alongside it the opening of Eliot's *The Love Song of J. Alfred Prufrock* (1917):

Bredon Hill

In summertime on Bredon
    The bells they sound so clear;
Round both the shires they ring them
    In steeples far and near,
    A happy noise to hear.   5

Here of a Sunday morning
    My love and I would lie,
And see the coloured counties,
    And hear the larks so high
    About us in the sky.   10

A.E. Housman

Let us go then, you and I,
When the evening is spread out against the sky
Like a patient etherised upon a table;
Let us go, through certain half-deserted streets,
The muttering retreats   5
Of restless nights in one-night cheap hotels
And sawdust restaurants with oyster-shells …

T.S. Eliot

1 Discuss with a partner the contrasts between these poems. Focus on:

- the different settings
- the different voices
- the differences in lexis and register
- the different verse forms
- the differences in what the poets are trying to do.

Read aloud the extract opposite from W.H. Auden's poem *1st September 1939*.

I sit in one of the dives
Of fifty-second Street
Uncertain and afraid
As the clever hopes expire
5   Of a low dishonest decade:
Waves of anger and fear
Circulate over the bright
And darkened lands of the earth,
Obsessing our private lives;
10   The unmentionable odour of death
Offends the September night.

Now read alongside it this extract from Hughes's *The Horses* (1957).

I climbed through woods in the hour-before-dawn dark.
Evil air, a frost-making stillness,

Not a leaf, not a bird –
A world cast in frost. I came out above the wood

5   Where my breath left tortuous statues in the iron light.
But the valleys were draining the darkness

Till the moorline – blackening dregs of the brightening grey –
Halved the sky ahead. And I saw the horses …

2 Discuss with a partner the contrasts between these poems. Focus on:

- the different settings
- the different voices
- the differences in lexis and register
- the different verse forms
- the differences in what the poets are trying to do.

3 Share your responses in class discussion. Then use the extracts from Eliot and Hughes to make a comparative analysis of *their* verse, using the same prompts as for 1 and 2 above.

Independent research

For further literary background to Ted Hughes, the best starting points are: *The Art of Ted Hughes*, Sagar, Cambridge 1978; *Ted Hughes, A Critical Study*, Gifford and Roberts, Faber 1981; and Hughes's *Letters*, ed Reid, Faber 2008. The letters are highly illuminating about the use Hughes made of his reading, especially of Shakespeare and Middle English poetry.

Independent research

Further research into the literary background to Eliot's poems will take you into some difficult areas – for example, his reading of French Symbolist poets of the 19th century such as Baudelaire, Laforgue and Verlaine; his collaborations with the American imagist poet Ezra Pound, especially on *The Waste Land*; and his reading of philosophy (notably F.H. Bradley) and anthropology (notably Sir James Frazer's *The Golden Bough*). The best starting points for this are: *A Student's Guide to the Selected Poems of T.S. Eliot*, Southam, Faber 1974; and *The Invisible Poet: T.S. Eliot*, Kenner, Methuen 1965.

Take it further

Set Eliot, Gunn and Hughes more firmly into their literary contexts by sampling poems from these Penguin anthologies: *Poetry of the Nineties* (for Eliot), *Poetry of the Thirties* and *Poetry of the Forties* (for Gunn and Hughes). Read the editors' introductions to these volumes to help you establish an overall perspective on developments in English poetry during the 20th century.

Biographical background: *Metaphysical Poetry and Selected Poems: Sylvia Plath*

There is a school of thought that argues that the student and critic have no business delving into the life of a writer. 'We have the poems/plays/novels: the life is not a legitimate topic for research, since the connections between life and art can never be known.' This is a matter you need to decide for yourself. The material below provides you with some biographical information about John Donne and Sylvia Plath to relate to their writing at your own, and your teacher's, discretion.

Activity 79

1 Read the following details about John Donne.

> Born into a Catholic family in Protestant England – went to Oxford University to read Law at the age of 11 – forbidden from taking a degree because of his Catholicism – squandered his large family inheritance on profligate living – secretly married Anne More, disastrously since her father
> 5   was Catholic – his career prospects were ruined – imprisoned on James I's orders but released after several weeks – went on to have 12 children – broke with his Catholic past in 1610 and won the favour of James I – took Anglican orders – appointed Dean of St Paul's in 1621 – never recovered from Anne's death in 1617 giving birth to their twelfth child – preached his
> 10 last sermon dressed in his shroud – died in 1631.

2 Read the following details about Sylvia Plath.

> Born to a German father and an American mother in 1932 – a student prodigy at Smith College, Massachusetts – a national winner of a fiction prize, which led to work as a guest editor for the magazine Mademoiselle on Madison Avenue – won a prestigious Fulbright scholarship to read
> 5 English at Cambridge University – met and married Ted Hughes: had two children – separated from Hughes in 1962 after he admitted an affair – took her children to live in a London flat – committed suicide in 1963 by gassing herself (she had attempted suicide twice before, once in her teens and once in her twenties).

3 In *Selected Poems*, Plath uses personal experience and feeling as the basis of much of what she writes. Donne's *Songs and Sonnets* and *Divine Poems* also give the strong impression of lived experience.

Work as a class. Find poems by each of these poets where biographical details might be thought to illuminate their subject matter and themes. In the light of these, discuss how far you should read a poem in terms of what you know about its writer's life.

Independent research

Further research sources for the biographical background to Donne and Plath include: *John Donne: Life, Mind and Art,* Carey, Faber 1983; *John Donne, the Reformed Soul – a biography,* Stubbs, Newton & Co, 2007; *Letters Home,* ed Aurelia Plath, Faber 1975; and *The Savage God,* Alvarez, London 1971.

Activity 80

With the advice and help of your teacher, research the biography of your poets. Then consider how far you can reasonably interpret their poems in the light of what you find out.

The context of reception

This sub-section helps you explore the reception of poems by literary critics and other readers.

Literary critical reception: *Thomas Hardy: Poems* and *The Best-loved poems of John Betjeman*

The title of the Betjeman volume above tells the story of his reception by readers and critics. Since his poems were first published in 1955, he has been highly popular with the 'ordinary reader', his work easily outselling that of every other poet in the 20th century. Until recently, however, he was given no serious attention by literary critics.

Hardy was a well-established, and highly regarded, Victorian novelist. After the controversy surrounding the publication of *Tess of the d'Urvervilles* and *Jude the Obscure*, he turned to writing poetry. Between 1898 and his death in 1928, Hardy published five volumes of verse amounting to more than 1000 poems – and no more novels. From then to the present day, his standing among both 'ordinary readers' and literary critics has been uniformly high.

Activity 81

1 Work in a small group. Read the following extract from a literary critic's evaluation of Betjeman in 2006.

> After spending time with Betjeman, most other modern poets seem curiously introverted, depending too much on self-generated production standards. Their work seems to lose sight of who they are and sets off instead on a great journey to the Land of Literature.
> 5 Reading the most respected modern poetry, you are immediately confronted by problems of comp-rehension which it takes another book to resolve. Betjeman, by comparison, competes along existing rules. He lays out his wares for us to judge by our own standards, not his … We don't need him on the syllabuses* because he has
> 10 taken out all the difficulty himself during the writing of the poem.
>
> *Hugo Williams*

*syllabuses: exam specifications

Look again at three poems by Betjeman that seem to reflect this critic's views. On the basis of these, say how far you agree that:

- there is little difficulty in understanding Betjeman's poems, even on a first reading

- he leaves it to readers to decide how to respond 'by our own standards, not his'.

As an A2 student, do you take the view that there is too little challenge in the poems to justify studying them in school? Give your honest opinion and explain it to your group.

Key terms

• transcendental

• nostalgia

Independent research

The best starting point for further research into Hardy's critical reception is *The Complete Critical Guide to Thomas Hardy*, Harvey, Routledge 2003. On Betjeman, the evaluation by Hugo Williams quoted above can be found in full in *The Guardian*, February 25, 2006. Otherwise, the best contextual sources are *John Betjeman, Letters: Volumes I and 2* ed Lycett-Green, Methuen 2006, and *John Betjeman*, a biography by Bevis Hiller, 2007.

2 Work in a small group. Read the following extract from a poet's and a literary critic's evaluation of Hardy in 1966 and 1986 respectively.

> He [Hardy] is not a **transcendental** writer, he's not a Yeats, he's not an Eliot; his subjects are men, the life of men, time and the passing of time, love and the fading of love ... When I came to Hardy it was with a sense of relief that I didn't have to jack myself up to a concept of poetry that lay outside my own life. One could simply relapse back into one's own life and write from it.
>
> *Philip Larkin*

> Hardy is the natural poet of a community whose natural modes of utterance are song and dance ... [however] his persistent locating of vision of community in the past can come perilously close to a disabling nostalgia or to a merely enervate sadness.
>
> *John Lucas*

Look again at three poems by Hardy which seem to reflect Philip Larkin's views. On the basis of these, say how far you agree that:

• Hardy's principal subjects are those that Larkin lists

• Hardy writes directly about common human experiences based on his own life.

Do you share John Lucas's view that Hardy's poems 'come perilously close to a disabling nostalgia' – that is, a wallowing in nostalgia that swamps the poem?

3 Share your responses in class discussion. Then discuss the possible reasons why both Hardy and Betjeman have always been popular with the poetry-reading public. As a starting point, consider these points:

• Their poems use simple lexis to explore everyday subjects and themes.

• Their poems are set in a recognisable time and place.

• Readers enjoy poems that take them back into their own past.

Activity 82

Adapt Activity 83 to your poets. For some, you will find there is a huge amount of critical reception that seems more substantial than the poems themselves. Be selective in how you use it. Remember that your focus is a *comparison* of the poems. You need to look at the different ways critics have approached and evaluated your poets over time, then decide how their views influence *your* understanding and judgements.

Take it further

Re-read the first four poems in your Hardy and Betjeman collections. Then write your own critical review of them for a quality newspaper of the present day, bringing out your personal response to the poems and making your own evaluation of them.

5 Tackling Section B of the exam

Part 5 gives you advice about how to prepare for and perform well in Section B of the exam. It shows you how to:

- understand the requirements of the question and plan your answer accordingly

- maintain a comparative focus throughout your answer

- include in your answer relevant material about context

- write your answer with the three assessment objectives in mind, particularly AO3

- write your answer in a coherent way and in a clear, fluent style.

What you have to do in the exam: a summary

1 You will answer the question that applies to your chosen topic area. It is worded in such a way as to allow you to use drama OR poetry texts in your answer. There is no choice of question.

2 You have to compare the use of linguistic techniques and literary devices by your two dramatists OR your two poets.

3 You have to comment on the way contextual factors help you to understand and interpret your two texts.

4 You have to show that you are using a combined linguistic and literary approach in the way you build up and write your answer.

Learn by heart points **2**, **3** and **4**. If you base your exam answer on them you will have done everything the question requires you to do.

Writing in the exam

This example question on the topic 'Family Relationships' is typical. Only the end of the first sentence, following the word 'present', will be different in your exam.
'Consider and evaluate the different ways writers of your chosen texts present the causes of conflicts in relationships.'
In your response, you should:
- critically compare the use of language techniques and literary devices
- comment on and evaluate the contribution made by the contextual factors to your understanding of your chosen texts.

Assessment objectives

Examiners use the following three assessment objectives for Section B.
AO1 – Select and apply relevant concepts and approaches from integrated linguistic and literary study, using appropriate terminology and accurate, coherent written expression.
AO2 – Demonstrate detailed critical understanding in analysing the ways in which structure, form and language shape meanings in a range of spoken and written texts.
AO3 – Use integrated approaches to explore relationships between texts, analysing and evaluating the significance of contextual factors in their production and reception.

Planning your answer

Stage 1: Making sure your material is relevant

You need to ensure that the answer you write is relevant to the examiner's question. Resist the temptation to reproduce an answer you have practised or learned, in advance.

Plan for at least 15 minutes. Start by underlining the key part of the question, which follows the word 'present' in the first sentence. Here are examples from all four of the topic areas, taken from the Sample Assessment Materials for this unit.

A Sense of Place

Consider and evaluate the different ways the writers of your chosen texts present people as trapped by the historical period in which they live.

In your response you should:

- critically compare the use of language techniques and literary devices
- comment on and evaluate the contribution made by contextual factors to your understanding of your chosen texts.

The Individual in Society

Consider and evaluate the different ways the writers of your chosen texts present an individual at odds with society.

In your response you should:

- critically compare the use of language techniques and literary devices
- comment on and evaluate the contribution made by contextual factors to your understanding of your chosen texts.

Love and Loss

Consider and evaluate the different ways the writers of your chosen texts present the need for love to be kept private.

In your response you should:

- critically compare the use of language techniques and literary devices
- comment on and evaluate the contribution made by contextual factors to your understanding of your chosen texts.

Family Relationships

Consider and evaluate the different ways the writers of your chosen texts present the causes of conflicts in relationships.

In your response your should:

- critically compare the use of language techniques and literary devices
- comment on and evaluate the contribution made by contextual factors to your understanding of your chosen texts.

Your next step is to create an answer plan in diagram form. (You can do this in your answer booklet, as long as you cross it out later.) You will have your own preferred form of diagram. Activity 85 uses one of many possible formats to illustrate this stage of planning.

Activity 83

1 Look carefully at the diagram below with a partner. It is an answer plan for the question on **Family Relationships** above. It uses the drama pairing *All My Sons* and *A Doll's House*.

Presentation of the causes of conflicts in relationships in *All My Sons* and *A Doll's House*

(Remember the question asks about how the writers <u>present</u> causes of conflict.)

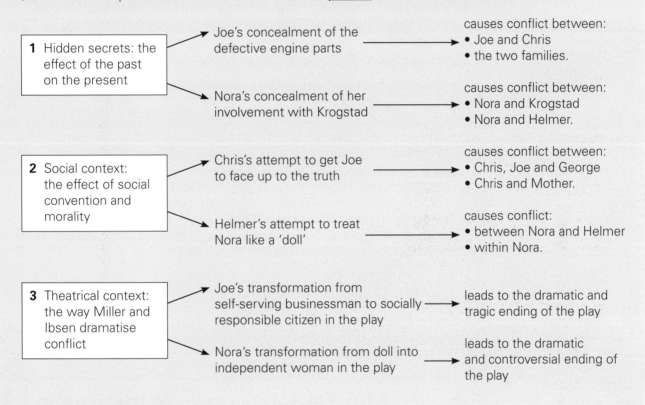

1 Hidden secrets: the effect of the past on the present	Joe's concealment of the defective engine parts	causes conflict between: • Joe and Chris • the two families.
	Nora's concealment of her involvement with Krogstad	causes conflict between: • Nora and Krogstad • Nora and Helmer.
2 Social context: the effect of social convention and morality	Chris's attempt to get Joe to face up to the truth	causes conflict between: • Chris, Joe and George • Chris and Mother.
	Helmer's attempt to treat Nora like a 'doll'	causes conflict: • between Nora and Helmer • within Nora.
3 Theatrical context: the way Miller and Ibsen dramatise conflict	Joe's transformation from self-serving businessman to socially responsible citizen in the play	leads to the dramatic and tragic ending of the play
	Nora's transformation from doll into independent woman in the play	leads to the dramatic and controversial ending of the play

Main focus
Theatrical context: the dramatic devices Miller and Ibsen use to present conflicts.

Compare the use of:

- **setting** – single sets, claustrophobic atmosphere – produces intensity and a feeling of entrapment

- **dialogue** – bruising and lengthy confrontations between characters – mode of argument: highly emotional exchanges, sometimes like a moral debate

- **idiolects** – clash of registers used by different characters, e.g. Chris and Mother, Nora and Helmer in the last Act

- **symbols and motifs** – strong use made of these, e.g. Larry's tree, the tarantella.

2 Produce as a class a variant of this answer plan for your own texts. Base it on the relevant question in the list above.

3 Use your completed plan to create the paragraphs for an exam answer. Write complete topic sentences for each paragraph. Leave the rest in note form.

Then discuss your paragraphs as a class. Once you are confident that your material is relevant, write in full the *first* of these paragraphs and any *one* other. Include specific reference to, and quotation from, the text.

Stage 2: Making sure you compare

Assessment objective 3 requires you to 'explore relationships between texts' – in other words, to compare and contrast them. It counts for 40 marks out of 60. Activity 86 helps you to ensure you keep comparison going throughout your answer.

Activity 84

1 Read through the whole of your answer plan from Activity 83. Check how successfully it highlights comparison by asking yourself the following questions.

   a Does it pay a roughly equal amount of attention to each text?

   b Does the first paragraph include comment on each text?

   c Does each subsequent paragraph make at least two comparative points?

   d Does the last paragraph summarise the main areas of comparison in the answer?

   e Are comparisons made *within* paragraphs or on the principle of 'one paragraph about text A, the next paragraph about text B'?

2 Share your findings with a partner. Constructively criticise the comparative nature of each other's answer plans in the light of the questions above. Make any changes to your plan you decide are necessary.

3 Read as a class the following two extracts from exam answers. Both writers are working at a high level.

The first extract is a paragraph from an answer on how two dramatists present people as trapped in the historical period in which they live. See the question on **A Sense of Place** on p 96.

> Brian Friel is very specific about the period in which 'Translations' is set: 'An afternoon in late August 1833 ... A few days later ...The evening of the following day'. David Hare is similarly specific: 'Stuff Happens' is a history play, which happens to centre on very recent history ...September 11th,
> 5   2001'. Both dramatists show how their characters are caught up in swiftly changing historical events. In 'Translations', Hugh is one the older generation of Southern Ireland who has been shaped by his nation's history ('The road to Sligo. A spring morning, 1798. Going into battle') but who is open to embracing the changes which the re-naming of Ireland by the English brings:
> 10   'We must learn those new names ... We must learn to make them our new home'.
>   Significantly, however, his son Manus is unable to do this, refusing to believe that a new culture can be grafted onto the old: 'I couldn't even go close to them. I just shouted something stupid – something like "You're a
> 15   bastard, Yolland"'. He is as trapped in the time in which he lives as strongly as President Bush and the Republican hawks are in 'Stuff Happens'. Bush is unwilling and unable to accept that the 20th century world order with America at its centre can ever change:
>   'I want you all to understand that we are at war, and we will stay
> 20   at war until this is done. Nothing else matters'.
> His policy is an all-out 'war on terror' whatever it costs. Any accommodation or negotiation with the perceived enemy is as inconceivable to him as friendship with the English is to Manus in 'Translations'.

The second extract is a paragraph from an answer on how two poets present an individual at odds with society. See the question on **The Individual in Society** on p 96.

> Both T.S. Eliot and Ted Hughes are ideologically 'at odds' with the society they depict in that they are strongly critical of the modern world. The 'individual' they present in this antipathetic relationship to society is the persona they create for particular poems. One of the speakers in 'The Waste Land', who might be Eliot himself, presents a view of London as
> 5 spiritually dead, inhabited by people who have lost all sense of purpose and direction in life: 'Unreal City, / Under the brown fog of a winter dawn, / A crowd flowed over London Bridge, so many, / I had not thought death had undone so many'. These living dead are like the lost souls in Dante's Inferno to which the poem implicitly refers. The colourlessness of their lives is suggested by the dull, monochrome imagery and their lack of volition by the sluggish, lethargic
> 10 rhythms. Ted Hughes is also 'at odds' with 20th century society, though for different reasons. The speaker in 'Soliloquy of a Misanthrope', who might be Hughes himself, states:
>
> > 'Whenever I am got under my gravestone ...
> > I shall praise God heartily, to see gone,
> > Complacency from the smirk of every man,
> 15 > And every attitude showing its bone,
> > And every mouth confessing its crude shire'.
>
> Modern man, Hughes suggests in this poem and in others such as 'Thrushes' and 'Macaw and Little Miss', has lost contact with his roots in the world of Nature. Instead of living, like the animals, purposefully and according to the promptings of instinct, he has intellectualised
> 20 himself into a shallow, effete condition where there is only 'complacency' in 'every attitude' and no attitude shows it 'bone'. The metaphor 'crude shire' in the extract above illustrates how Hughes's speaker wants modern man to re-connect with the earth, with the life of the senses rather than the mind, and resemble people in former times 'who grimace[d] / Under the commitments of their flesh'.

Hold a detailed class discussion about the way these writers:

- compare subject matter and theme

- compare the use of language in their texts

- use reference and quotation to illustrate their comparative points.

4 Use what you have learned from this activity to turn your answer plan into a full, carefully written exam answer.

Including material about context in your answer

Assessment objective 3 requires you to analyse 'the significance of contextual factors' in the way your texts are 'written and received'. Look back to Section B Part 2 or Part 4 of this book to remind yourself what 'contextual factors' are and how to distinguish between the contexts of production and reception.

Activity 85

1 Read the extract on the next page from an exam answer on the topic area **Love and Loss** which compares *The Glass Menagerie* and *Betrayal*. The writer is using the title: 'Consider and evaluate the different ways in which the writers of your chosen texts present love as a type of imprisonment'.

The theatrical context of these plays illuminates the theme of love as a type of imprisonment. For 'The Glass Menagerie', Tennessee Williams specifies a set which is meant to show how the characters are trapped in their own worlds of memory and illusion: 'In keeping with the atmosphere of memory, the stage is dim. Shafts of light are focused on selected areas or actors'.

5 The last few minutes of the drama are 'played as though viewed through sound-proof glass'. This makes clear that Amanda and Laura will never escape from their own private worlds. Amanda is imprisoned in her memories of the time when she was a 'southern belle' with an endless stream of gentlemen callers; Laura is imprisoned in her memories of Jim, her gentleman caller, who has left her forever with and in her self-created glass menagerie, in retreat from life. Only Tom

10 has access to the 'fire-escape' and even he, in his obsessive love for his sister, finds that he cannot really escape from the prison of the past:

Oh Laura, Laura, I tried to leave you behind, but I am more faithful than I intended to be'.

In productions of 'The Glass Menagerie', this atmosphere of entrapment has been highlighted by various stage devices. In one recent production, 'much of the action occurs behind

15 lacy curtains, so the cast members are often seen only in silhouette … this revival suggests that to recall the past is to see life as if it had occurred underwater, in some viscous sea through which people swim slowly and blindly' (Ben Brantley, theatre critic, 2006). Similarly, recent productions of Harold Pinter's 'Betrayal' have highlighted the way the main characters are imprisoned in their memories of a love triangle which has left them with 'an aching sense of loss' (Benedict

20 Nightingale, theatre critic). A 2008 production used a claustrophobic set based on the walls of rooms which sloped inwards and solid furniture which reminded one critic that 'memories don't fade; they grow more solid as they grow more distorted, and we bump into them whichever way we try to turn' (James Neilson, theatre critic). This reflects the feeling of entrapment which Pinter, like Williams, wants to create and which is enhanced by the way the play moves "backwards" in

25 time, as though the end of the story of Emma, Jerry and Robert in 1977 is less present to them than its beginning in 1968. Memory, as in 'The Glass Menagerie', imprisons people in a tunnel where the normal rules of time are suspended. It is interesting that Pinter, who rarely writes Production Notes, specifies that 'Betrayal can be performed without an interval'.

1 Discuss in a small group how well this response uses contextual factors to:

- interpret rather than describe the plays

- comment on the dramatists' purposes

- combine material on the contexts of 'production' and 'reception'

- make comparative points.

2 Choose *one* aspect of the context of your texts to include in an exam essay on a title you have not practised before. Working in a small group, discuss how you could build this into your answer without getting sidetracked from the essay title, losing your comparative focus or using too much space. Share your ideas in class discussion. Then write your 'context' section either as a class or by yourself.

Writing clearly and fluently

Look back to the advice on 'Improving your style and expression' on p 51 of this book. Absorb it again.

Activity 86

Use the essay title you devised for Activity 90 to write the first two paragraphs of an exam answer which compares the presentation of themes but which does not deal with context. Give yourself five minutes to plan. Then write these paragraphs without stopping to redraft. Concentrate on getting your thoughts down on paper in 15 to 20 minutes. Go over your writing straight away and improve its clarity and fluency. Read aloud your redrafted version to a partner and listen to them do the same. Be constructively critical of each other's style.

Read and compare the two extracts below. They are two versions of the same material. Extract A is a first draft written in 20 minutes. Extract B is a redrafted form, written with the advice of a teacher.

A

Thomas Hardy and John Betjeman are alike in writing about places they associate with happy times in their lives when they were younger than they are now. This is shown in 'The 'Varsity Students' Rag' when Betjeman is thinking back on being a student:

> 'Then we went to the Popular, and after that – oh my! I wish you'd seen the rag we had in the Grill Room at the Cri'

The bouncy rhythm in the quotation and the place names, which he uses a lot in his other poems, show his carefree happiness. It is also seen in 'Trebetherick':

> 'We used to picnic where the thrift
> Grew deep and tufted to the edge;
> We saw the yellow foam-flecks drift
> In trembling sponges on the ledge
> Below us …'

This poem uses more descriptive imagery than the first one. He says the sponges are 'trembling' which creates a clear picture. The letter 'f' makes alliteration in 'foam-flecks drift' which gives a lazy feeling to his picture of the sea on a sunny day. Therefore both as a child in Cornwall and at Oxford University Betjeman shows that his memories of places are happy ones.

Hardy also has a nostalgic feeling for places, although his happy memories are more tinted with sadness:

> 'Childlike I danced in a dream;
> Blessings emblazoned that day;
> Everything glowed with a gleam;
> Yet we were looking away!'

This is remembering his childhood when the alliteration of 'glowed with a gleam' shows everything was cast in a happy glow. He says that his childhood brought him 'blessings', which has a religious tone to it, and they were 'emblazoned' which makes them sound like the bright colours on a shield in heraldry. However, he did not at the time feel full happiness because 'we were looking away' so he wasn't fully appreciating the blessings. The exclamation mark at the end tells us that he regrets it with hindsight.

B

Hardy and Betjeman both write about places they associate with happy times in their youth. In 'The 'Varsity Students' Rag', for instance, Betjeman recalls his student days, using a voice which is jaunty and colloquial:

> 'Then we went to the Popular, and after that – oh my! I wish you'd seen the rag we had in the Grill Room at the Cri'

The exuberant, chant-like rhythm here suggests the carefree happiness he felt while at University. Betjeman uses proper nouns a great deal in his poems to evoke a specific time and place, as he does here. The reader is made to feel familiar with them by being positioned as a listener who is part of the culture and so needs no further information about 'the Popular' and 'the Cri'. Betjeman's recollection of happiness at 'Trebetherick' is expressed in a more formal, literary style but the poem conveys a similar pleasure in his surroundings:

> 'We used to picnic where the thrift
> Grew deep and tufted to the edge;
> We saw the yellow foam-flecks drift
> In trembling sponges on the ledge
> Below us …'

This is strongly visual, relying more on direct statement than on poetic devices, though the alliterative 'foam-flecks' and the swaying rhythm of the verse combine to evoke a sense of the Cornish seaside on a sunny day.

Hardy's nostalgia for places he associates with happy memories is, by contrast often tinged with sadness:

> 'Childlike I danced in a dream;
> Blessings emblazoned that day;
> Everything glowed with a gleam;
> Yet we were looking away!'

This, from 'The Self-Unseeing', is a recollection of his childhood at home. Looking back, he is keenly aware of 'blessings', suggesting a semi-religious sense of privilege, and the emphasis on the archaic verb 'emblazoned' gives the impression that his memories have for him the significance of history or legend, the word deriving from heraldry. However, his happiness is qualified by hindsight. From the perspective of an adult looking back, he recognizes that he did not fully appreciate his 'blessings' since 'we were looking away!'. Childhood happiness may 'glow' with a gleam' but its extent is only apparent in retrospect. The note of regret which this realisation brings is conveyed by the emphasis given to 'Yet' in the last line and the exclamation mark with which the poem ends.

1 Read the examiner's comments below on extract **B**. It is being assessed against AO1. Working as a class, assess extract **B** against AO2 and AO3.

> **AO1** *This is a fluent response which would be placed at the top of Band 3. The points made are carefully and systematically developed in a way which is easy to follow. Very good knowledge of concepts is shown and there is a sufficient range of literary and linguistic terminology. The expression is accurate and sentences are well-varied. The writer has a wide vocabulary. S/he is well able to convey some quite subtle insights at times. The two paragraphs are coherent, following a comparative structure, and the expression is concise. This is mature writing from an able candidate.*

Unit 4: Presenting the world

What you will do in the course

Unit 4 is the coursework unit for Edexcel A2 English Language and Literature. It builds on and extends your studies and reading for the AS units.

The emphasis in this unit is on your own independent research and reading around a chosen topic to develop your skills as a writer.

In this unit you will:

- choose a topic area and one **core text** as a focal point
- read widely around the topic
- use your study of your core text and your wide reading as a stimulus to create your own texts.

How you will be assessed

You will complete a coursework portfolio containing three pieces of writing, which will be worth a total of 80 marks:

- one piece of literary writing (21 marks)
- one piece of non-fiction writing (21 marks)
- one analytical evaluative commentary (38 marks).

Literary writing can be described as writing that derives from the writer's imagination and adopts a narrative approach, for example prose fiction, drama scripts and poetry.

Non-fiction writing is based on facts and includes reports and articles for newspapers, biography, obituary, popular science, travel journals and so on.

The word count for your portfolio is 2500–3000 words for your creative texts (approximately 1500 words each). For the commentary you are allowed 1000 words to cover both creative pieces.

You will notice from the tables on p101 that your literary and non-fiction pieces are assessed in exactly the same way and are worth a total of 21 marks each, and that your commentary is worth 38 marks. Your commentary therefore forms a significant proportion of your coursework portfolio.

The course

At A2 you will become more independent as you will be given opportunities to make personal choices and to follow your own ideas and interests. You will also be expected to make decisions about your wide reading and to find resources for yourself. You will, of course, have the support of your teacher, and opportunities to discuss your work and ideas with other members of your group.

At AS you were asked to choose from five prescribed topic areas; at A2 you have the freedom to choose any suitable topic, in consultation with your teacher.

You must choose one substantial core text to study in close detail. You have a free choice of a text in any genre, either literary or non-fiction. Your teacher will discuss this with you and will advise on suitable choices.

As in Unit 2 you will support the study of your chosen text with a range of wide reading in different genres and for a variety of audiences and purposes.

What you will do for your A2 coursework

Choose a topic

Choose a text in any genre
e.g. drama, fiction, non-fiction

Select wide reading to support your core text and to provide you with materials for research
*e.g. journalism, letters, diaries, historical and eye-witness accounts, stories, poetry, films,
TV and radio documentaries, web pages*

Assessment of your literary and non-fiction writing

Assessment objective		What this means in practice
AO1	Select and apply relevant concepts and approaches from integrated literary and linguistic study, using appropriate terminology and accurate, coherent written expression 10 marks (5 marks for each creative piece)	You will need to: • show that you can select suitable genres and approaches for your own original writing • be able to explain your methods when carrying out your research • use technical terms when you analyse and write about your own texts.
AO4	Demonstrate expertise and creativity in using language appropriately for a variety of purposes and audiences, drawing on insights from linguistic and literary studies 32 marks (16 marks for each creative piece)	You will need to: • show that you understand and can use the conventions of different genres in your own writing.

Assessment of your commentary

Assessment objective		What this means in practice
AO1	Select and apply relevant concepts and approaches from integrated literary and linguistic study, using appropriate terminology and accurate, coherent written expression 6 marks	You will need to: • show that you can select suitable genres and approaches for your own original writing • be able to explain your methods when carrying out your research • use technical terms when you analyse and write about your own texts.
AO2	Demonstrate detailed critical understanding in analysing the ways in which structure, form and language shape meanings in a range of spoken and written texts 16 marks	You will need to: • show evidence of your wide reading and research • be able to explain and comment on the literary and linguistic choices you made in shaping your material for your original writing.
AO3	Use integrated approaches to explore relationships between texts, analysing and evaluating the significance of contextual factors in their production and reception 16 marks	You will need to: • show understanding that your stimulus texts can be read and interpreted in different ways • show that you are aware that texts have many different layers • be able to explain the contexts and purposes of your own original texts.

Key terms

- core text
- evaluate

Across AS and A2

The Assessment objectives for this unit are the same as those for Unit 2, your AS coursework unit. You will apply the range of literary and linguistic concepts you studied at AS, making the step up to A2 by:

- doing more independent research than at AS
- extending the range and type of texts that you explore to stimulate your own writing
- writing in different genres from the ones you chose at AS.

Across AS and A2

Look back on the coursework pieces you produced for Unit 2 and consider *how* you wrote and *what* your choices of tasks and genres were. Then think about how you could venture into different areas for Unit 4.

How to succeed in English Language and Literature Unit 4

You will need to:

- take more responsibility for your own learning
- be prepared to read widely and to write in different ways
- reflect thoughtfully and consider what you have learned
- be organised and systematic
- communicate: take opportunities to share ideas with other members of your group
- **evaluate**: explore how others write and how you write yourself, and be able to say how a piece of writing works.

To gain high marks at A2 you need to show that you can:

- sustain a literary and linguistic analysis
- make judgements about the meanings of texts based on your literary and linguistic knowledge
- consider the effectiveness of texts in relation to the writer's/speaker's intentions
- demonstrate your ability to select and use the most effective techniques to suit your purposes and audiences in your own original writing.

A Approaching your coursework

In this section you will explore the issues relating to your A2 coursework and find out about the reading requirements for Unit 4. You will start to consider the types of tasks and approaches that would enable you to show your literary and linguistic expertise.

The title of the unit, 'Presenting the world', indicates that you can focus on any area of human experience that is represented in literary and non-fiction texts. The unit gives you the opportunity to work like a professional writer. You will choose your own subject matter, develop your research skills and find out about different ways in which you could present your subject. Your coursework will represent a journey where you have the chance to find a world that you wish to enter and explore.

1 Choosing your topic

You will begin by choosing a topic and a text linked to that topic, both of which are suitable for study at A2. You will decide on your topic and core text in consultation with your teacher; you may be studying the same topic as other members of your group.

To ensure that you have chosen a good topic, test it against the following questions.

- Does it offer enough scope – that is, does it provide opportunities for varied and substantial research?

- Is it manageable – that is, can you get access to the materials you will need to research it?

- Does it provide you with ideas for a range of possible writing outcomes, for both literary and non-fiction texts?

Below are some examples of suitable topic areas that would fulfil all these criteria.

- The impact of war on the individual
- Global epidemics and disasters
- Crossing boundaries
- Revolutions and dictatorships

How do you choose?

Start by considering these questions.

- What is there in your world and your experiences that particularly interests you?

- What fascinates you about other worlds and other people's lives and experiences?

Your choice of topic should give you the scope to research different times, places and cultures.

On the next page are suggestions for two routes by which you can start to explore possible topics.

Route 1: Starting from your own experiences

Begin by thinking about your own experiences and what interests you.

Activity 1

1 Copy the first column of the table below, and write your own responses in the 'Examples' column.

Personal profile	Examples
A2 subjects studied at school/college	English Language & Literature, Art, History
Sports and activities outside school/college	Basketball, guitar
Part-time work	Local supermarket
What do I like watching?	Football matches, DVDs, favourite TV programmes
What do I like listening to?	Favourite artists, radio programmes
What do I like reading?	Magazines, newspapers, novels
What do I like writing?	Short stories, online blogs

2 Working in a small group, share your personal profile with others and discuss the range of interests and experiences that you all have.

Now widen the scope of your discussion by extending from what is specific to you to a topic with more global implications.

3 Working in pairs, discuss aspects of your own life and experience that could be a starting point for your topic, such as the following.

• Your interests: if your passion is football you could widen the scope from your experience of European football to investigate the impact of the game in different countries. For example, in less economically developed countries such as those in South America, football can be an important means of advancement for talented young players.

• Your sense of national identity: you might begin by considering your own sense of identity, your family background and origins, and the cultural influences on your life, and then widen the scope to explore lifestyles in other cultures. For example, you could research and write about the experiences of migrant workers in the UK, or you could research different marriage customs.

Route 2: Starting from the bigger picture

Start with the bigger picture by thinking about global topics and themes that fascinate or intrigue you. For example:

• you may be interested in natural disasters and epidemics of recent years such as hurricanes, earthquakes, and global fears of pandemics. You might begin by considering the implications of epidemics in this country, such as cattle diseases and bird flu, and then go back in time to investigate the Great Plague and various kinds of writing about it.

• you may have been fascinated by your study of world wars in history lessons, and inspired and moved by war poetry. You could research current wars in Iraq or Afghanistan and consider the writing, both literary and non-fiction, that has come out of these conflicts.

Activity 2

Working individually or in a small group record your ideas about possible topics and how you would research them on a chart like the one below. Some topic areas and suggested approaches have been completed as examples. Add possible topics of your own.

Topic	Time	Place	Key events (add dates)	What people have written	What you could write (different genres)
Crossing boundaries/ transitions	Past Present	Emigration to the new world (the Americas and Australasia) Emigration within Europe	The Pilgrim Fathers, 1620 Convict ships sent to Australia (late 18th century) The Empire Windrush (Afro-Caribbean emigration to UK, 1948)	The Voyage of the Beagle: Charles Darwin Articles on immigrant workers in Britain (e.g. Chinese cockle-pickers, Eastern European agricultural workers) English Passengers: Matthew Kneale (novel about emigration to Tasmania) Our Country's Good: Timberlake Wertenbaker (play about English convicts in Australia) Testing the Echo: David Edgar (play about British citizenship)	Feature article: 'The benefits of a multicultural society' Editorial presenting an argument for or against a citizenship ceremony to celebrate being British Extract from a radio play with the theme of racial identity
The impact of war on the individual	20th/ 21st century	Siberia Eastern Europe Afghanistan Iran Iraq		The People's Act of Love: novel by James Meek First-hand accounts of people living in the danger zones (e.g. online news)	
Revolutions and dictatorships	Recent Past Present	Cuba	Resignation of Fidel Castro (2008)	Articles/ biographical material on Fidel Castro Journals and political writing of Che Guevara Our Man in Havana: novel by Graham Greene	

Choosing an angle of enquiry

Once you have chosen your topic you will need to narrow the focus to set up a particular angle of enquiry. Give yourself a focal point, a problem to solve or a question to ask when exploring your topic area. Be active – while you are doing your research and background reading you should also be finding out people's views, through interviews, questionnaires and informal conversations.

For example, you may be interested in the topic 'Crossing Boundaries'. When you think of this, what places and events come to mind? How have people written about it in different ways? Use the following prompt questions to think about your topic:

Topic

- Questions to ask about the topic
- What can I read?
- What can I watch?
- Who can I talk to?
- What can I write? Non-fiction Literary)

Choosing your core text

Selecting your core text is an important part of the coursework process as it is the starting point for your investigation of your topic.

Your core text should:
- offer scope for a substantial exploration of the topic
- stimulate your interest and imagination
- have enough themes and layers of meaning to suggest areas for research and wide reading
- give you ideas about different ways in which you could write.

The examples below describe two suitable core texts that fulfil these criteria.

Topic: Crossing Boundaries

Core text: *English Passengers* by Matthew Kneale. **Genre:** Prose fiction.

A fictionalised account of a nineteenth-century sea voyage transporting convicted prisoners and new settlers from Britain to Australia. The story is based on research into historical documents. The approach is via a series of intermingled narratives by a variety of characters.

Themes and issues include social status, religion, language, ethnic identity, racial discrimination, exploration of new territories.

Suggested linked wide reading: original diaries and letters of emigrants to the new world, historical archives, related literary texts such as *Our Country's Good* (drama by Timberlake Wertenbaker), modern accounts of emigration, case studies of twenty-first-century people who have settled in Australia/New Zealand.

Topic: Revolutions and Dictatorships

Core text: *China Road* by Rob Gifford.
Genre: Non-fiction.

An account of a journey along Route 312 which runs 3000 miles from Shanghai to the border of Kazakhstan. The approach is part reportage, part personal pilgrimage, part travelogue.

The theme is the rising power of contemporary China. Issues explored include China's history, geographical and ethnic diversity, reflections on Chinese culture, accounts of meetings with Chinese people.

Suggested linked wide reading: *Mao* by Jung Chang (biography of the dictator), *Wild Swans* by Jung Chang (fictionalised account of the life of three generations of Chinese women), current newspaper articles about the economic power of China, related television documentaries, investigative reports into the conditions of workers in Chinese factories, travel guides on China.

Exploring your core text and topic

Once you have chosen your core text, you can begin a process of reflection and interrogation to explore topics of interest to you and select wider reading that relates to your angles of enquiry.

Below and on the next page are examples of possible topics and core texts, with questions to ask. Whichever topic you choose you will need to reflect on your reading, think about the ways in which different speakers and writers have presented the topic, and then consider what *you* could write about it.

Topic: Football
Core text: *Football Against the Enemy* by Simon Kuper

- Question: Has the game of football provided opportunities for talented, underprivileged young people to escape poverty and oppression?

- Research: Read newspaper articles, research the impact of football in South America, search for relevant biographical information, e.g. *My Father and Other Working Class Football Heroes*: Gary Imlach – a mix of biography and social history – and the lively blog http://www.bangladeshfootballdoc.blogspot.com.

- Writing outcome (non-fiction): An extract from a documentary about the impact of the game of football on underprivileged young people as a route out of poverty, for example in Brazil or an African country.

Topic: Crossing Boundaries
Core text: *A Thousand Splendid Suns* by Khaled Hosseini

- Question: How do different cultures mark important events? Use your own experience and then move out to explore other cultures.

- Research: You may decide, for example, to focus on marriage rituals. Collect information about marriage rituals and customs in different cultures. Look for different perspectives; how are marriage customs presented in fiction and non-fiction? Find a specific area to investigate, e.g. the benefits of arranged marriages (read **editorials** and articles giving views for and against, interview people, read accounts of arranged marriages in fiction, e.g. *A Thousand Splendid Suns*, read real-life non-fiction accounts of arranged marriages, e.g. *The Bookseller of Kabul* by Asne Seierstad).

- Writing outcome (non-fiction): A persuasive magazine article arguing in favour of arranged marriages.

Key terms

- editorial
- stimulus text

Activity 3

Working in pairs, add another angle on the topic 'Crossing Boundaries'. Suggest possible **stimulus texts** and areas of research, and one or more writing outcomes.

Topic: European Identity
Core text: *Testing the Echo* by David Edgar

- Question: What is life like for young people living in Britain who have a mixed sense of identity – who may be only the second or third generation to live in England?

- Research: Read biographical accounts such as *Greetings from Bury Park* by the journalist Sarfraz Manzoor.

Topic: European Identity
Core text: *Testing the Echo* by David Edgar

- Question: What effect does emigration have on people's lives and sense of national identity?

- Research: Explore issues of emigration, immigration, customs and lifestyles. Begin with your own family and background, your own sense of national identity and factors that have influenced it. Extend to explore other people's sense of identity and how it is created. Research and find case studies of Eastern European immigrants in Britain (search the archives of national newspapers, watch TV documentaries, read related fiction, e.g. *The Road Home* by Rose Tremain, *Two Caravans* by Marina Lewycka).

Activity 4

Add your suggestions for both literary and non-fiction writing outcomes for the topic 'European Identity'.

Activity 5

Think about your own interests and make a list of possible topics that you would like to research and write about.

Don't be afraid to choose an angle that may be controversial; what matters is the quality of your research and your ability to produce convincing, well-written and interesting outcomes.

Across AS and A2

As you research and write your notebook, consider the links between your Unit 4 coursework and the other units; for example, you may be able to gain ideas from your wide reading for Unit 3. Remember that you will be building on the skills you acquired and the experiences you had when writing your AS coursework.

Your working notebook

The boxes labelled 'Your working notebook' throughout this unit are a prompt to record something in your notebook.

Your working notebook

You will need a clear system for recording details of your research and textual study and for making notes about your ideas. Keeping a notebook from the beginning of your work on Unit 4 will help you gather and make sense of your ideas, as well as assist you in writing your commentary.

Start your notebook at the beginning of your A2 course. Keep adding to the notebook as you progress through your coursework preparation. You will be able to refer to it when you are writing the first drafts of your creative pieces and, more importantly, the first draft of your commentary.

The idea is to keep a complete record of your reading and research, your initial ideas about texts, and the decisions that you make. This requirement to keep documentary evidence of your work in progress reflects the approach of professional writers and is an essential skill if you choose to pursue your studies at a higher level.

Here are some of the things that you can include in your working notebook:

- details of your topic area and core text
- details of anything that you read or watch with brief references to the different writing styles and approaches that you encounter (keep details of the sources, as you will need to include a bibliography in your coursework portfolio)
- ideas about new texts or particular stylistic approaches
- short pieces of preparatory writing – make notes about what worked well and what you particularly enjoyed doing
- notes on any significant decisions or changes that you have made, as you may wish to refer to them in your commentary
- details of any interviews: date, name of interviewee, and so on
- ideas for areas of investigation.

It might be a good idea to carry a tiny digital voice recorder to use as a convenient note-taker.

The working notebook is your private document – feel free to use colour-coding, sticky notes and so on to help you sort and retrieve information. You might like to think of it as the kind of documentary evidence that students of art are asked to produce to accompany their portfolio of work; but note that you will not be required to include the notebook in your portfolio.

Activity 6

Work in pairs or small groups. Look at the extract below and on the facing page from a student's working notebook and discuss what the notebook tells you about the following:

5

- the topic
- the core text and wide reading
- the possible writing outcomes
- the process of thinking, research and investigation
- the way in which the student has recorded ideas.

10

Topic: The Impact of War on the Individual

Main text: 'The People's Act of Love' by James Meek. Fascinating novel, different narrative perspectives, set in early 20th century Siberia, but seems like it's happening now. Must have done huge amounts of research but it's a great story of war and love.

Wide reading:
Reports on current wars: Iraq, Afghanistan. Articles by foreign correspondents and first-person accounts.

'Shuttered lives': Iraq through the eyes of its women (Independent 28/09/07)

'Treat us like you would your own': first-hand accounts by Iraqi interpreters (The Guardian 15/08/07)

Obituary of Dith Pran – the interpreter in Cambodia in 1960s; his story inspired the film 'The Killing Fields' (Independent 01/04/08)

15 Alan Johnston writes about the pressures of being a foreign correspondent: 'As you try to get out into the streets and see what's happening, the interview requests pour in: BBC News 24, World TV, World Service, Five Live. You scribble dispatches and try to stitch together telly and radio pieces as your manic day unfolds.'

20 He was kidnapped in Gaza in 2007. Good idea to read his autobiography?

Fiction: read some extracts from 'The Kite Runner' by Khaled Hosseini, set in 1970s Afghanistan. Different perspective from 'People's Act of Love' – sees events through the eyes of a 12-year-old.

Other reading in different genres?
25 Do some research on war in the past – letters/diaries
Good sites for research into WW2: Modern History Sourcebook, Imperial War Museum
Interview people who have had first-hand experience of war, read blogs posted by civilians living in war zones

30 Writing ideas:
literary:
interested in the lives of women in present-day Iraq – could re-shape interviews and first-hand accounts to write an extract from a narrative with a fictitious female protagonist. Liked the character of Katya, the student in 'People's Act of Love' who
35 carries an explosive device in her satchel.

non-fiction:
a journalism piece could be a good idea? a short, pacy article about what it's like for young people living in Iraq or Iran – contrast with life in England – look at differences doesn't have to be the most obvious angle, e.g. an article showing the advantages of
40 wearing the veil or of arranged marriages.

2 Managing your time

One of the biggest challenges with coursework is making effective use of the time available. This could be crucial in enabling you to achieve high marks. You need to identify early in the process how much time you have and exactly how you need to divide it up.

For your Unit 4 coursework you will probably have the equivalent of one term. This will give you about 36 hours of classroom time, which your teacher will choose to use in different ways. In addition to classroom time you will also need to use a substantial amount of time outside the classroom (your teacher will give you guidance).

Give yourself a definite timetable with specific amounts of time allocated to each aspect of your coursework. Allow about 25% of your allocated time for each of these key stages:

1 Reading and reflection   3 Writing your non-fiction text

2 Writing your literary text   4 Writing your commentary

Part of the step up to A2 is that you need to take more responsibility for organising your studies and managing your time. The best way to do this is to give yourself regular deadlines for completing sections of work.

Set mini-goals by dividing your work into what you hope to achieve each week. At the end of each week, look over what you have achieved and congratulate yourself when you can tick off completed items.

You could note deadlines for the following in a diary:

- submitting proposals for your coursework tasks and titles
- writing the first draft of your literary piece
- writing the first draft of your non-literary piece
- writing the first draft of your commentary
- time for peer feedback
- writing the final draft of your non-literary piece
- writing the final draft of your literary piece
- writing the final draft of your commentary and bibliography.

Dividing your work into manageable amounts will give you more control of the coursework process, and will enable you to enjoy your preparation and writing.

Activity 7

Below are examples of the action plans drawn up by two students (labelled A and B).

Work in small groups. Read through both action plans and make notes on how effective you think they are. Is anything omitted? Where do you think the plans could be improved?

Student A

Choose topic

Start research

Select main text; some quick background research to find related reading

5

Begin reading/study of text and do as much wide reading as possible – use TV, film, etc. to get further ideas

10

Make notes on main text and on wide reading

Give in writing proposals for both pieces

Write first drafts

15

Write commentaries

Do re-drafting and revising.

Student B

Time: approx 12 weeks

Week 1:
Choose topic and main text (with teacher's advice)
Start reading and make notes about initial ideas for writing
5 outcomes
Begin working notebook

Weeks 2–3:
Research and note-taking. Share ideas and decide on writing
Write proposals and discuss with teacher

10

Weeks 4–6:
Write first drafts with word counts – use working notebook to make notes for commentary
Ask people to read/advise on both pieces

Week 7:
15 Write commentary. Add word count.

Week 8:
Give in both pieces and commentary

Weeks 8–9:
Revise and edit with advice from teacher. Make sure word
20 counts are accurate.

Weeks 11–12:
Write final drafts of two pieces and commentary
Complete bibliography
Proof reading and final check.

3 Getting started

You have thought about your topic and texts; you have made some notes on initial ideas and possibilities; you have talked to your teacher and other people; now you must begin. How do you get started?

Some writers say that for them it is important to try to write something every day rather than waiting for inspiration. While you are taking notes as part of your research, try writing short amounts as ideas come to you. You can save these paragraphs of writing in a file and refer to them later.

Remember that the more you write, the better you will be (if you wanted to learn to play a musical instrument you would be prepared to practise every day, and the same is true of writing). Remember also that you need to read. Good readers make good writers. Read widely and often; find out and read the best examples.

Start by creating an overview and map out everything you need to do. The section headings in this book will help you.

Writing freely and creatively

Before you begin to give serious consideration to what you will produce for your final coursework pieces, you need to give yourself the opportunity to write freely and creatively for your own pleasure, without the concerns of assessment.

Activity 8

1 Try any of these exercises to unlock your creativity and give writing practice.

- Look back at the 'flash fiction' that you practised at AS (see Unit 2 in *Edexcel AS English Language and Literature Student Book*, page 112). Try this with non-fiction; write 150 words on a real-life topic.
- Use an image from a painting or music for inspiration for a fiction piece of about 150 words.
- Write about a recent event (national or local), giving your views.
- Write a creative response to the title *The First Time*. Write about 150 words.

- Find a newspaper or magazine article that you agree or disagree with and write a paragraph in response.
- Imagine someone is going to write a biography about you and is searching your house for information about you and your life. Use this information to write a paragraph (remember to write in the third person: he/she).
- Choose an extract from any text and adapt a section of it into a different genre. For example, turn a letter into an extract from a short story, or a biography of a famous historical figure into a short extract from a play.

2 Working with a partner, choose one of the short pieces of writing that you have done. Explain the genre, audience, purpose and context of your text to your partner.

Begin a table like the one below:

Genre	Flash fiction
Purpose	To entertain/inspire/amuse
Audience	Readers interested in creative fiction
Context	Magazine aimed at young male or female readers

3 Re-write your creative text using a different set of options – that is, change the audience, purpose and narrative voice – and add these details to your table.

4 Explore the differences in the effects created by the two texts.

4 Exploring the terms 'literary' and 'non-fiction'

If you have always thought of literary and non-fiction texts as being at opposite ends of a spectrum, you will find that the distinctions can become blurred.

If you are writing non-fiction, authenticity and accuracy are clearly important and this needs good research. But much fiction is also based on historical fact, or on particular real-life events, so how much accuracy is needed and when is it acceptable to speculate and introduce possibilities? For example, if you wanted to write a fictional account of an historical event, you would need to create characters and situations that seemed authentic. To do this you would need to research and acquire knowledge of the historical period.

Activity 9

1 Work in small groups. Make a list of as many types of literary and non-fiction texts as you can think of. Some ideas are given below.

> journalism, traditional fairy stories, memoirs, myths and legends, novels, diaries, poems, historical fiction, popular science, fiction based on events or real people, dramatisations of historical events, biography, reportage

2 Draw a line down the middle of a sheet of paper, and label the columns 'Purely imaginary' at the left and 'Completely factual' at the right. Use your list of types of texts to plot the genres across this scale.

Activity 10

Read the text to the right. It is an extract from *Tulip Fever*, a novel by Deborah Moggach. The novel is set in seventeenth-century Amsterdam and is based on the life of a famous Dutch painter of portraits, possibly Jan Vermeer.

As part of her research Moggach consulted books on art history and on the lives of the seventeenth-century Dutch painters, and she read letters from that period, including those attributed to Vermeer. In the novel, the painter has been commissioned to paint the portrait of a wealthy merchant and his wife.

Working in small groups, make notes in answer to these questions:

1 Where do you find evidence in the text of Moggach's research into the historical period?

2 What literary and linguistic features has she used to shape this material to create an authentic context and credible characters? Discuss your findings in your group and then make summarising notes on your discussion.

From *Tulip Fever* by Deborah Moggach

Behind his easel the painter is watching me. His blue eyes bore into my soul. He is a small, wiry man with wild black hair. His head is cocked to one side. I stare back at him coolly. Then I realize – he is not looking at me. He is looking at an arrangement to be painted. He wipes his brush on a rag and frowns. I am just an object – brown hair, white lace collar and blue, shot-silk dress.

This irritates me. I am not a joint of mutton! My heart thumps; I feel dizzy and confused. What is the matter with me?

'How long is this going to take?' I ask coldly.

'You're already tired?' The painter steps up to me and gives me a handkerchief. 'Are you unwell?'

'I'm perfectly well.'

'You've been sniffing all morning.'

'It's just a chill. I caught it from my maid.' I won't use his handkerchief. I pull out my own and dab at my nose. He moves closer to me; I can smell linseed oil and tobacco.

'You're not happy, are you?' he asks.

'What do you mean, sir?'

'I mean – you're not happy, standing.' He pulls up a chair. 'Sit here. If I move this… and this…' He shifts the table. He moves quickly, rearranging the furniture. He puts the globe to one side and stands back, inspecting it. He works with utter concentration. His brown jerkin is streaked with paint.

Whether fiction or non-fiction, texts in all genres aim to entertain and to establish a hold over their audience to ensure that they continue reading. As with literature texts, non-fiction texts will be deliberately shaped and crafted, and the writers will have made decisions about what to include and what to omit. Context, audience and purpose are vitally important.

In your research and preparation for both of your texts, you will be taking an approach similar to an investigative journalist as you search for ideas. It is interesting that many journalists – writers associated with non-fiction – use their experiences to write works of fiction.

One example is the journalist and war reporter James Meek. In an interview with an online magazine he discusses the differences between fiction, reportage and other types of journalism. He identifies imagination as an essential quality not only for writing fiction, but also for journalism and other types of non-fiction. Novelists use their imagination to delve into the infinite world of possibilities to find material for their narratives. But journalists and writers of other types of non-fiction need to use their imagination to decide where they are going to go, what they are going to research and who they are going to speak to. The table below summarises his ideas.

Fiction	Reportage	Journalism
Offers flexibility: can be pure fantasy or based on type of research done by journalists, shaped into a narrative Creating atmosphere is important but the location does not have to be specific	Events are reported while they are happening or immediately after they have happened Pieces have to be economical with words and written to deadlines – these types of reports are also referred to as 'stories'	Can be feature-writing, editorials, reviews, commentaries, sporting events – written with time to plan and reflect – or can be more impressionistic 'mood pieces' evoking atmosphere and the approach of feature writers is to look for 'the human story'; this can also be a narrative and the atmosphere of a specific location can be evoked as in fiction, but must be genuine

Activity 11

Work in pairs or small groups. Read the extract below, then answer the following questions using your knowledge of literary and linguistic techniques.

1 Identify the context, audience and purpose of the extract. Is it an article or an extract from a thriller?

2 Point to specific textual evidence for your decision, such as:
   • use of tense
   • sentence length and type
   • use of direct speech
   • inclusion of authentic detail.

> One of our drivers spotted him first – a stranger in fatigues who had slipped into the open-air restaurant by the Tigris River in central Baghdad and was watching us intently. Two other unknown men lurked in the background. It was dark, we had just finished three large dishes
> 5 of masgouf – roasted carp – and were sitting around a blazing fire.
> The driver took no chances. He came over and whispered in my ear: 'Mr Martin, we must go.' We were out of the restaurant in a trice, walking hastily to our two cars, our bodyguards with their pistols drawn. Within another minute we were speeding down Abu Niwas road
> 10 towards the safety of our heavily fortified hotel.

Independent research

Below is a list of fiction and non-fiction texts that involve a synthesis of imagination and factual detail to support further reading. **Fiction** *The Darkness of Wallis Simpson* by Rose Tremain (short story based on the life of Wallis Simpson, the woman responsible for the abdication of Edward VIII), *The Clothes on Their Backs* by Linda Grant (a novel about emigration and Israel), *The People's Act of Love* by James Meek (a murder mystery set in Siberia in 1919), *The Tenderness of Wolves* by Stef Penney (historical novel set in Canada but researched in the British Library in London), *Atonement* by Ian McEwan (a story of love and betrayal set in the Second World War) **Non-fiction** *Miracles of Life* by J.G. Ballard (an autobiography), *Stalin* by Simon Sebag Montefiore (re-creates the life of the Soviet dictator).

Take it further

When you have identified the text as either an extract from a thriller or journalism, re-write it in the other genre. Share your version with a partner and discuss the changes you made.

Journalists, especially those who write more reflective and impressionistic 'mood-evoking' pieces, often need to create atmosphere and to 'search for the human story'. To do this they employ stylistic techniques of descriptive writing that are also typical of the fictional genres.

Activity 12

Compare the literary and linguistic techniques used in the two extracts below. To guide your comparison, use the questions in Activity 11 and try to add more points of your own.

Text A is an extract from the reporter Martin Fletcher's account of his day in Baghdad.

Text B is an extract from *We Are Now Beginning Our Descent*, a novel by the journalist James Meek, which is set in Afghanistan.

Your exploration of these two texts should have helped make you aware of the links between writing journalism and writing fiction, in preparation for your own work in literary and non-fiction genres. The next activity is intended to help you consider what makes good journalism.

Text A

The streets are rutted, the buildings crumbling and dilapidated, the lampposts broken. Walls are pockmarked by shrapnel. Everything is covered in a fine brown dust. Someone somewhere is making an effort, however. Many
5 of the ugly concrete blast barriers have recently been decorated with brightly coloured murals of bucolic scenes.

Where Saddam's statue once stood in Fardous Square there is now a children's playground – the authorities' antidote to horror.

Martin Fletcher, *The Times*

Text B

From *We Are Now Beginning Our Descent* by James Meek

At first the road was a swathe of small, half-loose rocks embedded in soil that had become dust as fine as talcum powder. Once a second, the old Soviet army car jolted and lifted the passengers in their seats. The dust splashed off
5 the tyres of the Uazik in front as fluid as milk before spreading high and wide around them so that the day turned yellow and they bound their scarves tight across their mouths and nostrils. It was mid-October, and they were thousands of feet above sea level, and climbing, yet
10 the sun shone.

Activity 13

Below is a list of reporters and journalists currently writing in national newspapers and reporting the news on our television screens.

- James Meek
- George Alagiah
- Orla Guerin
- Frank Gardner
- Rageh Omaar
- Lyse Doucet
- Robert Fisk
- Alan Johnston

Choose one name from the list and do some research into what he or she has written and reported on. Read some examples of your chosen journalist's work and choose one piece to present to the class, giving reasons for your choice. This could be either a written article or a transcript of a television news report or documentary. Make sure you address the following points:

- What interested you about the work of this journalist?
- What did you find effective in his or her style of writing/reporting?

The next activity asks you to consider the question of accuracy in non-fiction texts by examining how one writer adapted and shaped her personal experiences to create a text for a wider audience.

Activity 14

Vera Brittain

The following two texts were both written by the writer Vera Brittain about her interview for Oxford University in 1914.

Text A is an extract from her diary, written immediately after the event.

Text B is an extract from her autobiography *Testament of Youth*, written some time later.

Text A

From *Chronicle of Youth: War Diary, 1913–17* by Vera Brittain

March 16th–20th Somerville College, Oxford

I found with my very first paper that I had been working on quite wrong lines, having read more books of criticism than the works of the writers themselves, which was what they wanted. Also I found out that all the women's colleges have now entrance exams, so without this one I cannot get in at all. Of course had I known that I should have been much more careful in preparation instead of trying to do it all alone. Also, this is the worst possible year for anyone to try to get into Somerville. Last year they had forty vacancies owing to the new buildings, but this year they have only 18, & 82 people trying for them!

On the Tuesday soon after breakfast we had our first paper. The moment I read mine, I realised that I could not have any chance at all. I was so petrified by the discovery that I sat staring for half an hour at the questions without writing a word, which of course made me unable to finish the 5 questions which we had to do out of nine. However, after thinking I would ask Miss Penrose to let me go home that afternoon, I forced myself to start, & wrote an answer to a question on Thomson & Cowper very inefficiently, with only half my attention, still thinking I would go home that afternoon. However I came to the conclusion that although I knew it was hopeless it would be quite amusing to stick it out, & though it is useless I am glad I did, for if I had proved myself to be afraid of failing I should never have respected myself any more.

Just after my paper I had an interview with Miss Darbishire, the literature don. She has a kind & clever face & I found her delightful. She asked me whom I liked best in my period to which I of course answered Wordsworth, & she seemed pleased to think I had discovered him for myself & also that I had worked alone & against opposition.

Text B

From *Testament of Youth* by Vera Brittain

I know of no place where the wind can be so icy and the damp so penetrating as in Oxford round about Easter-time. On my first intimidating night, the longing to thaw my stiff fingers tempted me to abandon even a frantic last-minute revision for that prolonged struggle to light a fire with which every Somerville student is familiar. My efforts were, of course, unavailing; the Oxford women's colleges have never had the means to afford the best drawing-room nuggets, and my previous experience with good Midland coal had not endowed me with the skill that I later acquired in wresting warmth out of a mass of dust, a few damp sticks, and some nobbly chunks of slate.

As Somerville did not then run to a large supply of hot baths – though I should have been too shy to appropriate one if it had – I spent the night in a shivering stupor, kept wretchedly awake by the misery of my frozen feet and the periodic clamour of unfamiliar bells. Consequently my first paper the next morning plunged me at once into panic, in which condition I sat for an hour without writing a word, desperately clasping and unclasping my hands under the table, and inwardly resolving that the moment we were permitted to leave the room, I would tell the Principal that I was returning home at once.

The subsequent course of my entire future probably depended upon the mere chance that something – perhaps my guardian angel, perhaps nothing more romantic than the warmth restored to my icy limbs by the stuffiness of the lecture-room in which we were working – suddenly made me decide to 'stick out' the ordeal for which I had prepared at such a cost of combat and exasperation, and to make the best of the job that had begun so badly. So, frantically seizing my pen, I started to write; any nonsense, I felt, was better than the blank sheets that would so forlornly typify my failure of imagination and courage.

All through the days of the examination, in spite of the three or four quickly-made friends with whom between papers I ate large teas in the town, I felt an unadapted alien to an extent that privately filled me with shame, and remember still the ludicrous shock from which I suffered after first meeting two or three of my terrifying competitors from East End or north-country High Schools.

1 Work in small groups. Read both texts and identify and list any differences. Look for both variations in content and differences in stylistic techniques.

2 What evidence is there to show that Text A was written spontaneously and that Text B was carefully crafted? You could consider the following features: different levels of formality, from casual to very formal; use of descriptive writing and scene setting; use of emotive vocabulary; deliberate shaping of a text to create tension.

3 Why do you think Vera Brittain re-shaped her diary entry for her autobiography? Identify and comment on specific features in Text B to support your ideas. Share your ideas with other members of your group.

This activity should have helped to increase your awareness of how non-fiction texts need deliberate shaping to have the same appeal for their readers as literary texts. You probably noted and discussed points similar to the ones below:

- non-fiction texts need more than mere facts to appeal to their readers

- writers of autobiography (and biography) need to make the subject three-dimensional by including contextual background detail

- writers of non-fiction need to re-craft raw material using carefully selected literary and linguistic features to create a rapport with their audience

- writing about events retrospectively will tend to lead to a different perspective.

Activity 15

1 Choose an event in your life that made a lasting impact on you. If you have recorded it in a diary entry, you could use this as your starting point. Produce a short written or spoken account of the event.

2 Listen to or read the account and decide how you would need to present it to make it suitable for a commercial autobiography or biography. Ask yourself these questions: what do I need to add; what, if anything, should I omit; which stylistic features should I use to create more impact and to interest my audience?

3 Now write the account of your own experience in approximately 250 words, as if it was an extract from your autobiography. Exchange accounts with your partner and discuss how well your crafted version has worked, adding ideas for further improvements.

Activity 16

The contemporary novelist Zadie Smith said that it could be seen as the duty of writers to please readers – to be clear, interesting and to entertain. The task of writers is not necessarily to represent things in the way readers already see them by playing on shared experiences, but instead to show what could be called 'one person's truth'.

In groups discuss how far you agree with Smith's principles.

Assessment objectives

In the short writing activity in Activity 15 you have addressed AO4 by demonstrating your expertise in writing appropriately for a particular purpose and audience. It is also an opportunity for you to address AO2 by explaining how your choices of structure, form and language have helped to shape your text and make it suitable for a wider audience. You need to give specific examples to provide evidence for your explanations.

To conclude this section you will carry out a small amount of research and complete two short pieces of writing, one of which will be literary and one non-fiction. This will give you an insight into what it feels like to research a topic and to illustrate how the same material can be shaped in different ways.

Activity 17

The topic for your research is 'Football: Is it more than a game?'

Read the two texts opposite and below and use them to stimulate ideas. As you read, consider the following issues.

- Angle: what is the perspective of each writer?

- Content: what does each writer say about football?

- Style: how do they each say it?

- Did you find anything interesting or effective about the ways in which these two writers approached the topic of football?

Text B is an extract from the introduction to a non-fiction text that explores the influence of football all over the world.

Text A is an extract from a newspaper editorial by Germaine Greer, which argues that football is an intrinsic part of a nation's cultural life.

Text A

Sport is perhaps the best way to demonstrate how culture works to enliven and leaven daily experience. We know that the Aztecs played ball games, and that the annual ceremonial games were of crucial importance in the cultural life of Mesoamerican peoples. Our reasons for risking bankruptcy in staging the Olympic Games are cultural. But sport does not simply bring people together; it also divides them, sometimes with murderous effect. What is perhaps more important is that, when well-managed, the battle on the pitch is a stereotyped outlet for aggression and conflict; this symbolic warfare inspires acres of newsprint, much of it better written than anything on comment pages.

Football unites all those people who love the game, whether in agreement or disagreement, at the same time as it divides the supporters of the different clubs. The more you know about the game, the deeper the enjoyment; the more passionately you support your club, the deeper your involvement. The amount of intellectual energy generated by football is unimaginably massive; the effect of such passion is to dramatise the lives of people who might otherwise be snared in disadvantage, poverty and disability, with very little to look forward to if not their club's promotion.

Germaine Greer, *The Guardian*

Text B

From Football Against the Enemy by Simon Kuper

No one knows how many football fans there are. World Cup USA 1994, Inc. has put out a booklet claiming that the TV audience for the Italian World Cup was 25.6 billion (five times the world's population), and that 31 billion are expected to watch the American World Cup.

These figures may be meaningless. For any recent World Cup final, you can find viewing figures that disagree by billions, and the same booklet claims that Striker, the World Cup's canine mascot, will have been seen one trillion times by the end of 1994. One trillion precisely? Are they sure?

But for certain, as the booklet states, 'soccer is the most popular sport in the world.' They say in Naples that when a man has money, he first buys himself something to eat, then goes to the football, and then sees if he has anything left to find a place to live. The Brazilians say that even the smallest village has a church and a football field – 'well, not always a church, but certainly a football field'. More people in the world go to prayer than to football matches, but otherwise there is no public pursuit to match the game. This book is about its place in the world.

When a game matters to billions of people it ceases to be just a game. Football is never just football: it helps make wars and revolutions, and it fascinates mafias and dictators.

Step 1 Reading and research

Do some quick research on the impact of football on your region or area and on the lives of individuals. Make some notes using internet sources, articles from local and regional newspapers, extracts from any relevant autobiographies, and short interviews/ discussions with people you know who have an interest in football.

Step 2 Writing tasks

Write one literary and one non-fiction piece inspired by the stimulus texts. Remember to choose a particular angle or focus and to have a clearly identified audience and purpose in mind, for example:

- for your non-fiction task, write an article for your local or regional newspaper about the significance of the game in your local community

- for your literary task, use the material to inspire a short extract from a novel for children aged 11–13 and which features a main character (either female or male) who is obsessed by football.

Aim to write approximately 250 words for each task.

Step 3 Feedback

Share your writing outcomes with other members of your group. To do this effectively, make sure that all the extracts are anonymous, mix them up and share them out at random among the group. Each group member should evaluate the text he or she has been given.

To be worthwhile, the evaluation process must be constructive and everyone must be prepared to accept that some aspects of their work may be more successful than others. Although it is difficult to assess honestly the work of your friends and peers, focused constructive criticism is the way to improve your writing and therefore to achieve higher marks in your final assessment.

Use these guidelines to evaluate the texts.

- Does the text have a clear genre and approach?
- Is there a clearly defined audience?
- Does the writer show awareness of audience by using suitable techniques to capture and maintain their interest?
- Were there any features of the text that you found particularly effective?
- Do you have any suggestions for improving the text?

Repeat the feedback activity and evaluate another text. At the end of the activity, the writer of each piece should have received feedback from two other group members.

Step 4 Discussion

Conduct a whole-class or group discussion about what makes good literary and non-fiction writing.

You don't have to reach definite agreement about this, but it will help you focus on the need to be acutely aware of the specific purpose and audience for each original text that you write.

Activity 18

1 Complete a table like the one below to record your ideas,

Fill in your choice of topic and main text. Find three examples of wide reading in literary genres and three in non-fiction genres (remember that for wide reading you can also make reference to film, TV, radio, stage plays and material accessed via the internet).

Topic:	Global Disasters and Epidemics
Main text:	A Journal of the Plague Year: Daniel Defoe
Wide reading 1:	An Inconvenient Truth (documentary film presented by Al Gore, 2006)
Wide reading 2:	Historical records of the plague in the village of Eyam, Derbyshire
Wide reading 3:	Article on climate change by Johann Hari in The Independent (04/08/08), 'The WMD that really should be worrying us'
Wide reading 4:	The Simpsons Movie (animated satire on climate change issues, 2007)
Wide reading 5:	Internet searches on related issues
Wide reading 6:	'The Great Global Warming Swindle' (Channel 4 documentary opposing current theories on climate change, 2007)

2 Share your ideas and get feedback from others in your group. This activity is important whether or not you are studying the same topic as others in your group. Note the range of genres and types of wide reading that other students have chosen.

Your working notebook

Copy your completed table into your working notebook.

Coursework checkpoint

Review what you have done so far, checking that you have completed these key steps.
1 Choosing your topic – are you satisfied that it meets all the criteria: Does it offer sufficient scope, Is it manageable, Will it provide you with ideas for writing tasks?
2 Choosing your core text – it should relate to your topic area and be substantial enough to provide you with interesting ideas to explore. If you are studying the same text as other members of your group, you will be able to share ideas for wide reading and your thoughts about possible writing outcomes.
3 Choosing some wide reading around your topic area – you will add to this during your research.
4 Thinking about your tasks – have you noted some initial thoughts about your writing tasks? Your wide reading and research will probably lead you to refine the title and the focus of your writing tasks.

B Reading and reflection

In this section you will be given advice and guidance on how to:

- study your main text
- develop a research plan
- find wide reading and resources around your topic area
- document your findings and ideas.

You will also be given the opportunity to compare and contrast different genres and approaches to writing, and to practise writing in different genres (a vital part of the coursework process). Although you may be eager to begin writing your creative pieces, it is essential that you devote time and thought to your reading and research so that you maximise your opportunities to write well-informed, original and expert creative tasks.

Reading and researching is not a passive process, as you will also be critically analysing the texts that you read, making notes, and trying out original writing ideas. You need to study your core text in as much detail as you would for an examination, but as this is a coursework unit you will have more freedom and flexibility in how to approach your reading and critical study. You will therefore be able to adopt different lines of enquiry and examine your texts from different perspectives.

Across AS and A2

The key skill you will be developing which takes you to advanced level is the ability to make critical judgements about meaning and tone in texts and to *evaluate* the effectiveness of different stylistic techniques. This relates particularly to AO2 and AO3, which will be assessed in your commentary. Remind yourself of what is required for AO2 and AO3 so that you can apply them to your close textual analysis, reading and research.

Key terms

- multi-modal

1 Reading across units 3 and 4

While you are studying for your Unit 3 examination it is likely that you will also be involved in preparing and possibly writing your coursework for Unit 4.

The two units assess similar skills, as both require you to:

- make connections between texts
- work independently
- read across a range of genres from different contexts.

It will make your progress through the units much smoother if you can see the connections and use your work for the two units to complement each other.

Wide reading: You will be reading texts from a variety of written, spoken and **multi-modal** sources for both units, so your awareness of genre conventions and your decisions about which genres to use for your own original writing could be influenced by your reading for Unit 3.

Style models: You will be introduced to many different style models during your preparation for Unit 4 and you will also encounter different styles and approaches through your reading for Unit 3.

Inspiration/ideas for written tasks: During your studies for Unit 3 you may find some inspiration or a starting point for a writing outcome that you can then integrate into your choices of coursework tasks.

2 Reading your core text

Once you have chosen your core text, you need to develop a plan for studying the text closely. Previously when you made a close study of set texts, you will have been working with the rest of the group and with considerable guidance from your teacher. Now, at A2, you will probably be making some independent decisions about the best way to study your core text and wide reading. You can, of course, ask your teacher for advice and you should take any opportunity to work with others in your group.

You do not have to take the most obvious approach to textual study. You can integrate tried and tested methods with different approaches to your reading. Previously you may have studied a text by beginning with a straightforward chronological reading. When you read your core text for Unit 4 you will also be thinking about how it relates to your topic and what ideas it could give you for your own writing.

Here is a suggested two-step strategy for reading your text, which you can use or adapt.

Step 1: Getting an overview

Begin by reading your text quickly and absorbing any initial responses and ideas to gain an overview of the text's genre, historical period or context, its main theme and how it is presented.

Below is an extract from an exemplar core text to give you a flavour of the text, followed by a student's overview of the text.

> **From *A Journal of the Plague Year* by Daniel Defoe**
>
> London might well be said to be all in tears; the mourners did not go about the streets indeed, for nobody put on black or made a formal dress of mourning for their nearest friends; but the voice of mourners was truly heard in the streets. The shrieks of women and children at the windows and doors of their houses, where their dearest relations were perhaps dying, or just dead, were so frequent
> 5 to be heard as we passed the streets, that it was enough to pierce the stoutest heart in the world to hear them. Tears and lamentations were seen almost in every house, especially in the first part of the visitation; for towards the latter end men's hearts were hardened, and death was so always before their eyes, that
> 10 they did not so much concern themselves for the loss of their friends, expecting that themselves should be summoned the next hour.

Topic: Global Epidemics and Disasters
Core text: *A Journal of the Plague Year* by Daniel Defoe

Genre	Novel written as a diary or record of events
Historical period and context	Published in 1722; describes the epidemic of the Great Plague of London in 1665
Main theme and presentation	The effects of the bubonic plague on the people of London; presented as a spontaneous record of reminiscences and observations

Step 2: Exploring in detail

Once you have an overview, you need to begin to explore the text in more depth. Depending on the length and type of your text, you could either read it through again in chronological order or choose specific sections. To give a focal point to your reading, use the following guiding questions to structure your study.

1 What do you feel is the main purpose of the text?

2 How does the writer's point of view influence the reader's understanding of the text?

3 What type of audience is the text aimed at?

4 What specific literary and linguistic techniques are used to shape meaning and to create effects?

5 How is your reading of the text influenced by your background, experiences and beliefs?

Your working notebook

Make a similar table for your own text and copy it into your working notebook. When you have explored these questions on your core text, write up all of this initial work in your working notebook. Remind yourself of the Assessment objectives for the commentary (page 103) and notice how you are already acquiring the approaches needed to demonstrate expertise in AO2 and AO3.

Assessment objectives

By interrogating your core text in this way you are applying your knowledge of literary and linguistic approaches (AO2) and demonstrating understanding of context, audience and purpose (AO3). If you select appropriate technical terminology and if you write accurately and coherently, you are also addressing AO1. As there is a total of 38 marks for your commentary, it is important that you prepare for it as carefully as for your two original writing tasks.

3 Devising your research plan

The focal point of your research plan will be to find a number of texts in different genres that relate to your topic area. There are three overlapping strands to your research:

Strand 1 Getting ideas:
You need to use your core text and wide reading to inspire you with ideas for the subject matter of your literary and non-fiction texts

Strand 3 Finding style models:
You need to explore and investigate different styles and perspectives to help with your decisions about your own writing. When you have decided on the genres for your creative tasks, you will need to read a variety of texts in those genres.

Strand 2 Researching content:
You need to research your topic area to ensure that the content of your own creative work is accurate and convincing. You will need to use different types of resources, such as books, internet searches, films and historical records.

Investigation and research should be your priorities at this stage in your coursework preparation. Remember that you should not be concerned with 'right' or 'wrong' answers. This unit is all about you making discoveries for yourself. As the American scientist Richard N. Zare, writing in a science periodical, said: 'Students often seem to value more the answer than the question. I think quite the opposite. The quest to answer a question is where the learning takes place, not the answer itself.'

Writing in your coursework

The quality of your research and your ability to ask questions are important factors in the success of your coursework. Evidence of careful preparation and willingness to ask questions and approach your topic with an open mind will be demonstrated in the quality of your three written pieces. Your reading and research into different genres and style models will help you to choose suitable approaches and should make you aware of effective literary and linguistic devices. Your questioning approach to texts will improve your critical analytical abilities and will equip you with the skills you need to write a successful commentary on your own original writing tasks.

4 Research pathways

Your research, reading and writing are all closely linked. The more reading, research and reflection that you do, the more you will narrow down the precise focus of your writing tasks, and the more you will be able to show your knowledge of writing in your creative pieces.

The diagram below illustrates the interdependence of each of these aspects of your coursework.

Main text
⬇
Wide reading – literary
⬇
Wide reading – non-fiction
⬇
Ideas for writing tasks
⬇
Narrow the focus of writing tasks with further research and reflection
⬇
Wide reading for literary style models
⬇
Wide reading for non-fiction style models
⬇
Refine writing tasks
⬇
Final coursework tasks

You have chosen your topic and your core text and you have already done some initial work on your core text. The following activity will get you started on your individual research around your topic area.

Activity 19

Find four texts that relate to your topic area and will add depth to your study of your core text. Use these texts as the basis for a presentation to other group members.

The four texts should be in different genres and can be literary or non-fiction (although a mix of both would add variety). The definition of a 'text' for your wide reading can also include films and recordings of television and radio programmes. A *multi-modal* text is one that involves more than one mode, such as a blog, which is written but employs spoken language features and is electronic.

For your research and choice of texts you do not need to restrict yourself in terms of time or place. For example, you could use historical accounts of emigrating to the new world as well as political speeches and documentary evidence from the past.

Below is an example of a topic and some types of text that you could choose for your presentation.

Your working notebook

When you have chosen your texts, record the details on a grid like the one above in your notebook. This will give you a visual check to ensure that you have chosen a variety of texts in different genres and modes, which offer different perspectives on your topic.

Topic: Crossing Boundaries
Core text: *English Passengers* by Matthew Kneale

Text	Genre	Mode
Text 1	Editorial from a national daily newspaper about migrant workers in Britain (e.g. 'A boon, not a burden', The Independent 09/09/08)	Written: print media
Text 2	First-person accounts of the experiences of emigration (source from internet searches, online diaries/blogs, memoirs, etc.)	Written, spoken or multi-modal
Text 3	Political speech on the topic of immigration	Written to be spoken
Text 4	Stage, TV or radio drama dealing with issues surrounding the attempts of young migrants to integrate into British society (e.g. Testing the Echo by David Edgar)	Spoken: performance text

Step 1
Do some initial research into what is available on your topic to support your study of the core text (use internet searches, libraries, ask for advice from your teacher, and discuss with other students).

Step 2
Once you have identified a range of possible resources, choose four texts related to your topic area to study in detail. The texts may have very diverse purposes and different effects on their audiences. If a text is lengthy (such as a novel), you will need to select an extract. If it is brief (such as a newspaper article), however, you may be able to refer to the complete text.

Step 3
Copy your chosen extracts from the texts and then analyse them, using the guiding questions you used for your initial study of the texts in Activity 17 (page 119).

Step 4
Make your presentation to the rest of the group.

- Introduce your texts.
- Explain your reasons for choosing each of them, especially how they relate to your topic and core text.
- Give a brief analysis of their individual approaches to the topic and their key stylistic techniques.
- Give your opinion as to how successful each text is in presenting a particular perspective on the topic.

Even if each member of your group is engaged in researching a different topic, this activity will give you more ideas and may widen your experiences of other genres.

5 Responding to texts in different ways

During your reading and research you need to think about and discuss the different ways in which readers receive texts. Understanding more about the relationship between writers and readers will help you focus clearly on your audience and purpose when you are crafting your own texts.

We all give meaning to what we read from our own personal experience and our experience of society. This means that we tend to make assumptions about texts. You need to avoid this by asking questions about the texts you are studying. Move away from who wrote it, when, and what for, to a more complex investigation of the context in which the text was written and how it could be received by different audiences.

For example:

- Who was the original audience?
- What was the original purpose?
- What is the writer's/speaker's attitude?
- What were the social and cultural contexts when the text was produced?

It is helpful to make the distinction between **reader-orientated** and **writer-orientated texts**.

In reader-orientated texts the reader and writer share expectations; the reader recognises the genre conventions and expects them to be adhered to. The writer provides recognisable signposts for the reader to follow. The reader therefore feels comfortable with the experience. Most fiction genres fit this category, a classic example being the romantic novels published by Mills and Boon; other genres of fiction also tend to follow a predictable structure, such as the Victorian novels of the Brontës and Charles Dickens, contemporary and classic crime fiction, and horror.

In writer-orientated texts the writer may decide to subvert the expectations of the reader or may want to experiment with different styles and approaches. This type of text involves more work on the part of the reader as it sets up challenges and the reader does not know what to expect next. This can, of course, make it a more satisfying read. Examples of contemporary fiction writings that are stylistically experimental and defy expectations are *Cloud Atlas* by David Mitchell and *American Gods* by Neil Gaiman.

As you study your core text and explore your texts for wide reading, try to read them in different ways. Ask yourself these questions while reading:

- Does the construction of a text make it difficult to read from any other perspective than that offered by the writer?
- Does a text allow for different interpretations depending on the audience?

Key terms

- reader-orientated text
- writer-orientated text

Across AS and A2

Remember that to make the step up to A2 you will need to *evaluate* the success of different approaches and techniques. You can base this both on how effective you feel the texts would be for the original intended audience, and on how well they have worked for you as an individual reader or viewer.

First-person narratives are usually difficult to read from any other perspective than that offered by the writer. They are specific ways of interpreting the world. Good examples are *Bridget Jones's Diary*, the fictional chick-lit diary by Helen Fielding, and the collection of poems in *The World's Wife* by Carol Ann Duffy.

Activity 20

The following text is the first verse of the poem 'Mrs Aesop' by Carol Ann Duffy, in which the imaginary wife of Aesop, the famous writer of fables, gives her opinion of her husband.

Identify the techniques that Duffy uses to encourage the reader to agree with the viewpoint of Mrs Aesop.

Mrs Aesop

By Christ, he could bore for Purgatory. He was small,
didn't prepossess. So he tried to impress. Dead men,
Mrs Aesop, he'd say, tell no tales. Well, let me tell you now
that the bird in the hand shat on his sleeve,
never mind the two worth less in the bush. Tedious.

Carol Ann Duffy

By contrast, a speech delivered by a Labour prime minister could be received and interpreted in different ways by an audience at the Labour Party Conference, an audience of the general public, an audience of mainly Conservative voters.

Audiences will respond differently to political speeches depending on their national, political and personal attitudes to the speaker and the topic.

When you are reading your core texts and the texts you have chosen for wider reading, think about the effect they have on you as a reader. For example, if your topic is 'Crossing Boundaries' and your core text is *A Thousand Splendid Suns* by Khaled Hosseini, which focuses on relationships in arranged marriages, you may be inspired to write an editorial arguing either for or against arranged marriages.

Activity 21

Read the following edited extract from a text on the topic of global warming.

1 Consider the different ways in which it could be received, depending on the convictions and attitudes of the reader. How would it be read by:

- a campaigner for an environmental organisation
- a person who doesn't drive a car
- a driver who owns a 4 x 4 car
- a producer of the *Top Gear* television programme?

2 How did you personally respond to the text, and how persuasive did you find it? Consider honestly how much this had to do with your existing attitudes and values.

THE BIGGER PICTURE

Car drivers are made to feel very guilty about the environment, but transportation isn't the only cause of global warming. In fact, the answer to climate change is just as likely to lie in your toaster or your fridge as it is in your car.

If you listen to popular opinion about global warming, it's easy to conclude that the car is public enemy number one. In 2007, the Intergovernmental Panel on Climate Change (IPCC) concluded that climate warming was 'unequivocal', and that it was more than 90 per cent likely that this was due to man's activity. There's little room left for doubt.

But if you're reading this with the aid of artificial light, then you'll be enjoying the benefit of the biggest man-made $CO2$ producer of them all – power generation. Which isn't to say that the environmental effects of cars are unimportant. But the truth is, there are plenty of other major sources of greenhouse gas that we must bear in mind.

Windows Of Opportunity

Unless you live in a hermetically sealed home, you're almost certainly occupying the global-warming equivalent of a sieve. British homes leak heat. Badly. They demand more energy than they ought to for heating, and they also waft heat directly out into the atmosphere. The country's 25 million homes caused 152 million tonnes of carbon dioxide to seep into the atmosphere in 2006 according to the Statistics Office. That's considerably more carbon dioxide than Britain's 26 million cars emit. And we have yet to see those who actively target four-wheel-drive owners rushing out to lecture the residents of Victorian homes about the evils of draughty sash windows.

Richard Bremner, *Audi Magazine*

Activity 22

Read the text to the right, which is an entry from the diary of Lady Marianne Brocklehurst written between 1854 and 1891. Marianne Brocklehurst made many visits to Egypt to acquire antiquities. Here she records her delight at having smuggled some precious artefacts out of Egypt. Consider her attitudes and values.

1 Is there evidence that she assumes her readers will share these attitudes and values?

2 How do you respond to the text as a 21st century reader?

3 How would you respond if you were curator of a museum of national antiquities in Cairo?

We hurried on board and with Mr Ralph's assistance got all our valuables, which were ready boxed, on shore. The guards unsuspectingly let them pass on their way to the Railway station, but the next lot which we had to pack and bring later, attracted their notice and we had to submit to all being turned out on the high road, lamps & kettles & blankets & all sorts of things. We grumbled openly but secretly rejoiced to think that our Mummy and our little friends were safely waiting for us at the station. At Alexandria we were equally fortunate & got everything bribed on board the steamer without difficulty, but that there is a good deal of chance about it, that we were lucky whilst others are not, has been since shown in the case of our friends on The Philae who had all their antiquities seized at Alexandria, and are doubtful if they will ever be able to recover them even with Mr Ralph's assistance.

6 Reading and writing in different genres

The following activity will help you to think about different ways of shaping material to suit literary and non-fiction outcomes based on the same topic.

Despite all the differences in genre and style between the four texts on war below, they are all contemporary and immediate. They all tell an old story in a new way.

Activity 23

Imagine that you have chosen the topic 'War and the Individual'. Opposite and on the facing page are extracts from four texts on the topic of war. They give diverse perspectives and approaches. Read each text and then explore and evaluate them by asking questions such as those you asked in Activity 17 (page 117).

You have deliberately not been given the sources of these four texts to enable you to test your knowledge of genre conventions and literary and linguistic approaches.

1 Below are descriptions of the four genres. Match each genre to a text, A–D, and give explicit reasons, based on your literary and linguistic knowledge, for your decisions.

a) a non-fiction narrative that gives a journalist's perspective on a country at war

b) a special report about living in a war zone

c) retrospective reportage from an observer

d) a fictional account of life in a war-torn area.

2 Discuss your findings in your groups. There may not be immediate agreement, but the purpose is to investigate the texts to give evidence for your decisions.

Text A

STANDING IN PIGEON SQUARE and surveying the surrounding hills, it is impossible to imagine any better terrain for laying siege to a city. High tree-covered hills roll up on all sides almost as if designed for concealing troops. As the traditional tin-makers patter away with their hammers in the old market and children slurp out of the spring water fountain there is little sign that, for more than a thousand days, no-one came in and no-one went out of Sarajevo. Since then there have been steady and prolonged efforts to return the city to the way it was.

But first our guide wants to remind us just what happened here in the early 90s. On a bumpy bus ride through its suburbs it is evident that reconstruction is slow. Pot-holed roads, abandoned, burnt-out or shell-hit buildings sit next to construction sites full of weary looking labourers. We stop on a gravel road half way up one of the city's eastern slopes.

Sani Kirslak was a young teenager when he and his family were trapped in the city by the encircling Serbian forces; now he runs tours of its siege past under the title of War, hope and reconciliation. He has taken us to a Jewish cemetery which overlooks a large proportion of the centre and gives an eagle-eye view of the bright yellow Holiday Inn which was home to international journalists during the siege.

This, we are told, was a favourite position for Serb snipers. They preferred looking west apparently for their morning sniping as any direct sunlight would stream down onto the city from behind them illuminating their targets. The headstones of the dead Jewish inhabitants of the cemetery would provide ideal cover from which to take pot-shots at anyone below brave, stupid or desperate enough to stray into open ground.

After describing to us what life was like in the siege and the indiscriminate and random nature of the violence inflicted on the people of Sarajevo, Sani asks if there are any questions.

'Were you happy that the foreign journalists stayed to report what was happening here?' someone ventures.

'Happy?' says Sani. 'I did not care. I was just trying not to get shot.'

Text B

Voices from the streets of Baghdad

Bashar Salam, 50
Christian, hotel receptionist

Nowadays everything is difficult: Bombs, mortars, kidnapping and you cannot get a job. No one takes care of the people because those in the government are busy making money for themselves and planning their own future, so we expect a dark future for ourselves.

Hamad Al-Jumaili
Sunni, lecturer at Baghdad University

The majority of the Iraqi people have found the past five years very hard and this is quite natural because we have been under occupation. It is the occupation that is responsible for everything. The future depends on whether or not the next Iraqi election produces a national government that unites people.

Haitham Sadiq Jaafar, 28
Shia, security guard

Recent years have been bad but they are not as bad as the years of Saddam. We are free now so we can perform our Shia holy ceremonies, while we were slaves under Saddam's regime.

Text C

The darkness stalked Omar Yussef, watchful and predatory. With each indistinct movement he perceived in the blackness, he halted and squinted into the dusty wind until he was sure he was alone. And he was. The streets were as empty as at the loneliest hour of night, though it was not quite eleven.

The dust cloud shivered in the ochre glow of the streetlights, as though all those who passed this way during the day surrounded Omar Yussef now, raising the dirt into the air with their silent tread. The wind sounded in Omar Yussef's ears with the same heavy rush as the waves of the Mediterranean, a hundred yards beyond the road. It was humid and his shirt stuck to his back.

Under the hum of the storm, Omar Yussef heard the sound of engines. Two jeeps came around the corner from Emile Zola Street. Their motors growled so loudly that is seemed as though they might be the source of the moaning wind.

The jeeps rolled to a halt in front of Omar Yussef. They were dark green and unmarked and their headlights were off. He made out the shapes of four gunmen inside each one, their assault rifles upright between their legs.

Text D

7 Writing crime fiction

Reflecting on and writing in a particular genre will enable you to address issues of research and the precise interplay between fact and fiction. It may also help you to learn about how professional writers carry out their research.

Below is the written record of an interview with the novelist Carla Banks, about how she plans and researches her novels. She has written a number of books in the genre of crime fiction, which have all involved a substantial amount of historical and geographical research. Here she is talking specifically about her novel *The Forest of Souls.*

Interviewer: How do you begin your writing – are there different stages in your planning?

Carla Banks: I usually start with a theme – what is the book about. This is often vague at the beginning, but firms up very quickly. For example, The Forest of Souls is about guilt and consequences.

Interviewer: How much time do you allow for research, in proportion to the time spent on the book?

Carla Banks: It depends on the book, but I would say that about 20 to 25 per cent of my time is spent on research.

Interviewer: What type of research do you do – where do you look? Who do you talk to?

Carla Banks: I use the internet a lot – this is always a good starting point. I talk to people who have experienced the things I want to write about, whether it's a serving police officer about the ways in which a specific crime would be investigated, or if it's a way of life I want to explore. I also like to visit the places I'm writing about. It's hard to write about somewhere you've never been.

Interviewer: What are the important things to remember when crafting a book which is fiction based on fact and real life?

Carla Banks: It's important to be true to the facts, and I think you need to be very careful when fictionalising real people. I prefer to use the historical facts as they stand, and leave it to the characters I have created to carry the narrative. If I read a book in which the writer has put words into the mouth of a real character, it pulls me right out of the fiction. I don't like it. In The Forest of Souls, I used events involving real people and I used their names, but this was seen through the eyes of Eva, and I didn't embellish the historical facts. I also didn't want to write anything that made resisting the Nazi occupation sound glamorous or exciting – there's a lot of 'Boy's Own' tosh written about the

resistance in Western Europe. In Eastern Europe, the people who did it were incredibly brave, but they faced a horrible, public death.

Interviewer: How would you describe the genre of this novel?

Carla Banks: It's not clear cut. It's certainly a crime novel – there's a murder and there's a mystery – but it's also contemporary fiction.

Interviewer: Do you have any advice for young people on researching and then selecting, using it in their writing?

Carla Banks: Research thoroughly. You need to know a lot about something to turn it into convincing fiction. If you understand the world you are writing about, then you will be able to create it on the page in a way that the reader can believe and accept. This is true even if you are writing fantasy. To allow the reader the 'willing suspension of disbelief', you have to give them a world that works, a convincing social structure, characters that act and speak in a way that makes them believable. Remember that just because you have researched it, you don't have to use it. Readers want a compelling narrative. If they wanted a factual account, they'd be reading non-fiction. You have to be selective. I talked in detail to people who had experienced bombing to get an idea of what it must have been like for the civilian population of Minsk when the Germans invaded. I wrote pages and pages, but in the end, I edited it down to two paragraphs. I sometimes think that the secret of writing is the art of deleting.

Interviewer: Are there any books or writers who have had a strong influence on you?

Carla Banks: I am a great fan of Dickens. His writing is incredibly atmospheric. I enjoy Barbara Kingsolver, Alison Lurie, Susan Hill, early Stephen King. I have always enjoyed ghost stories – M.R. James writes them better than anyone I think. I like subtle menace.

Activity 24

1 Discuss what you have learned from this interview about:

- good ways to research
- the importance of a sense of place
- influences on writers
- making crime fiction realistic.

2 Here is an edited extract from Carla Banks's novel *The Forest of Souls*. It focuses on an interview between an investigative journalist (Jake) and the character of the grandfather (Lange). Read the extract and then answer the questions below it.

Before you analyse the text you could remind yourself of Activity 10 in Section A on *Tulip Fever* (page 114), where you explored how Deborah Moggach used a specific historical period as the basis for a fictional representation of the life of a famous artist.

From *The Forest of Souls* by Carla Banks

'Many years ago.' Lange's brows drew together as he spoke. 'In the forest', he said. 'So beautiful. And in a clearing, the timber house and cherry orchard. There was no water, so Papa build a deep well. And Mama got better. And then I was born.' The room darkened as the sun went in. 'It's gone now, the orchard, the forest.'

Jake wanted to let the old man to stay in this moment of quiet reflection, but time was short. He pushed on. 'And this one?' he said, pointing to the photo of the young man in uniform. 'This is you?' It must have been taken in '38 or '39 – just before the outbreak of the war. Jake couldn't recognize the uniform.

But the old man seemed not to hear him. His eyes were focused on the photograph that Jake was holding out to him, but his face was blank. 'That winter, everyone is afraid. Fear makes people... made me...' He was looking directly at Jake as he spoke, but who or what he was seeing, Jake wasn't sure. 'I should not have done it,' he said. 'The bear at the gate... I was there.' He turned to Jake with a sudden intensity. 'I was there. And the little one...' Jake couldn't decipher what he said next. At first he thought the old man was speaking gibberish, then he realized that he had lapsed into another language – Polish? But it seemed oddly familiar to Jake.

The photographs dropped from the old man's hand. Jake caught them before they fell to the floor. 'Are you all right?'

Lange seemed to have forgotten Jake was there. 'Minsk', he said. 'It was in Minsk...' He was staring at his hand where the photograph had been.

---

a What evidence is there of historical research to create atmosphere?

b How would you characterise the narrative voice?

c Identify any literary or linguistic techniques that give the narrative *cohesion*, such as dialogue, reported speech, tense, imitation of spontaneous language features, descriptive writing, deictic references, implications for the plot, sentence length and type. For each feature that you identify explain how it contributes to the effect of the narrative.

8 Narrowing your focus

In the activity on the next page you will put into practice some of the ideas suggested by the interview with Carla Banks. This exploration will be suitable for any topic and core text, even if you are not going to write prose fiction for your coursework.

Carla Banks says that she starts with a theme. You already have your theme, which is your chosen topic area, and you have your core text for ideas and inspiration connected to the topic. What you now need to do is to narrow the focus to one particular aspect of your topic. For example, if your topic is 'Crossing Boundaries', you might wish to write about what it feels like to move into a country, area, or community that is unfamiliar to you and where you feel alienated, out of place or an outsider in some way.

Your working notebook

Write these questions and your answers to them in your working notebook. You will now be able to see the range of resources that are immediately available to you.

Your working notebook

Write a short commentary on your creative piece, noting any ways in which you have refined or adjusted the focus of your topic following feedback.

Activity 25

1 Ask yourself these questions:

  a What is there in your own experience that relates to this topic? (For 'Crossing Boundaries': Starting a new school, moving to a new area, emigrating to a different country, spending time abroad on an extended visit or exchange)

  b Where can you read about other people's experiences? (Autobiographies, biographies, travel writing, fiction – Victorian novels such as *Great Expectations* and *Jane Eyre*)

  c What can you watch? (Television documentaries on immigration)

  d Who can you talk to? (Friends or family members who were not born in Britain and came here as immigrants)

2 When you have chosen a particular angle or perspective, identify a target audience.

  Now write a short prose fiction piece related to your topic in approximately 250 words.

3 Introduce your original writing to the other group members, explaining why you decided on this particular perspective on your topic.

  Get feedback from your group on what was effective in your writing and ideas about how you could improve or refine your approach to your topic.

9 Finding ideas for your writing tasks

You may find inspiration for your task from many different sources connected to your topic. These could include a painting, a piece of music, a song lyric, a poem, a place you have visited or want to visit, a real-life event, letters or diaries you have read. Your starting point may even be a favourite genre that you want to write in.

The successful young horror novelist Rhiannon Lassiter was asked what inspired her writing.

Why did you decide to write a horror novel?

I didn't exactly set out to. But after several novels that have had science fiction or fantastical settings I wanted to write something that would take place in the real world. While I was staying in the
5   Lake District I found the scenery very evocative and the house where I was staying made me think about hidden rooms and old secrets. The story that grew out of that became very sinister and I realised that I wanted to write something frightening. Bad Blood turned out to be psychological horror about sinister secrets
10   hidden in a make-believe game.

What is it like to write horror novels?

I get very involved with stories, and with horror fiction you are not in control. Even as a reader or watcher, it's nerve-racking wondering what will happen when someone opens a door or
15   turns out a light or goes for a walk in the wood… I find it easier to write horror – where I am in control – than to watch or read it.

Activity 26

1 Make a note of the specific genres that you think you would like to write in.

2 Choose one of these genres and make notes on why you find it an effective way of presenting your chosen topic.

3 Present your ideas to the rest of the group.

You may find inspiration for your literary piece through a specific location.

Activity 27

1 Read the text below. It is an extract from a writer's impressions of a museum she visited in Egypt. She later used her experiences in her research for a novel aimed at children aged 8–12.

Discuss what it was about her visit to the museum that could have inspired a novel for young children.

> The world of the ancients unfolds. Ducks fly out of papyrus swamps; royal barques sail across the afterlife; the king's sarcophagus rests in the centre of the burial chamber. On one wall, 12 baboons sit on their haunches. Because of them, the locals call this place the Valley of the
> 5 Monkeys. It seems incredible, but we're a stone's throw from Luxor's Valley of the Kings, where hordes of tourists troop to and from their tour buses. Here, I gaze at the walls alone.
> Back in the taxi we give a lift to the tomb guardian who says there are jackals here and he sees them often, at night. He points out of the
> 10 car window. I realise these must be their tracks. 'Can we stop?' I ask.
> The driver obliges and I get out to inspect the ground. Sure enough, dog-like paw prints criss-cross the white limestone dust. I think of Anubis, the jackal-headed god of embalming, and his arresting black statue discovered in Tutankhamun's tomb. I shiver with pleasure.
> 15 Moments like this bring Egypt's history uncannily close to the present.
>
> Gill Harvey, *The Independent*

You will no doubt have noticed the appeal of the mysteries of the ancient civilisation, the very atmospheric setting of the tomb museum, and the sense of isolation and uncertainty that is created.

2 Now think of a place that has interesting or intriguing associations for you. This does not have to be an exotic location: it may be somewhere you have visited on holiday but equally it could be somewhere very familiar and close to home.

Introduce this location to the rest of your group and explain how you feel you could use it as a stimulus to write a piece on your topic.

Independent research

Read *Orphan of the Sun* by Gill Harvey, a novel for 8–12-year-olds based on life in ancient Egypt. Look for evidence of how her experiences travelling in Egypt helped her to create the setting and atmosphere of her novel.

10 Taking genre into account

It is important that you develop your understanding of genre and apply this understanding to your own original writing.

Activity 28

The following extended activity involves an analysis of three texts in different genres, plus three short writing tasks. The texts are a newspaper editorial, a **features article** and an **eye-witness account**.

1 Divide up the work between pairs and small groups, with each pair or group focusing on one text (A–C) and the associated task, and reporting back to the others.

2 Read and analyse your chosen group text, performing the following tasks as the basis for your investigation:

- identify and describe the features of the genre
- consider the purpose and intended audience
- explore and comment on specific linguistic and literary techniques, such as choice of lexis and syntax, use of discourse markers, phonological features, use of literary language
- comment on how the use of language conveys (either explicitly or implicitly) the attitude of the writer
- evaluate the likely success of the text in
  (a) meeting the reader's needs and
  (b) achieving authorial purpose.

3 The second stage in each activity is a writing task that links with your own topic and core text. You need to make a number of decisions before you begin writing.

- What is the mode of your text, that is, speech or writing?
- What is the field or topic?
- What is the perspective or angle that you wish to adopt?
- Which specific literary and linguistic techniques might be effective in contributing to the success of your text?

4 If you are asked to evaluate the work of another group member you should be prepared to make positive and clear suggestions about the good points of the writing, and how it could be improved.

Text A is an extract from an editorial about the war in Iraq, which appeared in a national daily newspaper.

Key terms

- features article
- newspaper editorial
- eye-witness account

Text A

The only lesson we ever learn is that we never learn

Five years on, and still we have not learnt. With each anniversary, the steps crumble beneath our feet, the stones ever more cracked, the sand ever finer. Five years of catastrophe in Iraq and I think of Churchill, who in the end called Palestine a 'hell-disaster'.

But we have used these parallels before and they have drifted away in the Tigris breeze. Iraq is swamped in blood. Yet what is the state of our remorse? Why, we will have a public inquiry – but not yet! If only inadequacy was our only sin.

Today, we are engaged in a fruitless debate. What went wrong? How did the people – the *senatus populusque Romanus* of our modern world – not rise up in rebellion when told the lies about weapons of mass destruction, about Saddam's links with Osama bin Laden and 11 September? How did we let it happen? And how come we didn't plan for the aftermath of war?

Robert Fisk, *The Independent*

The toppling of a statue of Saddam Hussein

Step 1 Textual analysis

a Read and analyse the text, completing a grid like the one begun below.

Features of the genre	• Attention-grabbing headline with rhythmic phonological features • Inclusive use of first-person-plural pronoun • Discourse markers 'but' and 'and', time references
Purpose and intended audience	• Persuasion; readers of serious news articles
Literary and linguistic techniques	• Rhetorical features of repetition • Rhetorical questions • Intertextuality (e.g. references to Churchill, Saddam, the Latin quotation)
How language conveys attitudes	• Emotive phrases, e.g. 'swamped in blood' • Attempts to provoke guilt, e.g. 'How did *we* let it happen?'.

b Debate how effective you think the text is.

Step 2 Writing task

Your task is to write a persuasive piece on any theme of your choice, linked in some way to your topic area and/or main text. Aim to write approximately 500 words.

a Complete a table like the one below to give you a framework for your text and to ensure that you have considered the essential aspects required. Details have been completed as examples.

Core text and topic area	*Lost in Translation* by Eva Hoffman; 'Crossing Boundaries'
Theme	Immigration
Genre	Non-fiction
Audience	Local community
Purpose	To persuade the audience of the advantages of welcoming migrant workers
Mode	Speech/appeal to local community or written article in local newspaper
Literary and linguistic techniques	Use of declaratives, imperatives, rhetorical questions, alliteration, paradoxical statements, subject-specific lexis

b When you have completed your writing, share it with at least one other member of the group and ask for comments about its effectiveness.

Take it further

Write a short analytical commentary (approximately 200 words) on the extract, commenting on how the writer's use of specific literary and linguistic techniques have contributed to its success.

Across AS and A2

Remind yourself of the work you did on rhetoric at AS and for Unit 3. In Unit 2 you explored the devices used for rhetorical effect in public speeches and other persuasive texts. Rhetoric is a way of speaking and writing that is designed to persuade. Text A employs a number of rhetorical features similar to those used in public speaking. The structure of a text can often have an impact on its rhetorical effect.

Text B is an extract from a retrospective reflection on the Munich air disaster of 1958, in which members of the Manchester United football team were killed. This article appeared in a national newspaper on the fiftieth anniversary of the tragedy.

Text B

A collective loss of life that sent shivers of shock round the world

A chilly February evening in the boarders' cloakroom in a school in the English midlands, some time between supper and prep. A 10-year-old boy is cleaning his shoes. Another boy enters and approaches him. 'Have you heard?' the second boy says. 'There's been an air crash and the Manchester United team are all dead.'

Perhaps this is the first of modern history's I-remember-where-I-was moments, a precursor to JFK and Lennon, Princess Di and 9/11. On February 6, 1958, however, the news has only just begun to find the means of spreading itself at speed through the global village. An international network exists, although it is a primitive and unreliable mechanism compared with the digital world of the future. This school, for example, has no television set. Not one of the boys yet owns a transistor radio, although a few have crystal sets, cobbled together from RAF war-surplus parts, used for listening to Buddy Holly and the Everly Brothers under the bedclothes via the static-drenched signal of Radio Luxembourg. So the news of the Munich crash arrives in imprecise, provisional dribs and drabs.

The effect, however, is instantaneous. The whole school seems to shiver.

Richard Williams, *The Guardian*

Step 1 Textual analysis

Read and analyse the text. Begin with audience, purpose and context as usual. Once you have defined these three aspects, consider the prominent and significant stylistic features of this particular text and how exactly they contribute to the achievement of the writer's purpose.

This is a news story and it is a type of narrative (the writer is, after all, telling a story), but he has adopted a particular perspective. What is it? What literary and linguistic features has he employed to create this angle or perspective?

To organise your thoughts, complete a grid like the one below.

Text	Article on Munich air crash
Audience	Readers of quality daily newspaper and those especially interested in the disaster; of specific interest to those who remember the event
Purpose	To revisit and re-create the atmosphere in the immediate aftermath of the tragedy
Context	A 21st-century re-telling of an event from the 1950s
Perspective	An emotive and moving recreation of the event
Examples of literary and linguistic techniques	Identify at least five techniques and comment on their contribution to the writer's intention of presenting the event in an emotional way

Step 2 Writing task

Choose any public event that relates to your topic area and has had a particular impact on you. It does not have to be a tragic event; it could, for example, be celebratory, such as a sporting achievement.

Write approximately 500 words in the style of an article in which you re-create the event and bring it to life for your readers.

Your working notebook

Write a brief commentary on your article in which you identify and explain your choices of key literary and linguistic techniques. You don't have to discuss everything; select the features you felt were particularly effective in the shaping of your text.

Text C is an extract from an eye-witness account of a nerve gas attack on the Tokyo underground in 1995. The attack killed eleven people and injured thousands of others. Police blamed members of a religious sect who believed that the end of the world was imminent.

Text C

The Cult of Death

Tokyo, March 1995

Takuhashi Kazumasa spent most of his working life on the underground railways. His colleagues say he was a hard-working family man; at the age of fifty, he would have been looking forward
5 to retirement from his job as assistant station master on the Underground. In the official photograph, he appears as a stocky bluff man with a wide smile and bright eyes; a man popular with his colleagues and the civil servants who
10 travelled with him on the Underground every morning. Some time after eight o'clock on a busy Monday last week, Takuhashi Kazumasa spotted some liquid which had spilled on to the train floor. Being the diligent man he was, he
15 immediately mopped up the fluid. Within minutes, Takuhashi Kazumasa was lying dead on the platform.

Across Tokyo similar scenes were being repeated. Men and women were staggering out of trains struggling for the open air of the above 20 ground, gasping for breath. Many of them were vomiting and rubbing ferociously at their eyes. Here, in one of the most sophisticated, cosmopolitan and technically advanced cities in the world, human beings were writhing and 25 convulsing like creatures possessed.

As word of the disaster spread through the city something close to a sense of group shock overtook the huge population of commuters who travel in and out of Tokyo every day from the 30 vast suburbs around the city. When I walked among commuters that evening, I sensed something approximating to disbelief. As one woman, a civil servant in the Foreign Ministry, put it to me, 'This kind of thing we expect to 35 happen in the Third World, maybe to happen in India, or even among the Arabs and the Israelis, but not to us here in Japan.'

Fergal Keane

Step 1 Textual analysis

Begin your investigation of the text by identifying audience, purpose, context and the writer's perspective. Then use your knowledge of literary and linguistic techniques to explore and comment on how the writer has re-created the scene for his audience. Identify and comment on the effect of at least three specific stylistic features.

Record your findings in a table like the one below.

Text	'The Cult of Death'
Audience	Educated adult audience interested in world news
Purpose	To give an immediate report of a tragic and disturbing event
Context	Tokyo, 1995; writer of the account witnessed the scene
Writer's perspective	Emphasises the human interest angle with a pen portrait of a named individual; this approach creates empathy
Literary/linguistic feature	Nominalisation: Takuhashi Kazumasa
Literary/linguistic feature	Adverbial discourse markers, e.g. 'Some time after eight o'clock', 'Across Tokyo'
Literary/linguistic feature	Use of direct speech

Take it further

Text C, 'The Cult of Death', was originally written to be broadcast on BBC Radio 4 for a series entitled *From Our Own Correspondent* where journalists working abroad make reports on important events. Read the text again with this idea in mind, and consider which stylistic features would make it particularly suitable for a radio audience.

Coursework checkpoint

By this stage you should have uncovered something, or several things, that are interesting, inspiring or intriguing about your core text and topic area.

You should have decided which particular aspects of your topic you would like to write about, then refined your ideas so that you have a specific angle or perspective.

Step 2 Writing task

a Choose any significant past event that interests you and links to your topic area. Do some research into the details of the event and read accounts by eye-witnesses.

b Use these factual details to shape a short fictional piece (such as an extract from a drama text or short story), in which you re-create the event using a fictional protagonist. Decide on the specific audience and purpose of your text and consider which literary and linguistic techniques would suit both the genre and content of your text. Aim to write approximately 500 words.

Before you begin writing your piece, record your initial decisions in a table like the example below.

Topic	Global epidemics
Genre	A fictional diary describing the Great Plague, written from the viewpoint of a 14-year-old boy living in London in 1665–66
Audience	Key Stage 3 students
Purpose	To re-create an historical event through a vividly imagined first-hand account, to both educate and entertain
Research for content and style	Content: Factual accounts of the Great Plague (internet searches and television documentaries) Style models: Fictional texts on historical topics for the specified age range, e.g. King of Shadows, a novel about Shakespeare's London by Susan Cooper, and The Roses of Eyam by Don Taylor, a stage play about a plague village in Derbyshire
Literary and linguistic techniques	First-person, past-tense narrative, use of simile to describe/evoke atmosphere, dialogue and/or direct speech, free indirect speech, some emotive lexical choices

c When you have completed it, share your text with other members of your group. Ask for feedback on how effective they found it and make a note of any suggested changes that you feel would improve your text.

Activity 29

To help you clarify your ideas about your two creative tasks, prepare a short presentation to other group members.

1 Write a script that takes about two minutes to read aloud. Focus on your choice of non-fiction task. Explain to your audience:

- Why you chose this task
- How it has been stimulated by (a) your core text and (b) your wide reading.

2 Allow some time for discussion. Your audience should look for and comment on the following.

- Are there clear links with the topic area and stimulus texts?
- Are the reasons for choosing the task valid?
- Is it a realistic and convincing task?

3 Use the feedback from your peers to help improve the focus. This will also help you to see whether the task and approach feel right.

4 Repeat the process with your fiction task.

Discussing these proposals with other members of your group will have helped you assess their strengths and possible difficulties. Remember that effective peer review is often the best way of assessing your work in progress.

You are now ready to make a proposal to your teacher. The following activity will give you guidance on how to do this.

Activity 30

1 Devise a coursework title for your non-fiction task, such as 'Football: a game without frontiers'.

2 On one A4 sheet, list your genre, purpose and audience, as in this example:

> Genre: A features article
> Purpose: To persuade that football is a game that breaks down boundaries and can bring together people of different nationalities and backgrounds
> Audience: A popular glossy magazine with a young male readership.

3 Write a brief explanation of how you will approach the task. List your core text and some areas that you have pursued for wide reading. Give the main ideas in a few bullet points.

4 Repeat the process for your fiction task, on another A4 sheet.

Assessment objectives

Look back over the work you have done in Section B and consider how it relates to the Assessment Objectives.

In your reading and research, you have:

AO1
✔ carried out some focused research on your topic area
✔ made an appropriate selection of texts in a variety of genres to demonstrate different perspectives on your topic
✔ used accurate and specific technical terminology in your analysis of texts

AO2
✔ shown evidence of wider reading/research on your topic
✔ given detailed explanations of how texts have been deliberately shaped or crafted
✔ shown your ability to be discriminating in selecting specific literary and linguistic features to comment on in a variety of texts

AO3
✔ shown your understanding of how texts offer different interpretations and perspectives on the same topic
✔ demonstrated your ability to (a) give a clear overview of a text and (b) read and analyse a text closely at word and sentence level.

In your writing tasks you have:

AO1
✔ selected an appropriate genre and shown that you understand the genre conventions
✔ used a clearly devised approach influenced by the style model of your chosen text

AO4
✔ shown your ability to produce fiction and non-fiction texts designed for specific audiences and purposes on your topic area.

C Writing your texts

This section gives advice and guidance on how to:

- plan your writing for your literary and non-fiction tasks
- draft, edit and revise your work.

You will also be given some examples of writing to discuss and assess against the Assessment objectives.

1 Planning your writing

For Unit 4 you have to produce two original pieces with a maximum word count of 2500-3000 words. One of these must be literary writing and one must be non-fiction. You will need to write creatively and imaginatively but within a very disciplined framework, paying attention to the word count and your specific choices of audience, purpose and genre.

Your two creative pieces do not need to be of equal length but each one must be long enough to provide a satisfying outcome. You can make decisions about the length of each piece based on the genre and purpose; for example, the opening chapter of a novel may require more words than an editorial or a political blog.

It is important to keep to the word count as those assessing your work will stop reading once the maximum word count has been reached. This means that if your work is too long you will not receive credit for all that you have written. Therefore although you will not lose marks by exceeding the word count, an excessive word count will disadvantage you.

To gain high marks for your A2 coursework you will need to allow time for detailed planning. The more care you take over your writing, the more successful you are likely to be in evoking the response you want from your readers.

There are three main strands to your writing: ideas, content and style.

- **Ideas:** These will emerge from your reading and research around your topic area, For example, if your topic area is football you may become interested in the power of the game to influence the lives of ordinary people.

- **Content:** For example, if you would like to write about football as an inspiring cultural phenomenon in a South American country, you may decide to write a reflective non-fiction article entitled 'The Boys from Brazil' about the famous Brazilian 1970 World Cup team.

- **Style:** At word, sentence and structural levels, your piece will display stylistic features appropriate to your choices of content and genre.

For both your literary and non-fiction tasks you need to have a good 'story' or narrative and you need to write in an interesting way. The following short activity develops this idea.

Activity 31

Take it further

Write another 100 words to complete the paragraph in Activity 31, in the genre of your choice.

Read the short extract opposite. It is the opening of a much longer text.

Consider the language and literary features the writer has used to evoke mood, and try to identify the genre of the text. Give reasons for your choice.

> The dark season accords well with Perugia, a moody city of huge medieval arches, underground labyrinths and steep and crooked cobbled lanes. Hallowe'en is in sight…

Focusing on style: Your non-fiction piece

You have completed your reading and research on your topic, you have chosen the angle or perspective that you wish to follow, and you have identified the genre that would best suit your purpose for your non-fiction piece.

You now need to consider how you are going to write in a particular style. If your topic is, for example, 'Crossing Boundaries', and if you feel very concerned about the scandalous use of child labour in garment factories in developing countries, you may wish to write a forceful editorial for a magazine aimed at young females who buy clothes from high street stores.

In this case, you would need to address the following issues.

Selecting your material

Although you may have collected a great deal of material at this stage, you will have to be discriminating and selective in what you choose as the basis for your content. For example, is it relevant to your chosen angle, is it interesting, does it illustrate the points you want to make?

Structuring your argument

Your argument needs to be clearly sequenced to lead your reader through the text. This means you need suitable paragraphing, clear indications of topic shifts, and effective grammatical links between paragraphs.

Choosing particular linguistic and literary techniques to suit your purpose

Consider what literary techniques you could use to intrigue and maintain the interest of your target audience. For example, for a highly persuasive piece you may want to use features of rhetoric such as rhetorical questions, imperatives, first-person pronouns, metaphor, and phonological techniques, whereas a piece of reportage may simply have the purpose of informing or raising awareness.

Writing your coursework

These tips for effective writing could apply to both literary and non-fiction texts. Write opening paragraphs and then write them again in different ways, read what you write out loud and think about how it sounds, try out your work on other people and consider what they say about it, don't try to use elaborate words or over-write; the best words are sometimes the simplest. Learn to use adverbs and adjectives sparingly (if you examine good descriptive writing, you will not find excessive numbers of adjectives), don't be afraid to use the techniques of writers you admire.

Activity 32

The text below is an eye-witness account of the bombing of the London docks in 1940. The writer has deliberately made use of a number of literary features to bring the event to life.

1 Read the text and make a copy of it in which you highlight or underline any examples of: (a) figurative language, (b) evocative or emotive vocabulary, (c) the writer's personal response.

2 Re-write the text by removing these features and presenting it as a simple factual account.

3 Explore the differences between the two versions. Consider how the factual approach could be used as the basis for a different type of writing, such as a historical record of events.

From *London Docks Bombed* by Desmond Flower

September 7 1940

Suddenly we were gaping upwards. The brilliant sky was criss-crossed from horizon to horizon by innumerable vapour trails. The sight was a completely novel one. We watched, fascinated, and all work stopped. The little silver stars
5 sparkling at the heads of the vapour trails turned east. This display looked so insubstantial and harmless, even beautiful. Then, with a dull roar which made the ground across London shake as one stood upon it, the first sticks of bombs hit the docks. Leisurely, enormous mushrooms of black and brown smoke shot with crimson climbed into the sky…

Independent research

For examples of narratives written from the perspective of a child, read the novels *Spies* by Michael Frayn and *The Go-Between* by L.P. Hartley.

Focusing on style: Your literary piece

Your literary piece is another opportunity to express your ideas and feelings about, and attitudes to, the world. Fiction is often inspired by historical and global events that fire the imagination.

For your fiction piece you need to consider these issues:

- your choice of genre, such as prose fiction, drama script, radio play
- your narrative approach or structure
- your choice of literary and linguistic techniques.

Even if you are writing in the genre of prose fiction, you do not have to take the most obvious approach. Consider the following suggestions.

You could try writing as a persona in another gender. The successful contemporary novelist Rose Tremain frequently writes first-person narratives in the voice of a man (see *Restoration*, a set text for Unit 1). Or you could try writing from the perspective of a protagonist who is much older or much younger than you. This does not mean that you have to write in the first person; you could, for example, make use of free indirect speech with very little authorial intervention, or you could employ a retrospective first-person voice so that a detached adult voice presents experiences as a child.

Adaptations and transformations

You may wish to take an existing story and do something else with it. Many writers of fiction turn to myths and old stories as inspiration for their narratives and re-shape them by updating them.

In *The Penelopiad*, novelist Margaret Atwood re-tells the ancient Greek story of *The Odyssey* by shifting the focus to centre her narrative on the character of Penelope, the wife of Odysseus. Atwood calls this 'the creative retelling, the sudden reversal' – bringing to the foreground of the narrative a female character who occupies a minor position in the original and giving her a voice of her own.

Atwood argues the case for re-shaping myths as she claims they can still tell us living truths. 'They are a big map of the human-ness of human beings, and they lay out the full range of human desires and fears… the basic stuff – love, hate, death, life, famine, plenty, the fates of souls, creation myths, what will happen at the end of the world – those are all fixtures'. She adds that language and narrative are 'the most important human inventions'.

The journalist and novelist Clare Boylan decided to complete an unfinished novel by Charlotte Brontë. Brontë had begun the novel, originally called *Emma*, in the 1850s and discarded it after two chapters. Boylan began with background research into Charlotte Brontë's letters and writings; she then retraced Brontë's steps through London, the location for the story, walking from Euston to Soho, the City and East End. Using Brontë's own style and phrases and creating an accurate sense of the period, Boylan produced her own new text, *Emma Brown*, a plausible revision of an incomplete work.

Some novelists show their admiration for other writers by devising sequels to famous works. Susan Hill was fascinated by Daphne du Maurier's *Rebecca* and imagined what happens later to the first-person narrator by writing a sequel entitled *Mrs de Winter*. To do this it was necessary for Hill to study du Maurier's stylistic techniques and characterisation and imitate them in her new text.

If you are interested in basing your own literary piece on an existing text, try the next activity.

Independent research

Read *The Penelopiad: The Myth of Penelope and Odysseus* by Margaret Atwood. Read also *The World's Wife*, a collection of poems by Carol Ann Duffy, which presents well-known classical and mythological narratives about famous men from the viewpoint of the women in their lives.

Activity 33

Think about the core text that you have studied for this unit. Would parts of it be suitable for transformation or adaptation into a new genre? How would the new genre be effective in presenting an interesting and original perspective on the topic?

Record any ideas you have in a table like the one below, which gives an example of a possible text and adaptation. Share your results with other group members, then add to your list any genres you had not thought of.

Original text and genre	Adaptation	Reason for choice of new genre
101 Poems Against War	Performance text	Gives me the opportunity to present the ideas and mood of several poems in dramatic form; could reach a wider or different audience as a drama text. Would need to consider the conventions of the new genre.

Your working notebook

Copy the table into your working notebook. If you decide to produce an adaptation you will be able to refer back to these ideas when writing your commentary.

Assessment objectives

By adapting a text you would be addressing all of the Assessment objectives.

In your new text:

- by showing your ability to select a suitable new genre and approach (AO1)
- by demonstrating your knowledge of the conventions of the new genre by choosing effective literary and linguistic strategies to suit your audience (AO4).

In your commentary:

- by providing a clear and convincing rationale for your choice of new genre (AO1)
- by showing evidence of your wide reading and by providing an analytical explanation of how you shaped your new text (AO2)
- by demonstrating your understanding of the different interpretations and perspectives offered by your stimulus texts (AO3).

Planning for success

You can gain high marks for your A2 coursework if you have a strong sense of purpose and you:

- choose a specific angle or perspective on your topic
- choose a clearly defined audience
- choose a genre that you feel comfortable with and that will allow you to demonstrate your expertise
- achieve a clear, sustained voice
- write with genuine interest and conviction
- make use of a range of appropriate and effective literary and linguistic techniques.

Across AS and A2

Your study of voice for Unit 1 should help you decide how you want to relate to your audience. For example, a first-person voice in the present tense usually has more energy, whereas a third-person voice in the past tense will sound less breathless, although could still have pace.

2 Drafting, revising and editing

Your first draft

Leo Tolstoy

All professional writers produce drafts of their work. It is said that Leo Tolstoy wrote *War and Peace* eight times and Ernest Hemingway wrote *A Farewell to Arms* 39 times. Obviously you would not either want or be able to write endless numbers of drafts, but at least one first draft is essential.

Remember that your first draft is not a polished piece. At this stage your concern should be to write as quickly and productively as possible. You have done your reading, research and reflecting, and you have explored and discussed different possibilities and approaches. Now it's time for you to write and create a world of your own.

The award-winning novelist Pat Barker writes her first draft as quickly as possible 'to sustain a sense of tension by writing fast'. Other writers prefer to write carefully in short amounts.

It may suit you to begin by writing some ideas on paper in pen or pencil, but try to get your work onto a computer as soon as possible. This will give you a permanent record of your writing and you will be able to make changes easily. It is vitally important that you save your work as you write and back up your document regularly.

As you complete the first draft of each task, print out a copy and, if possible, take a short break from it so that you will be able to read it over with fresh eyes. The contemporary novelist Jeanette Winterson suggests making an audio recording of the first draft then replaying it to listen to it. She says: 'You can cheat the eye on the page, but you can't cheat the ear.'

As you replay and listen to your work you can make notes on what you would like to improve. For example, you may feel that the narrative voice needs to be changed from omniscient third person to first person in order to gain more involvement with a character, or that a character in a literary piece would work better with a different age or gender.

Listening to your texts will also help you to assess the effectiveness of your chosen approach and your use of stylistic devices.

Ask for feedback from your peers and test out your work on members of the target audience. It is vitally important at this stage to check that you are meeting the Assessment objectives.

Activity 34

Your working notebook

When you have discussed your work with your partner, use the feedback to make any changes that you think would improve your written pieces and make notes on these changes in your working notebook. This will help you to write your commentary.

Work in pairs to carry out an evaluation and peer review. You should each have a copy of the Assessment objectives for (a) the literary writing and (b) the non-fiction writing.

1 Start by exchanging the first draft of either your fiction or non-fiction pieces. Read your partner's work carefully and note on the text where you feel the writing has met particular Assessment objectives.

2 Evaluate the text using the following questions for guidance.
   - Is there a clear link with the topic, core text and wide reading?
   - Does the writing show understanding of the genre conventions?
   - Does it have a clear audience?
   - Does it employ suitable techniques to appeal to the audience?

3 Discuss your comments with your partner and suggest ways in which the text could be improved.

4 Now repeat the process with your other creative piece.

Revising and editing your first draft

Once you have written your first draft and received comments from your teacher and members of your group, there will almost certainly be changes that you wish to make.

Revising and editing are both valuable processes as they make you think about what you have written and how to find the most economical and effective way of expressing yourself.

There are a number of different processes involved when you revise your first draft:

- making deletions
- making amendments
- proof reading for accuracy.

The following activity illustrates how a professional novelist drafts her work.

Activity 35

1 Read the two texts below. Text A is an extract from the first draft of a contemporary novel. Text B features the same episode in the published version.

The story concerns an Australian-Lebanese teenage girl, who is confused about her identity because she's straddling two cultures as well as growing up with a very protective father.

Text A

He grins and as much as I try to resent him, I can't bring myself to walk away. He makes me feel like a salty summer beach breeze. Like a sail boat bobbing
5 up and down on the harbour under a cloudless day. I talk to him, I've read him, and it's like fish and chips in butcher's paper and fizzy lemonade in a glass bottle. All I want is for us to start over as
10 Timothy and Jamilah.

'So, do you want to dance?' he asks me.

Text B

'Can I ask you something?'
'Yeah.'
'Who am I talking to? Jamilah or Jamie?'
I smile and look into his eyes. 'Jamie's gone,
5 Timothy.'

He suddenly steps forward, grabs both of my hands and kisses me on the lips. Then he leans back, still holding my hands tightly in his.

I'm stunned. It feels like an electric shock. Like
10 every cell in my body is on fire with the excitement of it. I feel like jumping up and down with delight. I feel like laughing. He makes me feel like a salty summer breeze. Like a sail boat bobbing up and down on the harbour under a cloudless day.

15 But then, out of the corner of my eye, I catch Bilal looking our way from across the room.

2 Identify and comment on the changes that the writer has made from the first draft to the published version. Consider the organisation of the text and the writer's choices of language and literary features. Try to provide reasons for her changes.

3 Now go back to your first draft and decide whether there is anything you would like to add, delete or change. Highlight your texts on screen with any areas that could be edited. If you save the original version as well as the edited version, you will be able to refer to the two documents and compare them when you are writing your commentary.

Across AS and A2

Remind yourself
of the editing skills
you needed when
completing your
coursework at AS
(see *Edexcel AS
English Language and
Literature Student
Book*).

You may also need to revise your work to meet the correct word count (see Section B, page 140). Working within a disciplined word limit is a real-life task.

If you have exceeded the word count in your first draft for either of your pieces, ask yourself these questions:

- Does every word work, or are there any small, unnecessary words that I could cut out?
- Have I repeated any words or phrases without a good reason?
- Have I chosen the best words for what I mean and want to say?

3 Assessing the texts

This section gives you the opportunity to assess some exemplar texts against the relevant Assessment objectives.

Activity 36

You will need a copy of the Assessment objectives grids for the creative tasks.

The text below is an example of a student's work that has been annotated with comments by an assessor.

The text relates to the topic 'War and the Individual', and is an extract from a short story intended to be included in an anthology of anti-war writing.

1 Try to link the comments of the assessor to the relevant Assessment objectives (AO1 and AO4).

2 How successful do you feel the text is in meeting its purpose of presenting the destructive and damaging effects of war on the individual? Give reasons for your judgement.

Immediate opening to capture the reader's attention

Sets the scene and gives the context

Alliterative effect of repeated letter

Effective use of demonstrative pronoun

Personification

Metaphorical language

Phonological technique of sibilant sounds

Omission of the definite article increases pace

Moves from metaphorical to reference familiar everyday features

Minor sentence with question to involve the reader

Premodifying adjectives

> Presenting the World: War
>
> The resounding noise of emptiness lingers in the air, in every possible gap in the mind, in the dark and isolated rooms that allegedly provide comfort. As I roll from place to place, nothing seems to remain a constant other than this blackness. When the bombs obliterated everything in the radius of a mile, I was fortunate to survive, unlike so many others.
>
> That day will always rewind and repeat itself in my head. The moment that peace became just a word; a word that could never again be a reality. The blackened sky howled tears of fire and shells and with them my life was shredded like so much of the landscape. The flames rose and smoke whispered until it silently snaked down throats, slyly suffocating. Screams were muffled by the noise of the crumbling buildings as they fell to the ground, bodies underneath. Our community was blasted apart: the church, the post office and the primary school with the children's gas masks still sealed in their boxes in the hope they would never be used.
>
> As I squinted into the intense white light, eyes blinking to adjust, the unlikely possibility that I was still alive never crossed my mind. Heaven or hell? Yet that intermittent electronic noise and the shooting, agonising pain

running through my legs was not heaven. This was a painfully clean hospital, buzzing with activity. Prim nurses flitted around. Groaning, I dared to look at my limp body and prayed it would all be all right. The staff talked but I did not understand. They did things to my body that I did not understand. They used medical terms that I did not understand. Reality and unconsciousness became entwined, merging to become one and the same thing as drugs took control.

> Reiterates pain reference with different context

> Syntactic repitition to show state of mind

> Moves back to abstract description

Legs carry your weight and take you where you need to be. They can be used as tools of leverage, as a prop and as something to support you. Without them, the outlook on life was bleak and this was my realisation as time passed. As it dawned on me, the grim truth that I had lost both legs in such a selfish act of war, I felt anger and hatred. Blood red hatred for the political reasoning behind the combat that seemed so pointless. In years to come, history books will publish pages and pages, with a small paragraph devoted to the number of lives lost, the numbers injured, and we will all just become statistics. The desperate pain that was caused to so many mothers and wives who lost husbands and sons, parents whose children were crushed, young people whose dreams were shattered, will be reduced to an inky print on an ageing textbook.

> Triadic structure

> Emotive lexis

> List of three again

> Tone more reflective as approach becomes retrospective

You cannot summarise the lifetimes of devastation that war causes, yet people will continue to try.

> Pronoun implies reader involvement

Twenty years on, I still feel trapped in the day the bomb destroyed our community. I stare and become speechless, lost in anger and lack of understanding.

> Ends with emotive and abstract expression

3 Read the concluding comments of the assessor relating to the extract above. Find evidence for these comments in the text. Do you agree with them?

Assessor's comments

AO1: A suitable choice of genre for a literary task, with a fictitious first-person narrative response to the topic of war. Adopts a descriptive approach with an anonymous narrator; shifts from abstract reflections to more realistic scene setting. Evidence of awareness of historical period implies research.

AO4: Involves the reader and attempts to maintain interest through a number of strategies: the immediate starting point, use of evaluative adjectives, emotive lexis, metaphorical language and phonological techniques. Maintains a tone of anger and disillusionment. The shift to the more retrospective comment at the end is thought-provoking. The ending leaves the reader to consider the issues.

Activity 37

The extracts on this and the facing page are for you to assess. Work in pairs or small groups.

1 Using the appropriate assessment grid, find specific evidence of where the writers have met the Assessment objectives.

2 How effective have you found each text in terms of the ways in which the writers have chosen to present their topic?

Text A
Topic: Football
Genre: A journalism blog

The text is an extract from a blog written by a young student journalist who visited a sports academy in Bangladesh to report on the importance and the future of Bangladeshi football.

Wednesday, 6 June 2007
Ed's diary – Day 12

In the afternoon Waj and I filmed the boys training and arranged with Tipo (head coach) to carry out all our interviews tomorrow morning. Then, with an hour left to go of the afternoon session, I
5 decided to put the camera down and just watch the boys train. Their passion for the game and their desire to learn and improve is amazing.

Since I've been here I've watched them get up at around 6.30 am every morning and train for at least three hours, rest in the early afternoon, and then train for another three hours in the early evening… never has their enthusiasm waned. They just love to play football – I guess for some of
10 them this really is the opportunity of a lifetime and they know it.

Ed's diary – Day 14

Today we were interviewing Jintu's father, a rickshaw driver, at his home just outside Dhaka; Shobu's father, a successful banker living in a high-rise apartment in the city; and Milan (the assistant coach) at the national football stadium in the city, ahead of a premiership clash.

15 First up was Jintu's house. It took close to two hours to get there, the final stage of the journey taking us along more dirt tracks than tarmac, passing hundreds of make-shift homes of bamboo and corrugated iron sheets as we went.

Along a main street we suddenly ducked through a tiny doorway in a large metal fence and were led along a narrow alley, thick with mud and lined with dirty tumbledown walls. Every so often we'd
20 pass an open doorway, revealing a one-roomed house no bigger than 10 foot by 10 foot that more often than not played home to at least five people.

By the time we arrived at Jintu's house we'd gathered a large group of followers fascinated by the camera and the presence of a tall lanky European.

Jintu's mother, father, and baby brother were there to greet us, and despite being as poor as they
25 were, had laid out a full breakfast spread on their dining table, squashed into their one-roomed house. I couldn't believe it. We gratefully crowded around the tiny table and enjoyed hot chicken patties and fresh mango.

Following our late breakfast we set up outside the house for an interview. By now the whole community had gathered to watch, making a great backdrop to interview Jintu's dad against. It took
30 about ten minutes. As we all piled back into the people carrier to leave we were yet again surrounded by a large crowd, many of them calling Jintu's name. We'd turned him into a local celebrity and he was loving every minute of it.

Text B
Topic: Crossing Boundaries
Genre: A features article

The text is an extract from a newspaper article written by a journalist who was asked to take part in a television documentary.

Last summer, I was asked to take part in a television programme, 'Women in Black'. The makers said they wanted to shatter stereotypes and show the empowered, modern, young, cool Muslim woman (presumably because we haven't gone off the rails like the modern, young, British, uncool Muslim man). Would I take part? 'Of course,' I said. Am I not empowered and modern and Muslim and cool? Hell, yes.

So I met the production team and one of the women (not Muslim, by the way) pulled out a little camera and filmed me saying, among other things, how irritating it is that non-Muslims act surprised that I'm Muslim just because I choose not to cover my head.

It went well, I thought, and so they said. But – and this was quite a big but – they were a bit concerned about my appearance.

'Your dress is quite Western,' they said ruefully. I was wearing jeans and a short-sleeved top (yes, I really do remember what I was wearing that day. How could I not? I thought I was going to be famous and on TV), but I was hardly scantily clad. So much for the empowered, modern, young, cool Muslim woman; turns out what the BBC really wanted was an authentic, well-covered one instead.

You see, burkas make good TV.

Text C
Topic: War and the Individual
Genre: A fictional diary of a young Iraqi girl

The text is an extract from the fictional diary of a young Iraqi girl written during the invasion of Iraq.

Wednesday July 18
Another car bomb exploded in the market today. The force of it broke the last window in the house that hadn't already been shattered by the reverberations. The missile that fell on the house next door blasted one of our walls clean off a few weeks back. Now those bastard Americans watch us cook, sleep, get dressed. It isn't enough that they're here turning our people against each other, killing our friends with their 'friendly fire' and patrolling our streets like Iraq's some sort of fucking colony. It makes me sick. Hearing George Bush and his arrogant promises. He doesn't know what it is to live each day wondering if you'll ever see the next. If the once beautiful sunset now veiled in an impermeable shroud of artillery smoke will be the last you'll ever see. And I'll bet he's never had to walk down streets having to turn away from the children disfigured by shrapnel playing in the wreckage of their neighbour's home. What has happened to humanity?

Sunday July 22
Haven't written for a few days because Ali was caught up in a run-in between British officers and Iraqi insurgents at the Basra checkpoint. Ali was shot through the shoulder but the hospitals are crammed so he's here, propped up against a pile of sacking in the kitchen. He's in agony. I can see it in his eyes when Mum tries to clean his wound. With what though. I mean, the water supply is turned off most of the day, as is the electricity. And many basic foodstuffs are hard to come by. You can't even leave the house these days without fear of arrest or I don't know… death? Can't think like that though, Mum says. She still goes to market every day. She's so sure of herself. I can feel the blood pounding through my ears when I'm walking through town. I'm scared.

Friday July 27
Ali died last night. I don't know what to write.

Coursework checkpoint

By the end of this section you should have:

- planned and written the first drafts of your literary and non-fiction pieces
- used peer feedback to evaluate and review your texts
- revised and edited your first drafts
- assessed some exemplar texts against the Assessment objectives.

D Writing your commentary

This section gives you advice and guidance on how to write and structure your commentary. You will also have the opportunity to assess some exemplar commentaries.

The maximum word count for your commentary is 1000. It is important that you do not exceed it. The advice that you were given about word counts and editing in Section C (page 140) applies just as much to your commentary as to your creative pieces – when the maximum word count is reached the assessor will stop reading and you will not receive credit for any extra work.

Assessment objectives

Your commentary is worth 38 of the 80 marks available for your A2 coursework. It is assessed against AO1, AO2 and AO3, so you will need to show that you are able to:

- select appropriate literary and linguistic approaches and use technical terminology accurately (AO1 – 6 marks)
- show understanding of the ways in which structure, form and language shape the meanings of texts (AO2 – 16 marks)
- use integrated approaches to explore the relationships between texts, considering and evaluating the influence of contextual factors (AO3 – 16 marks).

Across AS and A2

At AS you produced two commentaries, one for each of your original tasks. At A2 you have to write an analytical evaluative commentary in which you discuss both pieces. This may entail making some comparisons between them. *Evaluative* means that you will discuss how you attempted to achieve your objectives, reflecting on what you learned from your research and wide reading, and explaining how you used this knowledge to help you to write your creative pieces.

1 Purpose of the commentary

The purpose of the commentary is to give you the opportunity to:

- discuss both your literary and non-fiction tasks and the approaches that you have taken
- show the relationship of your creative tasks to your topic area and core text
- discuss and comment on your choices of literary and linguistic features
- show evidence of your wide reading and research.

Activity 38

Below are extracts from students' commentaries that illustrate each of the points above.

1 Which of the above purposes does each commentary illustrate?

2 What do you learn about these extracts that relates to your own commentary?

> **Text A**
>
> After reading J.G. Ballard's autobiography 'Miracles of Life', I became interested in what life was like for people involved in WW2 in the Far East. I decided that the best way for me to use the ideas I had gained from my research was to write a persuasive article entitled 'Why we must never forget' for my non-fiction piece.
>
> I wanted to find a much more personal angle for my literary piece and I like the quick impact of the dramatic genre so I decided to write an extract from a play for radio about a Japanese prisoner of war.

Text B

My core text was 'A Journal of the Plague Year' by Daniel Defoe and my topic was global epidemics. As the focus for my non-fiction task I chose to write about the growing problem of obesity in the western world by writing an informative and persuasive article for a free daily newspaper. I wanted to be more imaginative in my literary task so I wrote about the survivors of a deadly virus, in the form of an extract from a drama script for television.

Text C

On a textual level I have used a relatively informal register in my reportage text as shown by colloquialisms, compound words and contractions, as these reflect the sociolect of my target audience of 18–25-year-olds and give the otherwise serious text a pacy, vibrant tone.

Text D

When writing my editorial on the war in Iraq I was influenced by the articles of Johann Hari and Robert Fisk as well as by the first-person accounts of ordinary people living in Iraq which I found through internet searches.

For my short story on war I found inspiration in war poetry and diaries and letters written by soldiers.

2 Structuring your commentary

The following guidelines are suggested to help you organise and present your commentary effectively; however, it is not mandatory to use this precise format.

It is a good idea to start with a *rationale* or *explanation*, briefly explaining:

- your reasons for your choice of genres/types of text
- the contexts of each text
- the titles
- the types of audience you are aiming at.

The main part of your commentary will be your *analysis*. In your analysis you should:

- explain briefly how your creative pieces are linked to your stimulus texts
- discuss how you attempted to achieve your objectives, using specific examples from your own writing supported by reference to the source texts
- reflect on your wide reading. Make references to texts or types of writing that influenced your content, style and points of view.

Your *evaluation* is the conclusion of your commentary. In it you should reflect on the extent to which you achieved your objectives, any difficulties or challenges that you met, and how you set out to overcome them. This does not involve making vague claims about how successful you were. It means giving precise examples of the decisions that you took, mentioning specific aspects that you felt worked well, and changes that you made following feedback.

Take it further

Read the following evaluation and discuss how effective you think it is.
"When I read my fictional text about living in Iraq I realised that the first-person narrative voice sounded unconvincing as it was just me writing about me, so I decided to create a character based on my wide reading about the Iraq war and to present this character via a third-person narrative interspersed with interior monologue. That approach seemed much more effective".
When writing your evaluation, do not make bland statements such as 'I was successful' or say 'If I had more time…'. Do explain why and how your tasks were pleasing and made you feel that you had achieved something. You could even discuss your ideas for what you would like to do if you were to extend this type of study and research to a higher level.

3 Writing your first draft

Refer to your working notebook while you are writing your first draft. The entries you made in your notebook while preparing your creative tasks will now give you a good point of reference when you plan your commentary.

If you intend to compare and contrast the approaches of your two creative tasks, it is more effective to thread your comments throughout rather than taking each text in turn. You can use grammatical links to act as discourse markers, such as 'however', 'by contrast', 'similarly'. This is also more economical when you are considering the word count.

To help you compare your texts, use highlighters to flag up points of difference and comparison on your two texts (you can do this on the computer screen or on hard copies).

When you write your commentary, think about your reader. Your two creative tasks each had a specific audience and in the same way your commentary will have the assessors as your audience. Write clearly and organise your commentary in logical paragraphs, using the level of formality that you are accustomed to using in examination essays.

Read your first draft of your commentary aloud and make any necessary alterations to improve its coherence.

Activity 39

1 When you have completed the first draft of your commentary, use the checklist below to ensure that you have addressed all the requirements.

✔ Have you given a clear rationale/explanation for your choice of approaches and the significance of your chosen genres?

✔ Is there evidence of your wide reading and research?

✔ Have you made some evaluative comments about the style and influence of your stimulus texts?

✔ Have you made your purposes clear?

✔ Can you make some comparisons between the genre and approach of your two pieces?

✔ Have you shown understanding of the characteristic stylistic features of your chosen genres?

✔ Have you made use of appropriate technical terminology?

✔ Is your commentary coherent and interesting?

2 Exchange your commentary with your partner's and assess it against the checklist above.

- Does it meet all the criteria?
- Are there any gaps, or areas that need clarification?

When you have received feedback from your partner you will be ready to complete the final draft of your commentary.

4 Writing your bibliography

Your last task is to add a bibliography to your commentary.

You were advised to include a bibliography with your AS coursework. It is even more important that you produce an accurate, well-presented bibliography for your A2 coursework, for the following reasons:

- It helps to relate your final coursework pieces to your topic and core text.
- It provides evidence of your research and wide reading.
- It shows that you have taken time to document your sources while preparing for your original writing.
- It is good academic practice and will prepare you for similar tasks if you choose to take this subject to a higher level.

Begin with your core text and then list the books, articles, films, TV/radio programmes and websites that you used in the course of your research and that have given you ideas about style or content.

When you list books you should include the following, arranged alphabetically by author's name:

- author's surname and initials
- year of publication of edition used
- full title of the book
- edition of the book, if there is more than one
- place of publication
- publisher.

Entries for books should look like this:

> Hornby, N., 1992. *Fever Pitch*. London: Gollancz
> Keane, F., 1996. 'Farewell Hong Kong' from *Letter to Daniel*. London: BBC Books

When listing articles and reports, you should include these details:

- name of the writer
- publication
- title of the article
- date.

Entries for articles and reports should look like this:

> Joseph, P. 'The boys from Brazil: On the trail of football's dream team'. *The Independent Extra*, 10 April 2008

List websites at the end, for example:
http://www.bangladeshfootballdoc.blogspot.com

5 Assessing commentaries

Activity 40

On the next two pages are extracts from commentaries on the three exemplar texts you were given to assess in Section C. It might be helpful to photocopy the commentaries so that you can annotate them.

1 Use the checklist you applied to your own work (page 152) to find evidence that the requirements of the commentary have been addressed.

2 Assess the effectiveness of each commentary against AO1, AO2 and AO3. Note any aspects that you feel are particularly successful and make suggestions for any that could be improved.

Text A

Bangladesh football blog

Extract from introduction

I became interested in how football can be a positive and motivating force in the lives of underprivileged young people and so I decided to use my two pieces of creative writing to explore this in very different ways. The best way of recording my experiences of visiting the Bangladesh Sports Academy seemed to be a diary in the form of a blog as this gave me an economical method of describing my experiences.

Extract from analysis

I have used characteristic features of the diary/journal genre, with dates, times, names, etc. There are many deictic references to people I met and places I visited but I have tried to explain these briefly to keep my readers involved as my aim was to get them to share my experiences and impressions. My language choices were influenced by my desire to communicate my admiration for the commitment and vitality of the young people and the enthusiasm and warmth that we found in their communities, e.g. I have used abstract nouns like 'passion' and 'desire'. I emphasised their commitment by using a negative structure, 'never has their enthusiasm waned'.

I used some typical features of journalism like noun phrases in apposition to give quick, economical descriptions of who people were, e.g. 'Jintu's father, a rickshaw driver', 'Shobu's father, a successful banker'.

Adverbs were important in providing discourse markers for my readers as I took them on my journey, e.g. 'Along a main street', 'By the time we arrived'.

I deliberately used an informal, elliptical style typical of modern media presentations to suit the blog genre – people who read blogs expect them to be quick and pacy, e.g. 'First up was'. This quick, elliptical style with many deictic and personal references is very different from my other piece, my short play about a young English kid who fights to be allowed to pursue his passion for football. Both of my pieces were inspired by my core text, Simon Kuper's Football Against the Enemy, and I gained ideas about possible approaches from researching different types of journalism like features articles, blogs, news reports, etc. I had enjoyed reading Nick Hornby's novels about football and thought it would be interesting to use similar ideas in a different way by writing a short dramatic piece. My audience for my play was more specific as I was aiming it mainly at 12–14-year-olds, whereas I think it's more difficult to define the audience for a blog as it's in the public domain of the internet and people of any age may read it.

Text B

Features article

Extract from introduction

I decided to write a features article (which I imagined might be published in a magazine aimed at young women) as a response to my topic of 'Crossing Boundaries' as I feel strongly that even the people who claim to be open-minded and liberal in their attitudes often resort to prejudices and stereotypes themselves.

I had read and researched many features articles and I admired the forceful approach of journalists like Germaine Greer and Polly Toynbee, among others.

Extract from analysis

My idea was to use a satirical approach to convey my feelings so I used a number of literary and linguistic features typical of this sort of provocative journalism, e.g. my use of parenthesis to make an ironic aside and to add extra detail ('presumably, because we haven't gone off the rails', 'yes, I really do remember', 'not Muslim, by the way') and my use of the conjunction 'But' for emphasis in 'But – and this was quite a big but'. I used the throwaway comment 'So much for' to indicate my disappointment.

To get my readers involved I have used questions and a type of interior monologue so that they could share my feelings. Listing is a prominent feature of my article as I use it in an ironic way to convey my main points about stereotyping: i.e., I use a lengthy asyndetic list of adjectives to premodify the noun (Muslim) woman and then I repeat the process as an ironic contrast to show the stereotype of the young Muslim man.

I was influenced in my choice of clothing as the focal point of my topic by my reading of The Bookseller of Kabul, Reading Lolita in Tehran and A Thousand Splendid Suns, where Muslim women are often defined by their clothes.

Text C

Fictional diary of a young Iraqi girl

Extract from introduction

I decided to write a features article. My topic of War and my reading of war poetry, diaries and letters got me interested in the situation of ordinary people and how they cope with trying to lead normal lives in a war zone.

I had read extracts from Baghdad Burning in my AS year and when I began to study war for my A2 coursework I was reminded of how much I had admired the writer's style. I think the genre of the diary is a good one to use because it shows the passage of time and the way that daily life can be interrupted by traumatic events.

Extract from analysis

I wanted to focus in particular on the lives of young people of a similar age to myself and so I decided on a fictional diary for my literary piece. For this I adopt the fictional persona of an Iraqi girl and I write in the first-person narrative voice. I deliberately use an elliptical style, typical of diaries, to begin my entries, e.g. 'Haven't written for a few days', and I use contractions to imitate the informal nature of spoken language.

The ideas for the content I got from my reading of articles and news reports and watching televised news reports on the war in Iraq, but the approach could be used to describe any war in any time. I was also influenced very much by the war poetry I read where I found figurative language used effectively to show the destructive force of war, e.g. 'the once beautiful sunset now veiled in an impermeable shroud of artillery smoke'.

I used short sentences frequently to create tension and to increase the pace, e.g. 'He's in agony', 'She's so sure of herself'.

From my reading of published war diaries I thought it would be a good idea to end each entry with a language technique that had a strong impact, e.g. the rhetorical question 'What has happened to humanity?' and the short, declarative 'I don't know what to write'.

I wanted to make a contrast in approach with my non-fiction piece so I decided to use my research and wide reading to write a speech against war where I could take a more factual approach and be more forceful and explicit.

Extract from evaluation

I feel that I have learned a lot about the different ways that war can be presented. I was aware that I needed to do background research to make my fictional diary sound convincing, but I think I could have made it more authentic by adding details of specific places and events that actually happened. My initial idea to write a chapter from a novel proved too difficult and I realised that a diary would be a more suitable genre to portray a situation that is on-going.

Coursework checkpoint

You should now complete the final draft of your commentary. Check that your coursework portfolio contains the following:

• one literary piece   • one non-fiction piece   • one commentary with bibliography.

Glossary

abstract nouns [page 18]
the names of things which have no physical qualities, e.g. 'happiness', 'fear'

abstract vocabulary [page 43]
lexis which describes ideas, feelings or states of mind

active voice [page 18]
a grammatical structure in which the subject performs the action of the verb, e.g. 'Rooney shot fiercely from twenty yards'

alliteration [page 73]
the repetition of the same initial sound in a sequence of words

assonance [page 74]
the repetition of the same or similar vowel sounds in a sequence of words

ballad [page 79]
a poem that tells a story or describes a series of events, originally sung by a strolling minstrel

blank verse [page 59]
a form of unrhymed poetry written in iambic pentameter

characterisation [page 59]
the means used by a writer to describe a character's personal qualities (note that 'characterisation' refers to the techniques of the writer, not to the character in question)

chronology [page 70]
the arrangement of narrative events in order, beginning with the earliest events and moving forward in time

coherence [page 32]
the structure of a text to give clarity and internal consistency. A coherent text is one that 'makes sense'.

colloquialisms [page 17]
expressions from everyday speech, typically found in spontaneous conversation and in writing which reproduces this

colloquial lexis [page 22]
informal language typical of speech

concrete nouns [page 18]
the names of things which have physical qualities, e.g. objects and places

connotation [page 34]
the ideas, feelings or associations that a word suggests in addition to its primary, literal meaning

contextual factors [page 82]
the external circumstances affecting the content and form of a text, e.g. social and cultural influences, the writer's personal history, literary traditions, stylistic conventions

consonance [page 74]
the correspondence or near correspondence of consonant sounds in a sequence of words e.g. "tittle-tattle"

deictic language (deixis) [page 17]
a term for words or expressions that rely on context to give them meaning, e.g. 'this', 'that', 'here', 'there'

domestic drama [page 55]
a drama with a specific, localised setting, typically based on the family

dual / multiple time scheme [page 70]
the use in a narrative of more than one time-scale, e.g. events describing the present combined with events describing the past

ellipsis [page 61]
the omission of part of a sentence that can be understood from the context

emotive language [page 14]
words used to arouse strong feelings in the reader or listener

expressive language [page 25]
a general term for language in a written text which comes close to ordinary, everyday speech

explicitness [page 28]
a clear and unambiguous statement of meaning

external / internal viewpoint [page 34]
the perspective of the writer or narrator in a text: an 'external' viewpoint is detached and objective, an 'internal' viewpoint is involved and subjective

extended metaphor [page 77]
a comparison which is built up progressively in the course of a text (see also 'semantic field')

figurative language [page 17]
words that are used metaphorically in order to construct a comparison

formal language [page 17]
language with an impersonal register, incorporating standard English vocabulary and correct grammar

genre [page 10]
a type of writing with its own characteristic form and style

graphological features [page 14]
the visual aspects of a written text; the way a text looks on the page

heightened language [page 82]
language that is deliberately exaggerated for effect, more intense than the surrounding text

iambic pentameter [page 74]
a poetic rhythm with five strong and five weak beats to the line: di Dum/ di Dum/ di Dum/ di Dum/ di Dum

idiolect [page 59]
the term for an individual's unique language use in speech or writing

idioms [page 17]
colloquial or slang expressions

informal language [page 17]
the use of non-standard English, dialect or colloquial lexis

impersonal register [page 17]
language use which is formal in style and tone

implicit [page 28]
an implied or indirect statement of meaning (see also 'connotation')

jargon [page 22]
words or expressions specific to particular subjects, e.g. the law, science, religion

lexis [page 10]
the total set of words in a language, often called the 'vocabulary' of a language

literal language [page 17]
language which states the fact of something and nothing else (also termed 'denotative' language)

linguistic framework [page 17]
a toolkit used to examine the way spoken and written language works

lyric [page 79]
a short poem or song written in the first person expressing a particular emotion or sentiment

manifesto [page 82]
a declaration of a writer's or speaker's beliefs, typically found in texts with a political theme

minor sentence [page 32]
a sentence that lacks one or more of the normal clause elements, e.g. 'Great song! Brilliant'

modal verb forms [page 32]
auxiliary verbs that indicate possibility ('I can do this'), obligation ('I must do this', 'I should do this') or prediction ('I will do this')

modifiers [page 32]
words which describe a noun (adjectives) or a verb (adverbs)

motif [page 66]
a recurring distinctive idea running through a text, such as an image or a symbol, a word or a phrase, to highlight a central theme

narrator [page 70]
the person telling the story, either the writer or a character in the story

narrative viewpoint [page 32]
the perspective established by the writer or narrator of a text

non-fluency features [page 61]
aspects of spontaneous speech such as false starts, fillers and hesitations which indicate that it is unplanned

non-standard punctuation [page 22]
punctuation which does not follow the normal rules of grammar

onomatopoeia [page 73]
a word whose sound imitates what it describes, e.g. 'buzz', 'pop'

orthography [page 37]
standard English spelling

parallel action/plot [page 66]
a literary device where two sets of events are followed alternately in the course of a narrative

part-rhyme [page 74]
inexact or imperfect rhyme, where one sound is echoed by another similar sound

passive voice [page 18]
a grammatical structure in which the subject is acted upon, e.g 'The goalie was left helpless by Rooney's fierce strike'

persona [page 74]
the identity adopted by the writer of a text

personal register [page 17]
a form of language specific to an individual or character in a text

personal pronouns [page 18]
words which stand for named characters in a text, e.g. 'I', 'me', 'they', 'them'

perspective [page 14]
the way that a writer views something; his/her point of view

phonological features [page 73]
the sounds of words which combine to create meaning, e.g. alliteration, assonance, consonance

poetic language [page 25]
a general term describing lexis which is used imaginatively and which typically foregrounds simile and/or metaphor

polemic [page 32]
an argued or investigative text in which the writer/speaker sets out to shape an audience's opinion, often about a moral or political issue

positioning [page 77]
the technique a writer uses to place the reader in relation to what is being said, in order to guide their response

premodification [page 18]
the use of adjectives or adverbs in advance of the head word in a phrase, e.g. 'That's a lovely dress', 'I'm really sorry'

primary audience [page 10]
the principal audience/readership to which a text is addressed

public drama [page 55]
a drama which has a broad social setting and which typically deals with social or political themes

production (context of) [page 82]
the circumstances in which a text is produced, e.g. historical, social, cultural

prosodics [page 43]
the use in a spoken text of pitch, volume, pace and rhythm to give emphasis [page]

psychological drama [page 55]
a drama which explores the state of mind of a central character or a group of characters

reception (context of) [page 82]
the circumstances in which a text is read/heard and responded to by its audience

reiteration [page 18]
the repetition of rhetorical devices to highlight a central theme in speech or writing

rhetorical devices [page 43]
the linguistic techniques used to influence an audience in a spoken or written text

register [page 10]
a form of language suited to a particular situation or social context

semantic field [page 77]
a group of words drawn from a particular area of experience, e.g. food or colours

sentence forms [page 18]
sentences defined according to their grammatical structures: simple, compound, complex

sentence types [page 18]
sentences defined according to the purposes for which they are constructed: declarative, imperative, interrogative and exclamatory

social realism [page 82]
a literary genre which presents a view of society from an objective standpoint

specialised lexis [page 32]
terminology drawn from a particular field of knowledge or interest, e.g. medicine, literature, cookery (also termed 'field specific' lexis)

stage conventions [page 70]
theatrical devices, e.g. the division of a play into acts and scenes, the use of a narrator, lighting and sound effects

standard punctuation [page 22]
punctuation which follows the normal rules of grammar

subordinate clauses [page 32]
clauses which function as nouns, adjectives or adverbs in complex sentences

superlative adjectives [page 43]
adjectives formed by the addition of the suffix '–est' or the prefix 'most' to existing adjectives, e.g. 'cleverest', 'most beautiful'

sub-plot [page 66]
a secondary sequence of events in a story, running parallel to the main plot

sub-text [page 61]
the implied or suggested meaning of a text, as opposed to its explicit or overt meaning

symbol [page 66]
a literary device by which one thing is used represent something else, e.g. a concrete object like a bomb can be used to represent an abstract idea like hatred

syntax [page 10]
the ordered arrangement of words in a sentence

syntactic parallelism [page 18]
the juxtaposition of similar grammatical structures for emphasis or contrast, e.g 'The time for talking has passed; the time for action is now'

taboo language [page 17]
lexis that is considered inappropriate or offensive in certain social circumstances

term of address [page 25]
a set phrase used by one person to address another, reflecting the nature their relationship, e.g. 'the right honourable gentleman' in a formal speech, 'Hi Amy' in an e-mail

theatrical time [page 55]
a dramatist's use of chronology which does not reflect real time 'by the clock'

theme [page 73]
the principal ideas or issues raised by the story in a narrative or drama

transactional language [page 25]
a general term to describe lexis which is mainly factual and used to convey information

triadic structures [page 18]
lists of three, used for effect most typically in a formal speech, e.g. 'This nation is proud, this nation is resourceful, this nation will not be defeated'

values [page 13]
the writer's/speakers beliefs or moral stance in relation to the topic

vernacular [page 73]
an everyday form of language, specific to a region or country

Published by Pearson Education Limited, a company incorporated in England and Wales, having its registered office at Edinburgh Gate, Harlow, Essex, CM20 2JE. Registered company number: 872828

Edexcel is a registered trade mark of Edexcel Limited

Text © Pearson Education 2009
First published 2009

12 11 10 09
10 9 8 7 6 5 4 3 2 1

British Library Cataloguing in Publication Data
A catalogue record for this book is available from the British Library
ISBN 978 1 84690 246 8

Typeset by Redmoor Design, Tavistock, Devon
Picture research by Ann Thomson
Cover photo © Edexcel
Printed in Great Britain by Henry Ling Ltd., at the Dorset Press, Dorchester, Dorset

Picture Credits
The author and publisher would like to thank the following individuals and organisations for permission to reproduce photographs:
13 Getty Images: Henry Guttmann. **23 TopFoto:** Gary Lee/UPPA/ Photoshot. **45 TopFoto:** ©1999/TophamPicturepoint. **46 Getty Images:** Gerti Deutsch/Picture Post. **55 TopFoto:** Pete Jones/Arena PAL. **79 Getty Images:** E.O.Hoppe/Mansell/Time Life Pictures. **117 Getty Images:** Hulton Archive. **134 Getty Images:** mirrorpix. **144 Getty Images:** Time life Pictures/Mansell. **153 Photolibrary.com:** All other images © Pearson Education

Every effort has been made to contact copyright holders of material reproduced in this book. Any omissions will be rectified in subsequent printings if notice is given to the publishers.
We are grateful to the following for permission to reproduce copyright material:
Carla Banks (Danuta Reah) for an extract from an interview discussing her novel *The Forest of Souls*, reproduced with permission; Extracts from The Queen's speech on 5 September 1997 after Princess Diana's death; extract from abdication speech of King Edward VIII, 11 December 1936; and Queen Victoria's diary on 1 May 1951 © Crown copyright; Curtis Brown for an extract from 'The Head Boy' published in *Some People* by Harold Nicolson, 1927, 1996 edition, reproduced with permission; Edward Danson for an extract from "The Beautiful Game: Finding a Beckham of Bangladesh" 6 June 2007 blog entries http://bangladeshfootballdoc. blogspot.com reproduced with permission; Faber & Faber for the poems "1st September 1939" by W. H. Auden from *101 poems against war* eds M. Hollis & P. Keegan Faber & Faber, 2003; "Landscapes I New Hampshire" by T.S. Eliot published in *The Wasteland and Other Poems*, T.S. Eliot; extracts from the play *Stuff Happens* by David Hare and Faber and Faber, 2006; The poems "Snowdrop" and "The Horses" by Ted Hughes from *Selected Poems of Thom Gunn and Ted Hughes*, Faber & Faber, 1982; extract from the play *Betrayal* by Harold Pinter, Faber and Faber, 1998; the poems "Crossing the Water" by Sylvia Plath from *Selected Poems, Sylvia Plath*; and "The Love Song of J. Alfred Prufrock (1917)" by T.S. Eliot from *Prufrock and Other Observations*, Faber & Faber, 2001, reproduced with permission; Faber & Faber and The Agency for extracts from the play *Translations* by Brian Friel, Faber and Faber, 1981, reproduced by permission of Faber & Faber and The Agency (London) Ltd copyright © 1981 Brian Friel. All rights reserved and enquiries to The Agency (London) Ltd 24 Pottery Lane, London W11 4LZ info@ theagency.co.uk; Jonathan Greatrex for an extract from "War, hope and reconciliation", reproduced with permission; Guardian News & Media Limited for extracts from "Munich 58: A collective loss of life that sent shivers of shock round the world" by Richard Williams both published in

The Guardian 2 February 2008; "I'm the wrong kind of Muslim for the TV" by Huma Qureshi *The Observer* 27 April 2008 copyright © Guardian News & Media Limited 2008; HarperCollins Publishers Ltd for an extract from *Bad Blood: A Memoir* by Lorna Sage, Ebury Press, 2005, reprinted by permission of HarperCollins Publishers Ltd copyright © Lorna Sage 2005; Tony Harrison for the poems "Long Distance II", "Turns" and "National Trust" by Tony Harrison published in *Tony Harrison Selected Poems* by Penguin Books, 2007 copyright © Tony Harrison; Independent News and Media Limited for extracts from "Our legacy is a dark and forbidding place of militias" by Kim Sengupta *The Independent* 19 March 2008; "The only lesson we ever learn is that we never learn" by Robert Fisk *The Independent* 19 March 2008; and "Murder in Italy" *The Independent* 15 September 2008 copyright © Independent News and Media Limited 2008; Mary Jay for material, reproduced with permission; John Murray (Publishers) for the poem "Death in Leamington" from *Collected Poems*, by John Betjeman © 1955, 1958, 1962, 1964, 1968, 1970, 1979, 1981, 1982, 2001. Reproduced by permission of John Murray (Publishers); The Labour Party for an extract from Tony Blair's speech at the Labour Party Conference, September 1997, reproduced with permission; Navajivan Trust for an extract from Mahatma Gandhi's speech on 23 March 1922, 'Non-violence is the first article of my faith' published in *The Penguin Book of Historic Speeches* (Penguin, 1996), ed Brian MacArthur reproduced with permission by Navajivan Trust; new**books** for an extract from an interview with Rhiannon Lassiter published in new**books** magazine November/December 2007, Issue 42, reproduced with permission; The New York Times for an extract from "A 'Menagerie' Full of Stars, Silhouettes and Weird Sounds" by Brantley, B published in *The New York Times*, 23 March 2005, copyright © 2005 The New York Times. All rights reserved. Used by permission and protected by the Copyright Laws of the United States. The printing, copying, redistribution, or retransmission of the Material without express written permission is prohibited; NI Syndication Limited for extracts from "Shaffer's variation on a theme" by Irving Wardle *The Times* 27 July 1973; the Theatre Review of "Betrayal" by Benedict Nightingale *The Times* 23 January 1991 and "One day in Baghdad" by Martin Fletcher, *The Times* 30 January 2008 copyright © NI Syndication Ltd 1973, 1991, 2008; Northstar Publishing for an extract from "The Bigger Picture" by Bremner, R., *Audi Magazine*, reproduced with permission of Richard Bremner and Northstar Publishing; Oxford University Press for extracts from the play *A Doll's House* from *Four Major Plays* (2008) by Ibsen, H edited by James McFarland by permission of Oxford University Press; The Patton Society for an extract from the speech by General George Patton to soldiers of the US Third Army in 1944 on eve of D Day. Kindly granted by Charles M. Province, The George S. Patton, Jr. Historical Society. Copyright © 1984. www.pattonhq.com; Penguin Books (UK) Ltd for extracts from the play *Equus* by Peter Shaffer published by Penguin Books, 1997 copyright © Peter Shaffer, 1973; The Random House Group for extracts from *Dickens* by Peter Ackroyd, published by Sinclair-Stevenson; *The Blair Years* by Alastair Campbell, 2007, published by Arrow Books; and *The Fixer: A Story from Sarajevo* by Joe Sacco. Reprinted by permission of The Random House Group Ltd; Sheil Land Associates Ltd for an extract from *The Glass Menagerie* by Tennessee Williams, published by Penguin. Copyright 1945, renewed 1973 by The University of the South. Reproduced by permission of Sheil Land Associates Ltd; The Society of Authors, on behalf of the Bernard Shaw Estate for a letter from George Bernard Shaw to Stella Campbell, January 1918, published in *The Oxford Book of Letters*, Oxford University Press, 2003 copyright © The Society of Authors, on behalf of the Bernard Shaw Estate; and Telegraph Media Group Limited for an extract from "Radcliffe's naked talent makes Equus a hit" by Charles Spencer *The Telegraph* 2 March 2007 copyright © Telegraph 2007.

In some instances we have been unable to trace the owners of copyright material and we would appreciate any information that would enable us to do so.